Multimedia in Practice

BCS Practitioner Series

Series editor: Ray Welland

BAXTER/LISBURN   Reengineering information technology: success through
empowerment
BELINA ET AL   SDL with applications from protocol specification
BRAEK/HAUGEN   Engineering real time systems
BRINKWORTH   Software quality management: a pro-active approach
CRITCHLEY/BATTY   Open systems – the reality
FOLKES/STUBENVOLL   Accelerated systems development
GIBSON   Managing computer projects: avoiding the pitfalls
GODART/CHAROY   Databases for software engineering
HIPPERSON   Practical systems analysis: for users, managers and analysts
HORROCKS/MOSS   Practical data administration
LEYLAND   Electronic data interchange
LOW   Writing user documentation: a practical guide for those who want to be read
MACLEAN ET AL   Analysing systems: determining requirements for change and
development
MONK ET AL   Improving your human–computer interface: a practical technique
O'CONNELL   How to run successful projects
THE RAISE LANGUAGE GROUP   The RAISE specification language
RICE   VMS systems management
TANSLEY/HAYBALL   Knowledge based systems analysis and design
THIRLWAY   Writing software manuals: a practical guide
VERYARD   Information coordination: the management of information models, systems
and organizations
VERYARD   Information modelling: practical guidance
WALLMÜLLER   Software quality assurance: a practical approach
WELLMAN   Software costing

Multimedia in Practice

Technology and applications

Judith Jeffcoate

Prentice Hall
New York   London   Toronto   Sydney   Tokyo   Singapore

First published 1995 by
Prentice Hall International (UK) Limited
Campus 400, Maylands Avenue
Hemel Hempstead
Hertfordshire, HP2 7EZ
A division of
Simon & Schuster International Group

Printed and bound in Great Britain by
Redwood Books, Trowbridge, Wiltshire

Library of Congress Cataloging-in-Publication Data

Jeffcoate, Judith
    Multimedia in practice : technology and applications / Judith
Jeffcoate.
      p. cm. — (BCS practitioner series)
    Includes bibliographical references and index.
    ISBN 0-13-123324-6
    1. Multimedia systems. I. Title. II. Series.
QA76.575.J44   1994
006.6—dc20   94–42324
                                        CIP

British Library Cataloguing in Publication Data

A catalogue record for this book is available from
the British Library
ISBN 0-13-123324-6

---

1 2 3 4 5 99 98 97 96 95

For Gwen

Contents

Part II   Technology

Editorial Preface

The aim of the BCS Practitioner Series is to produce books that are relevant for practising computer professionals across the whole spectrum of Information Technology activities. We want to encourage practitioners to share their practical experience of methods and applications with fellow professionals. We also seek to disseminate information in a form that is suitable for the practitioner who often has only limited time to read widely within a new subject area or to assimilate research findings.

The role of the BCS is to provide advice on the suitability of books for the Series, via the Editorial Panel, and to provide a pool of potential authors upon which we can draw. Our objective is that this Series will reinforce the drive within the BCS to increase professional standards in IT. The other partners in this venture, Prentice Hall, provide the publishing expertise and international marketing capabilities of a leading publisher in the computing field.

The response when we set up the Series was extremely encouraging. However, the success of the Series depends on there being practitioners who want to learn as well as those who feel they have something to offer! The Series is under continual development and we are always looking for ideas for new topics and feedback on how to further improve the usefulness of the Series. If you are interested in writing for the Series then please contact us.

Multimedia is an area which is now taking off with the decreasing price of the technology. This book introduces the uses, benefits and problems of multimedia. The basic technology of multimedia is explained with references to relevant literature. There are examples of applications and a glossary of terms, in case, like me, you get lost in the acronyms! If you want to find out what multimedia is about and what it has to offer then this is an excellent place to start.

Ray Welland
Computing Science Department, University of Glasgow

Editorial Panel Members
Frank Bott (UCW, Aberystwyth), Dermot Browne (KPMG Management Consulting), Nic Holt (ICL), Trevor King (Praxis Systems Plc), Tom Lake (GLOSSA), Kathy Spurr (Analysis and Design Consultants)

Author's Preface

The primary objective of this book is to provide guidance for business managers and project leaders who need to introduce multimedia technology into their applications. This is a complex task, because multimedia is not a single technology. It stands at the point of convergence of several streams of development in the computing, communications and video industries.

In recent years multimedia has been the subject of a great deal of hype and counter-hype. The term is now being used in a number of different ways by disparate groups of people. These groups range from developers selling courseware for the computer-based training market, through consumer electronics companies selling video games for the home entertainment market, to the proprietors of multiple media (newspapers and TV channels, for example) in the publishing sector.

What all these uses have in common is the concept of multiple ways for people to communicate with each other. 'Multimedia' is about extending channels of communication between people to involve all their senses - sight, hearing and touch. Specifically it is about using the computer to manage and integrate these channels. Today's computer systems can handle text, graphics and images as well as alphanumeric data. The 1990s will see this capacity expanded still further - bringing audio and video into everyday use.

How to use this book

Whilst most recent books on multimedia have concentrated in detail on the use of one technology (such as DVI) or one platform (such as the Apple Macintosh), this book provides an overview of the full range of technologies and platforms available. It also describes how these can be used in applications that people use in their everyday lives, at work and at home.

Parts I and III do not require any previous knowledge. They can be read by non-computer personnel and are also suitable for undergraduate students. Part II, which outlines the basic components and technologies, requires some familiarity with computer architecture. It is suitable for computer personnel who are interested in multimedia and final year students who have completed a previous course on information technology. Part IV, which discusses the impact of multimedia on the development of applications, is intended for managers planning multimedia projects.

Part I   Multimedia today

Following a brief review of the current and future use of multimedia, the first part of the book defines multimedia systems as those computer platforms and software tools that support the interactive use of audio, still image and video. It shows how these new types of data can be used to enhance a wide range of existing applications. For example, voice annotation, photographs and video clips can be added to traditional business applications such as personnel databases and insurance claims processing. More importantly the introduction of multimedia technology will enable new applications, such as desktop conferencing.

Part II   Technology

Multimedia applications depend heavily on the integration of subsystems and components. This part of the book starts by providing an overview of the impact of multimedia on the main functions and architecture of computer systems: data capture, storage and retrieval, processing, output generation and communications.

Several widely available platforms now offer some support for multimedia. Chapter 5 discusses the impact of the Multimedia PC (MPC) specification before describing the facilities provided by Apple Macintoshes, IBM PCs and Unix workstations. It also outlines the features of enhanced operating systems such as QuickTime, MS Windows 3.1 and Presentation Manager 2.0.

Chapter 6 discusses the choice of authoring tools for building applications. Information systems based on hypertext can be extended to include a wide range of data types. The result - hypermedia - provides a new approach to information access. The chapter closes with a review of the high-level standards required to cover the organisation of multimedia data.

The three following chapters deal with issues that concern specific multimedia data types - image, audio and video. They cover the capture and compression of each type and summarise the relevant standards.

Methods and media for storing and retrieving multimedia data are described in Chapter 10. The technology covered includes magnetic media, videodisk and the series of specifications for compact disk.

Multimedia puts additional pressure on communications systems. The final chapter in this part covers types of information flow, together with bandwidth requirements. The development of appropriate services for local and wide area networks is outlined, with the likely impact of narrowband and broadband ISDN.

Part III   Applications

The third part of the book describes the actual and potential applications of multimedia technology, illustrated by examples drawn from the real world.

The early use of multimedia was largely for off-line training and education using interactive videodisk and standalone players. Some companies are now turning to Just-in-time (JIT) training as an alternative to off-line systems. In addition to embedded help facilities in software packages, JIT includes on-line help desks for mainframe systems.

Multimedia is also being used in kiosks - point-of-information and point-of-sale systems - to communicate information to the public and more recently to carry out transactions. As with computer-based training, early kiosks were developed as standalone systems using interactive video. Recent developments use CD-ROM and may be networked.

Document image processing has now been available for some years. DIP systems, based on workflow software, used by insurance companies, banks and building societies, can be extended to include voice annotation and video clips. In contrast high-quality imaging is used in applications such as health care and publishing.

The advent of the Multimedia PC and MS Windows 3.1 makes possible business audio and animation in desktop applications (e.g. business presentations, help facilities in WP and spreadsheet packages). These will familiarise users with multimedia and will raise expectations for office automation. Future applications will include multimedia mail and real-time desktop conferencing with audio and video.

The last chapter in this part discusses the future of multimedia in the home, from video games on compact disk, via interactive television, to the future of information services on the home PC.

Part IV   The impact of multimedia

The final part of the book focuses on a number of key issues which managers should consider when planning a multimedia project.

The human-computer interface is an area that has often been neglected by MIS departments. The satisfactory use of multimedia requires a high level of skill in the design of the user interface. Training software engineers to understand design issues, although necessary, will not be sufficient. Managers need to build mixed teams, including staff with a background in videographics.

Multimedia is not a standalone technology, but part of a number of significant developments in computing. Chapters 19 and 20 discuss two other technologies - object-orientation and groupware - that are likely to be combined with multimedia in applications.

Legal issues, especially intellectual property rights, will play an important role in the development of multimedia systems. The book closes with an outline of some of the problems of which developers should be aware.

Acknowledgements

This book draws on the research that I have carried out over the past five years for a series of reports published by Ovum. I am grateful to Ovum for allowing me to make parts of that research available to a wider audience. In particular I would like to thank Eirwen Nichols for her help and support over the years. I would also like to thank my fellow researchers and co-authors - Keith Hales, Man-Sze Li, John Matthews, Iain Stevenson, Alison Templeton and Stephen Timms.

During the course of that research I received much help from many individuals in companies in Europe and North America who are involved in multimedia either as users or suppliers. I would like to extend my thanks to them once again. I am particularly grateful to Linda Ljungstrøm at Danish State Railways for additional material in Chapter 13 and to Alan Mumby at Julia Schofield Associates for advice on design issues and for the photograph in Chapter 18. Other photographs were kindly provided by Asymetrix, Packard Bell, PictureTel and Sun Microsystems.

I would like to thank those who reviewed this book for their helpful suggestions on ways to improve the coverage and style. I am grateful to Viki Williams, Ann Greenwood and Jill Birch at Paramount Publishing International for their help in guiding me through the process of creating the book.

Milton Keynes   Judith Jeffcoate
July 1994

Part I

Multimedia in use

Many people think of multimedia as a solution in search of a problem. Yet the technology underlies applications that we already use at home, in the shops and at work. This use will increase steadily during the 1990s. From home entertainment, through training and education, health services and financial advice to business communications, multimedia will shape our lives for better or worse.

The first part of this book introduces the reader to multimedia systems - systems that support the interactive use of audio, still image or motion video. These new channels of communication have already been used to enhance existing applications such as computer-based training, information systems in shops and the routine processing of documents in the office. These changes will encourage users to expect multimedia features in other applications. A new range of personal computers, equipped with cameras and linked to the telephone system, will make it possible for us to see as well as to hear people thousands of miles away. Such radical changes in technology will affect many of the ways in which we do business. In the home interactive television will open up new opportunities for entertainment and information services.

The challenge for managers is to understand the potential benefits of multimedia, whilst remaining alert to the risks. High development costs, copyright problems and confusion over conflicting standards mean that companies that wish to introduce multimedia must proceed with caution.

CHAPTER 1

Introducing multimedia:

today and tomorrow

This introductory chapter gives the reader a flavour of what can be done using multimedia today, both at work and at home, before taking at look at some predictions for the future.

1.1   Multimedia today

It is customary - almost obligatory - to start books and articles on multimedia with a description of the future, say in the year 2001. Yet this is hardly necessary. Multimedia is with us today. Let us look for a moment at what is available right now, to those with the money and knowledge, through a day in the life of a modern couple in the mid-1990s.

Sarah is a product marketing manager for a multinational company. She is attending a two-day course on management skills at her company's training centre in the Cotswolds. In the past, the course was held at company headquarters in Des Moines and took four days to complete, in addition to the time spent travelling. Because the course has been put onto interactive videodisk she can now learn at her own rate - and without the need to travel abroad. The material on the disk includes interviews with the company's Chief Executive and several senior members of staff. It will be studied by every one of Sarah's rank in the company, ensuring that they receive a consistent view of company policy.

Whilst Sarah is out of the office, an important meeting is taking place back at head office in London. Because the training centre has installed a videoconferencing system, linked to London and Des Moines, Sarah can take part in making the key decisions.

Sarah's husband Richard and their two children are joining her for the weekend after the course. She uses a point-of-information system at her hotel to help her plan their activities. The computer-based system contains text and photographs that describe all the local attractions. From this she is able to identify a Wildlife Park that they can visit and to print off a map with directions and details of opening hours and prices. On the Saturday morning before they arrive she goes to a local store to look for a new washing machine. Although the shop has only a few models on display, one manufacturer has provided a point-of-sale system - another computer that can display information on the company's full range of kitchen appliances. From this information Sarah is able to select a couple of machines that meet her requirements. Once again she prints out details to discuss with Richard.

Meanwhile back in the family home, Richard has been entertaining their two children. His son has a new interactive video game - a cartridge that runs on a console connected to the TV. After losing badly at this, Richard helps his daughter with her homework - a study of animal behaviour which involves the use of a new encyclopaedia on a compact disk that she can play on the family's home computer. The disk contains short video clips showing animals in the wild and recordings of different animal noises. Later on Richard uses the computer himself for an interactive language learning session - a new Japanese for Business course, also on compact disk - before talking to his mother in Scotland over the videophone. Richard works from home, so once the children have gone to bed he downloads the latest electronic mail and news from the Internet. It includes a new piece of software for displaying images on the computer screen, which he plays with for a while before going to bed himself.

1.2   The future of multimedia

Multimedia applications are currently undergoing an important transition. During the 1980s custom-built applications were created using interactive videodisks - optical storage units that contained audio and video in analogue form. These applications - usually training or information systems - could be accessed on standalone computers equipped with a videodisk player, TV monitor and sound system. Although the quality was good, the systems were very expensive to develop and could not be integrated with modern networked computer systems.

Developments in digital technology at the beginning of the 1990s encouraged the creation of multimedia 'titles' - compact disks containing audio and video in digital form that could be played back on a personal computer, equipped with a compact disk player, a sound board and speakers. Because information on the disks is held in digital form, it can be processed, stored and transmitted over computer networks. At present these networks are not designed to cope with such large volumes of data. However, by the end of the decade improvements in networking technology will mean that multimedia can be relayed over local and wide area networks and played back on most personal computers and many home televisions.

1.2.1   Multimedia at work

How will these changes affect the lives of people at work? Let us take a look at Sarah's day in the year 2001. The company has now put its training courses onto compact disks. These are held on a central information server. Sarah no longer needs to leave her office to take part in a course. Instead, whenever she has a short break, she can call up any course over the network and view it on her personal computer. This now incorporates a small built-in video camera, microphone and speakers. Sarah can take part in a videoconference with anyone else in the company from her desk by using the computer to find the correct telephone number in the directory and set up the call. During a conference with her manager and another colleague in Rome she opens up a spreadsheet containing her latest sales projections. This appears on all three computers at the same time. The team members can work together on the figures until they are satisfied. Once the spreadsheet is complete, Sarah sends a copy of the final version, together with her audio commentary, by electronic mail to a colleague in Des Moines.

During her lunch break Sarah goes down to her local shopping centre. In the banking hall she uses a video kiosk to contact a financial advisor at the bank's head office in Leeds. The advisor calls up information on a range of savings policies for Sarah to consider. Next she goes to a grocery kiosk, which she activates using her smart card. The screen displays her last week's shopping list. Sarah normally orders the same basic groceries each week, but she can change the list by touching items on the screen. This week there is a special offer on certain wines. Touching the screen brings up details of the offer - price, quantity, nutritional value and country of origin - together with a promotional video, which Sarah hastily closes down. After she has made her selection and confirmed her choice, the system processes the order automatically, deducting the money from her account and arranging for the groceries to be delivered to her house at the date and time she has chosen.

1.2.2   Multimedia in the home

Traditional entertainment in the home has taken a number of forms. Music, speech and moving images have been distributed on a variety of analogue media: sound on vinyl disks, moving images on videotape and both by broadcasting. What all these have in common is that there is very little opportunity for interaction with their users - often referred to, in derogatory terms, as 'couch potatoes'. The digitisation of data will allow consumers an increasing amount of control over their entertainment systems in future, as the audio and video facilities with which they are already familiar will be married to computer technology.

What will Richard's evening at home be like by the year 2001? The main change is that he and his children are no longer dependent on material they have purchased on disk. His son can download a video game over the telephone line or select a film from one of the hundreds of satellite and cable channels now available. His choice from a list of the Top 20 movies is scheduled to start within 10 minutes. Richard's daughter can access her encyclopaedia on-line, over an Internet that has been expanded and upgraded to handle multimedia information. Richard needs to buy a new set of golf clubs. To do this he uses his interactive television to access an electronic shopping mall. Virtual reality makes it possible for him to move about in this mall, looking at the latest shop window displays until he comes to the sports shop. He enters this to view a selection of options. One of these offers a special promotion, accompanied by a video of the latest Open Golf tournament. Encouraged by this, Richard places his order. He follows this by mailing a videogram that the children have made for their grandmother's birthday before switching to one of the many sports channels, which offers coverage of the evening's football match from Milan. Richard uses his remote control device to select the camera angle, commentator and sponsor that he prefers and settles down for the evening.

Summary

Multimedia is already available in applications that we use every day at home and in the office. Predictions for the future suggest that this use will increase and - most importantly - that it will move from simple standalone systems to shared systems on local and wide area networks. The personal computer on the desktop and in the home office, the telephone and the television set will all undergo major changes. The differences between broadcast services such as entertainment and telecommunications services such as telephone calls will become blurred.

CHAPTER 2

What is multimedia?

This chapter provides a definition of multimedia - the interactive use of audio, still image and motion video in addition to text and graphics. A basic multimedia system is a personal computer that has been enhanced to support these new data types. Using such systems, developers will be able to enhance existing applications, by including photographs or voice annotation, for example. The most recent multimedia computers have video cameras and audio telephony that will enable users to conduct real-time videoconferences from their desks and share information over networks.

2.1   Towards a definition

Multimedia information systems make use of many different ways of communication (or media). These can include text, record-based data, numeric data, graphics, image, voice and video. Many applications are multimedia in the sense that they use more than one of these forms. A desktop publishing package, for example, supports both text and graphics. The term 'multimedia' is generally used, however, to describe more sophisticated systems - particularly those that support moving images and audio - and that is the sense in which I shall use it in this book. The common factor is that each of these new forms of communication is essentially generated outside the computer. Speech and music, photographs and video have to be converted from analogue to digital forms before they can be used in computer applications. In contrast text, graphics and even animations are created on the computer and thus do not extend its use. Some people refer to audio and video, together with animation, as time-sensitive, dynamic or continuous media. However, these terms have not achieved the widespread popularity of multimedia.

> A computer platform, communications network or software tool is a *multimedia system* if it supports the interactive use of at·least one of the following types of information - audio, still image or motion video - in addition to text and graphics.

Multimedia systems are potentially of great value to organisations. They can make available in electronic form the vast information resources that are currently on paper. They can automate meetings and enrich telephone conversations. Suppliers of computer systems are greatly increasing the nature, volume and structure of information supported by their systems. Both suppliers and users can develop an infrastructure for the many business processes that mainstream management information systems (MIS) do not yet support. More importantly, perhaps, computer systems can begin to store and manipulate more of the variety of information formats we use every day.

Multimedia has now become commercially feasible as the price of specialised hardware, such as cameras, optical storage and processors, has fallen. Multimedia is effectively an infrastructure technology, characterised by the ability to handle very diverse data types. It is used to improve electronic information representation, storage and manipulation in a wide range of applications, the most important of which are described in Part III of this book.

2.2   The elements of a multimedia system

A multimedia system combines elements that are familiar from the worlds of film, video, broadcast television, music and telecommunications as well as computing. Early systems consisted of the following basic components:

- a processor, typically a personal computer or workstation that has been enhanced to handle audio and video;
- a variety of methods by which the user can interact with the system, such as keyboard, mouse, joystick or touch screen;
- a screen that can display high-quality still images and moving video as well as computer-generated text, graphics and animations;
- speakers to allow speech and music to be output;
- a microphone;
- a way to play back pre-recorded source material, usually from some form of optical disk, such as a compact disk.

In the mid-1990s a new generation of systems has started to appear on the market. These new personal computers include a video camera and audio communications to enable videoconferencing to take place on the desktop (see Figure 2.1).

2.3   Why do we need multimedia?

Human beings are very good at handling information. We are surrounded by it all the time. On your desk you may have letters, forms, brochures containing descriptions and photographs of new products, magazine articles and a copy of this book. All of these contain information that you have no difficulty in accessing. However, if you wanted to store all of this information in your personal computer, you would have considerable problems in storing and retrieving it because your existing software packages are very limited in the kind of data they can handle.

To illustrate the nature of these limitations, consider a simple application - a personnel system that contains information about the members of your staff, their skills and the training courses they have attended. If you use a computer database to hold this information, it will probably support a range of basic data types including:

- numeric (e.g. staff number);
- character string (e.g. surname, course title);
- alphanumeric (e.g. course code);
- Boolean (e.g. male or female);
- date (e.g. date of birth);
- text (e.g. description of a particular course).

Each item of information is held in a field of the correct data type. The fields make up a record that contains all the information relating to one person. However, this list of basic data types is inadequate. There is no way of holding documents such as letters and application forms or images such as photographs. With a scanner we can capture such images and, given the right database, hold them in storage and display them on the screen or print them out. Document image processing systems now provide such features.

Images alone will not bring the people to life. Suppose we can extend the personnel system to hold other types of information - a recording of each person's voice, even a short video clip - and suppose the computer has the facilities to play back that recording and the video clip. Then we have a true multimedia system.

The personal computer, with three basic tools (word processor, spreadsheet and database), has already been able to automate the bulk of repetitive clerical tasks (typing, accounts and filing). Businesses are looking for ways to automate other activities and multimedia technology can provide some of these ways. For example, voice annotation, photographs and video clips can be added to traditional business applications such as insurance claims processing. More importantly it will make possible new applications. The number of 'knowledge workers' in the business

Figure 2.1   *Personal computer with video and audio*

community is expanding rapidly. Such people require access to information, tools to enhance creativity and support for small project teams. Multimedia can be used to enhance the work that they do. Live audio and video links will allow workers in dispersed project teams to take part in desktop conferences - 'virtual meetings' in which each participant can hear and see the others, can share applications, transfer files and compare images. Multimedia will revolutionise the way we work in the 1990s.

Summary

This chapter defined multimedia systems as those computer platforms and software tools that support the interactive use of audio, still image or motion video. The latest generation of personal computers will expand the range and quality of media available. As a result users may request multimedia features in all their computerised work. Existing applications, such as personnel databases, may be modified by incorporating new combinations of information to make them more powerful. New applications, such as real-time video communications, will become feasible. Such applications will require both additional development effort and changes in office practice and organisation.

CHAPTER 3

Using multimedia:
applications, benefits and problems

During the 1980s some large organisations adopted interactive video for their computer-based training systems. The same technology was later used in point-of-information and point-of-sale systems. As the cost of hardware has come down, multimedia has started to make an impact on the development of information systems. This influence will expand during the 1990s to all desktop software. Presentation packages and just-in-time training are already available. These will be followed by multimedia communications - electronic mail and collaborative computing. The use of multimedia can provide benefits both in economic terms and through improved quality. New business opportunities will open up. Development costs will remain high, because multimedia applications require a wider range of skills than conventional systems. Social and psychological barriers must be overcome to ensure that workers feel comfortable with the new technology. Legal problems, especially copyright issues, will impede progress.

3.1   Who is using multimedia?

3.1.1   Early users

In the first chapter of this book I described some advanced uses of multimedia. However, the typical user in the business community today is a large multinational corporation with a distributed workforce that it has to train. Indeed it used to be suggested that there were only three uses for multimedia: 'training, training and training'. This is because most of the multimedia applications that were developed during the 1980s were training and education systems for large corporations, government departments and military installations. Such computer-based training (CBT) systems were typically large customised projects, designed and built by professional courseware developers, often in specialist consultancies. They cost anything from £30,000 to £250,000 to develop, because they required the use of professional authoring tools and powerful workstations that were capable of capturing audio and video. Delivery platforms consisted of a personal computer, with a videodisk player and add-in boards to support the capture and display of audio and video information, costing around £7,000.

Towards the end of the 1980s some point-of-information (POI) and point-of-sale (POS) applications (known collectively as kiosks) started to appear in banks, travel agents and department stores, museums and art galleries. For example, one local authority in the UK installed POI systems to provide a wide range of information about the council and its services, including a 'What's on' in the county feature. The system incorporated graphics and sound, with a touchscreen, and was designed to appeal to people who were diffident about using computers. For many users these systems will have been their first contact with multimedia.

Although the majority of multimedia systems were used for training or kiosks, some were used by professionals in a number of specialist markets that require the ability to handle video, animations and very high-quality images. These applications included professional videographics in film and broadcasting companies; computer-assisted publishing (CAP); and specialist image processing applications such as medicine, remote sensing and seismography. Typically these were comparatively small systems based on the use of high-performance, high-cost equipment and tools.

3.1.2   Multimedia in the 1990s

Most applications to date have been developed by training or marketing departments. MIS departments have yet to become involved in multimedia, though the time has now arrived when they should do so. The appearance on the market of products that support the storage, retrieval and transmission of high-quality still images opens the way for a variety of extensions to existing applications. For example, document image processing (DIP) systems already handle still images - usually of business documents such as letters or forms. These can be enhanced by the introduction of audio - voice annotation, for example - and moving images such as video clips. In the same way, vendors in vertical markets such as computer-aided design (CAD) will add support for multimedia to their existing product lines, for example as part of their on-line documentation.

Multimedia is now available on standard computer platforms. Organisations which replace their existing personal computers every four years must therefore consider carefully whether to move to platforms that will support multimedia versions of standard software packages in future. Desktop presentation packages are already available. These allow staff without professional videographics skills to build applications that incorporate animations, audio and video clips. Their impact is expected to be similar to that of desktop publishing in the 1980s. Users will be able to access information that is stored in multimedia databases, both on-line and on optical disks. Already an increasing number of companies are using compact disk-read-only memory (CD-ROM) as a distribution medium for software as well as for database information. Sun Microsystems, for example, has put its entire third party software catalogue onto disk, including demonstration versions of some of the packages.

During the 1990s multimedia will be fully integrated with personal computers and workstations, allowing users to receive audio instructions, pictures and animations that explain how to carry out a complex command. Such just-in-time (JIT) training will enhance existing help facilities in standard spreadsheet or word processing packages. In the second half of the decade the expansion in multimedia communications will create opportunities for other applications such as mail and groupware. Existing electronic mail packages will be enhanced to incorporate new data types. Users will be able to include voice commentaries, photographs and video clips within the mail messages that they send to other users. Present-day videoconferencing systems are expensive and often require specially equipped studios. With one of the new video PCs, in contrast, users can open up windows on their desktop machines and talk directly to colleagues over a network. More importantly they will be able to share documents. As one user modifies the document on-screen, the changes will appear on the copy of the document on the other user's computer. Multimedia will play an important part in software that supports co-operative working - commonly known as groupware.

3.2   Benefits of using multimedia

Organisations that use multimedia systems can experience both economic benefits and qualitative benefits. Perhaps the most attractive reasons for using multimedia - and the hardest to assess - are the new business opportunities that may open up. This section outlines the benefits experienced and expected from the use of multimedia in four key areas.

3.2.1   Training

Although multimedia systems were initially very expensive to develop, early users of training systems reported overall economic benefits from the use of the technology. Successful organisations need to maintain high levels of staff training and development. Through reductions in the expenses associated with holding conventional training courses, the costs of developing a multimedia training system can be recouped within a few years. These savings in training costs are achieved because:

- each course can be used by many more people;
- time spent away from the office, including travel time, can be reduced;
- employees can work at their own pace so the average training time per employee is reduced;
- full-time classroom instructors are no longer required;
- expensive demonstrations can be used without jeopardising safety.

Because the best instructors prepare and take part in each course, the quality of courses may also be improved. Both the content and quality of courses will be consistent across the whole organisation. Furthermore it is likely that students retain more from interactive multimedia training than from traditional classroom courses. A study for the British Audiovisual Association showed that people retain 10 per cent of what they see, 20 per cent of what they hear and 50 per cent of what they see and hear. Seeing and hearing are essentially passive. In contrast people retain 80 per cent of what they see, hear and do. Interactive multimedia training courses are essentially active - they encourage students to act and react as well as watching and listening.

The same approach has been adopted in the field of education where interactive multimedia can be used in the classroom at all levels from primary school to university. An early example was the Domesday Project, developed by the BBC with funding from Esprit. A set of two interactive videodisks contained data on the life of the United Kingdom in the 1980s, including contributions from over a million people.

Distance learning projects can also benefit from interactivity. In the past these courses were supported by materials such as audio cassettes and videotapes, distributed to students by post, and by terrestrial broadcasts of television and radio programmes. Feedback from students was by means of post, telephone or meetings with tutors. In future satellite broadcasts of studio discussions will be supported by live feedback from students over audio or videoconferencing links.

3.2.2   Sales

In the retail field multimedia is changing the traditional methods and concepts of marketing. Both consumers and retailers benefit from the consistency of information that results from the introduction of point-of-sale systems. The benefits to the retailers are savings on space, inventory and distribution, estimated at up to 50 per cent of retail profit. Retailers can afford to bring more products to market and to explore alternative sales channels. Some see the introduction of shopping kiosks as a way of regenerating the high street, attracting customers back from out-of-town shopping malls.

Benefits to the retailer may be matched by problems for the rest of society. For example, the introduction of remote consultations using video communications on personal computers, coupled with the drive for banking over the phone, will radically transform the banking industry. It may well lead to the closure of many high-street branches, with the consequent loss of thousands of jobs.

3.2.3   Communications

The economic benefits of multimedia are not confined to training systems. Savings in travel time can also be achieved through the use of videoconferencing systems. One customer reported a saving of $42,000 in the first three months that was achieved by avoiding a total of 35 trips - the payback time for return on investment in this case was less than 10 months.

In the future desktop videoconferencing is expected to provide better communications between persons separated by space and time who need to work together on common projects. For example, the use of video communications will enable support staff at a manufacturer's headquarters to view the internals of an aircraft at a line station and offer immediate advice, streamlining the entire maintenance operation.

In addition to the economic benefits of videoconferencing, social benefits may arise through the conservation of natural resources and reduction in pollution levels as unnecessary travel is eliminated, improving the quality of life. A pilot project in California shows that telecommuting by state employees has led to an average reduction in the total distance travelled of about 40 miles for each day spent away from the office (Lee 1993). These reductions were in peak hour travel with consequent implications for the need for new road building programmes.

Early studies conducted in the 1980s predicted that teleworking would become very widespread. For example, the National Economic Development Office (NEDO) estimated that by 1995 between 10 and 15 per cent of skilled workers in the United Kingdom would be engaged in telework, increasing to between 15 and 20 per cent by 2010. However, a review of recent studies suggests rather a pattern of gradual, evolutionary growth with teleworking increasing amongst the self-employed rather than in the corporate sector. Whilst individuals surveyed showed a marked interest in decentralised work at home - as many as 23 per cent in the UK - decision makers were noticeably reluctant to let this happen. As few as 2 per cent in the UK would decentralise data entry and 6 per cent would decentralise word processing. The main reasons for this reluctance included the high level of resource requirements and the supervisory problems in managing a remote workforce (Fothergill 1993).

This finding is reinforced by a report for the UK Department of Trade and Industry (DTI), which identified two key misconceptions amongst company managers:

- the view that teleworkers will be more difficult to communicate with and to manage;

- the expectation that unsupervised teleworking will lead to reduced productivity.

In contrast the evidence from both teleworkers and experienced employers is that teleworking can lead to improved productivity and enhanced communications (Mitchell 1993). These conclusions were based on the existing use of electronic networking for interpersonal communications and on related technologies such as groupware. By providing better communications between remote workers and the office, multimedia may go some way to bridging the gap between the aspirations of workers and the anxieties of management.

Improved communications will also have an impact on the employment prospects of particular groups such as the long-term unemployed, mature people, women returners, single-parent families, people in rural communities and the disabled. The European Commission has conducted research into the use of telematics (defined as the fusion of computing and telecommunications) to assist such groups. Under the Fourth Framework programme, this research will be expanded to include the use of multimedia technology and applications.

3.2.4   Medicine

Multimedia can offer organisations the opportunity of business diversification and expansion by opening up new business opportunities. For example, a number of hospitals in the USA are investigating ways to offer new radiology services based on the transmission of images. These opportunities may come in the form of providing 'value-added imaging' in which the hospital supplies a service for the primary interpretation of X-rays and other images to clinicians and other health centres. This will enable its picture archiving and communications system (PACS) to become a revenue centre in its own right. At the same time, the provision of such services will encourage these new customers to refer their patients to the hospital, thus increasing its revenues from its mainstream activities. The primary benefit of these changes will be better communication of results. Clinicians will no longer need to visit the radiology department, leading to decreased demand for filing in the film library and fewer disruptions in the reading areas. The quality of consultation between radiologists and clinicians should also improve.

In a more radical example, surgeons can use three-dimensional images created from magnetic resonance imaging (MRI) scans of the human body to practise complicated procedures such as brain tumour removal and reconstructive surgery. Better planning of surgical routines will cut medical costs and lead to fewer complications. The time required for investigative surgery on victims of car accidents and patients with genetic defects will be reduced.

3.3   Problems with multimedia

Despite the real and potential benefits just outlined, the adoption of multimedia by businesses has been very slow. There are several reasons for this reluctance. Some early users seriously underestimated the costs of developing a multimedia system. These costs reflect both the complexity of the technology involved and the need to acquire the rights to use a large volume of material, usually owned by someone else. The quality of some of these early systems proved to be disappointing as well. The developers had not understood the need to use skilled designers for the interactive and audiovisual elements in their systems.

As we shall see, some of these problems remain unresolved. Other, newer problems are likely to arise in future. For example, there has been little investigation about how users will react to the prospect of video communications on the desktop. How acceptable will it prove? What codes of behaviour should users adopt? What about the environment - will noise and movement in the background prove too distracting?

3.3.1   Investment costs

Against the positive economic benefits outlined above must be set the high cost of implementing a multimedia system. Though the cost of technology is falling steadily, the cost of development work remains very high. Such work typically requires the assistance of one or more third party suppliers as very few organisations have the requisite design skills available in house. Experience shows that most managers underestimate the skills involved, the need for a new approach to product management and the length of development time.

Unlike most other computer-based systems, multimedia involves a high proportion of information (usually referred to as its *content*) in a form that is very expensive to create and maintain. This is exacerbated in many cases by the need to pay royalties or fees to the owners of copyright, since the ownership of much audiovisual material is likely to lie outside the organisation.

3.3.2   Technical barriers

Multimedia is surrounded by a barrage of new terminology, often involving strings of acronyms, that are confusing to users. Many new and relatively untried technologies are involved. Managers should be aware that they will need to upgrade their infrastructure to provide:

- personal computers or workstations that can support and manage multimedia data, including real-time video;
- new file servers that can manage large volumes of data stored on optical or

magnetic media;
- new software tools, and new versions of old software tools, that can handle multimedia;
- local area networks that can transmit multiple concurrent streams of multimedia data;
- connections between local and wide area networks for the transmission of voice, video and data.

The need to network multimedia applications will cause particular problems. Such applications are characterised by the need to transmit large volumes of data, often time dependent, in continuous streams over local and wide area networks. Different types of data - audio and video, for example - must be synchronised and delivered in real time to applications on the desktop.

The lack of standards has made it difficult to ensure compatibility between the user's equipment and that of the distributor of information. An application developed on one platform (say an Apple Macintosh) will not run on a different machine (an IBM PC, for example). Networking the application will exacerbate this problem. The establishment of genuine international standards for fax machines meant that the user could send a document to any machine anywhere in the world and be sure that it would be transmitted correctly. Similar standards are urgently required for distributed multimedia applications to allow workers in different companies to communicate and collaborate successfully.

3.3.3   Social and psychological barriers

As we have seen, self-employment and teleworking have increased over the last few years and are expected to continue to grow though the social and psychological aspects of distributed working are not well understood. A study of the experiences of a group of self-employed people in the publishing industry who were using telephones and PCs to work at home identified some of the problems (Stanworth 1993). The least liked aspects of telework were loneliness, isolation and the lack of contact with both clients and other members of the profession. Telephone contact was felt to be qualitatively little substitute for meetings with clients. These workers felt cut off from the social world of publishing and felt deprived as a result. Social problems were seen as more significant than the negative economic aspects of self-employment and teleworking such as fluctuating earnings and workload. The use of videophones may improve the quality of social interaction for remote workers, though involvement in collaborative projects is likely to prove more satisfactory than one-to-one communications.

Similar problems are likely to arise with other forms of distributed work. For example, training and problem-solving sessions are often held off site. In such sessions members of staff, freed from the pressure of dealing with queries and telephone calls, can concentrate on the job at hand. Such off-site meetings also encourage staff to work together, increasing bonding and building teams.

In the office constant interruptions may also make it difficult for people to use interactive training materials on the desktop. In practice it may be necessary to create quiet areas for training sessions.

The typical office environment does not support the kinds of multimedia interaction we have been discussing. The need to share offices and, still more, the trend to open-plan offices means that there is a high level of background noise and movement. This already makes it difficult to make telephone calls - lengthy calls have to be made from a quiet room or at home. The use of a desktop videophone is likely to exacerbate this problem, since participants will be further distracted by movement in the background, which in turn may cause the picture to degrade. Some people will see the videophone as unnecessarily intrusive and feel uncomfortable at the thought that they are visible to the caller - there may even be renewed pressure from management with regard to dress codes in the office!

3.3.4   Legal problems

One of the barriers to the growth of multimedia applications has been concern about the ownership of content. Most developers will already be aware of the need to identify and contact the owners of copyright of all the material that forms the content of their applications. If a company that develops a multimedia application reproduces the whole or a substantial part of a copyright work, without the permission of the copyright owner, it will infringe the owner's rights. Copyright law protects literary, musical, graphic, artistic and other works. A copyright owner whose rights have been infringed can sue for damages. Even if only a small portion of the multimedia product infringes these rights, the owner can seek to have the entire product withdrawn from the market. Problems may also arise concerning intellectual property rights in applications where multimedia networks are used to support collaborative work.

A further set of questions, similar to those that arise in electronic data interchange (EDI) applications, is posed by the networking of multimedia. These relate to contract formation, confidentiality and the accuracy of the information communicated. Claims for liability may arise out of the use of multimedia networks to provide professional advice or through the provision of incorrect or misleading information. Security and control of access to information are required to ensure the integrity of data. Networked multimedia applications are likely to be subject to more than one regulatory framework - to both telecommunications and broadcasting regulatory bodies, for example. Applications that include real-time video communications are also likely to cross international boundaries, thus becoming subject to different legal systems.

Summary

Multimedia in the form of interactive video has been used effectively in computer-based training systems and more recently for retail information systems. Reductions in cost will make the technology widely available by the end of the decade. Early users have reported substantial economic benefits, such as reduced travel expenditure, as well as qualitative improvements in knowledge acquisition. However, high development costs and confusion over standards, together with unresolved social and legal issues, have delayed the adoption of multimedia applications on a wide scale. Despite these problems, multimedia has the power to change many of the ways in which we do business. Part II will show that the appearance of cheap multimedia computers mean that MIS managers must now take multimedia seriously.

References

[Fothergill 1993] A. Fothergill, 'Facts and figures: teleworking research in the last decade', *European Journal of Teleworking*, vol. 2, no. 1, pp. 15-20.

[Lee 1993] S. Lee, 'California dreamin': the California Telecommuting Pilot Project and its relevance to Europe', *European Journal of Teleworking*, vol. 1, no. 4, pp. 4-8.

[Mitchell 1993] H. Mitchell and E. Trodd, *DTI Teleworking study 1992-1993: Final report*, DTI/TWKG/93.03.

[Stanworth 1993] C. Stanworth and J. Stanworth, 'Saved or damned? The growth of freelance teleworkers', *European Journal of Teleworking*, vol. 1, no. 4, pp. 9-15.

Part II

Technology

Multimedia is not a single technology. It is a group - a large group - of infrastructure technologies with widely differing origins. Building a multimedia application is partly a matter of integrating these technologies. Managers must therefore be familiar with at least the main features of each one. They should know which subsystems and components will be required to support it and be aware of the relevant standards - or lack of standards - that may apply to its use.

Part II provides an overview of the impact of multimedia on the main functions and architecture of computer systems. It first reviews the main platforms and tools that support the development and delivery of multimedia applications. Image, audio and video have been identified as the three most important multimedia data types. A chapter is devoted to each of these in turn, to review the different technologies involved in their capture and processing. What all multimedia data has in common is the large volumes of storage that it requires. A further chapter surveys the wide range of available storage media

A major handicap is the great demands that multimedia places on communications systems. Until very recently most multimedia applications ran on standalone single-user systems. This set them apart from the mainstream of computer networks. The time is approaching when this isolation must end. The final chapter in this part deals with the developments in local and wide area networks that will be necessary to support multimedia communications.

CHAPTER 4

System components

Many of the difficulties that arise in developing multimedia systems do so because multimedia is not a single technology. Rather it is the convergence of many different technologies that have reached differing degrees of maturity. This chapter sets the stage for the rest of Part II by outlining the key functions of multimedia computers, which differ from those used in the development of traditional information systems. They involve the capture, editing and playback of a range of data types that originate outside the computer.

4.1   Converging technologies

It is now quite conventional to describe multimedia as lying at the convergence of three or four separate industries, namely computing, telecommunications, entertainment (in the form of film and television) and publishing. Certainly it has attracted considerable interest in all of these areas. Currently this convergence is encouraging companies with very different backgrounds to work together. Other companies have been formed specifically to take advantage of the opportunities provided by the combination of such different spheres of interest.

However, the emergence of multimedia in the 1990s can also be seen as the convergence of a large number of technologies, some of which have been evolving steadily throughout the past century. These technologies range from the invention of optical disks in the 1920s to the development of digital signal processors in the 1980s. Most new technologies spend many years of comparative isolation in university research departments or corporate laboratories. It may be 20 years before commercial products that support the technology start to appear on the market. During this long gestation the technology continues to evolve independently, both of other new technologies and of real-world systems.

Early adopters will purchase the first products. They, typically, are not too bothered about conforming to standards or integrating their prototype applications with legacy systems. It is only when the new technology has to be introduced into mainstream computing that serious problems of compatibility arise.

This is the stage at which multimedia has arrived. In its early years multimedia was isolated from mainstream computing. Training or marketing departments generally developed the earliest applications, using outside consultants and by-passing the MIS department. This picture is now starting to change. As a result multimedia systems are expected to fit into conventional systems development and perform to the same standards.

The manager who wants to develop a multimedia application is faced with a bewildering array of incompatible products, evolving international standards and novel equipment that includes cameras, speakers and microphones. In this chapter I will describe the role of these items in the development and delivery of multimedia applications. Subsequent chapters look in more detail at platforms and software, describe the underlying technology and review the relevant standards.

4.2   Functions and subsystems

There are many simple multimedia platforms on the market at present. A basic delivery system such as that illustrated in Figure 4.1 might consist of:

- a personal computer with a high-resolution bitmapped screen;
- a CD-ROM drive, which may be standalone but is more likely now to be incorporated into the computer;
- speakers and a microphone;
- one or more adapter boards to decompress and play back audio and video material;
- software support including device drivers for the adapters and runtime libraries for the development tools used.

In order to create a multimedia application a development system providing additional support is required to perform specialised functions and to control all the disparate part of the system. Such a system might include:

- one or more adapter boards to capture, digitise, compress, manipulate and edit audio and video material;
- a software toolkit to develop applications, support editing of audio and visual material and supply device drivers for the adapter boards;

Figure 4.1 *Personal computer for multimedia*

- software libraries for basic functions, application programming interfaces (APIs) and system support;
- authoring tools for specific applications - the equivalent of a desktop publishing (DTP) package such as Ventura;
- libraries of clip art, music and video.

This multimedia development system must perform three main functions, as shown in Figure 4.2. These functions are data *input* from sources such as cameras or musical instruments, application *development*, and data *output* to some delivery medium such as a videodisk or CD-ROM.

The main differences between a multimedia system and a conventional one lie in the nature of this data. Conventional files typically consist of small blocks of data that the computer can handle with comparative ease. The relation between these blocks is generally not dependent on time. Multimedia data in contrast usually consists of very large files that contain a single image or a continuous audio or video sequence. These files must be handled in one piece. In the rest of this chapter we will look at the impact of this new type of data on the main multimedia functions.

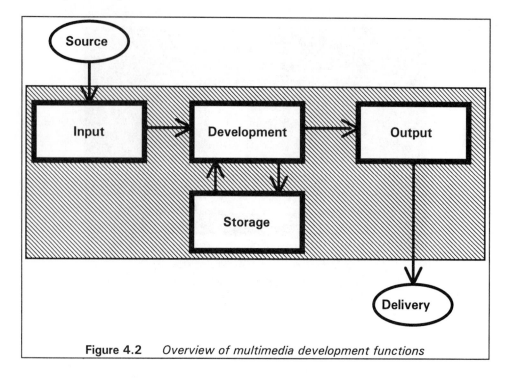

Figure 4.2   *Overview of multimedia development functions*

4.2.1   Input

Figure 4.3 illustrates the relation between the main data input functions. These consist of the capture and compression, processing and monitoring, and finally storage of the data. All the multimedia data types that we have been discussing so far are produced outside the computer. Consequently the first and most important step will be to identify the *source* of each item of information. This source may be live, such as a musical instrument or video camera, or pre-recorded such as an audio cassette or videotape. In either case the input data stream that is *captured* by the computer will be in analogue form - it will be composed of a continuously varying signal. So the next action that the system must perform is to convert this signal into a series of discrete numerical values that can be manipulated by the computer - in other words it must *digitise* the data. Converting the analogue signal into digital form not only makes it easier to handle in the computer. It also makes it possible to process the data, eliminating any unwanted distortions introduced by the recording equipment.

In practice most multimedia systems will be composed of a wide range of different data types from many different sources. Existing images may be imported

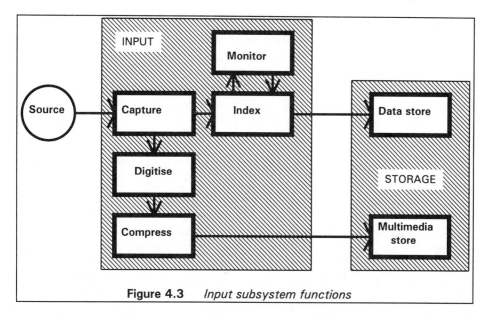

Figure 4.3   *Input subsystem functions*

as files in an industry-standard format such as TIFF (Tagged Image File Format), developed and supported by Aldus and Microsoft. Still images such as documents or photographs are normally captured using an optical scanner or a camera. The type of camera will vary according to the source material and the level of detail that is required. High-resolution images such as colour photographs of paintings or X-rays will require special equipment. All the images are digitised so that they may be reduced to arrays of bits - binary information that can be stored in the computer.

Music and speech may be captured live from a microphone connected to the computer or from pre-recorded tapes, cassettes or compact disks. In each case a sound digitiser is used to capture and digitise the analogue sound signal.

Audiovisual material can be input in a standard format (e.g. composite or S-VHS formats for NTSC or PAL colour television standards). Input devices include video cassette recorders (VCRs), camcorders, videodisk players, TV tuners and video cameras. Video digitisers should be able to accept analogue signals from any of these devices and digitise them. Single frames can be 'grabbed' and stored as still images.

After it has been captured, the input data must be filed. In order for this to happen in an orderly way, each file must be *indexed*, assigned a storage address and transferred to permanent storage - probably on an optical disk. The user will need software that enables him or her to name and index each item in turn. The index information is generally stored in a separate database, often on the hard disk, whilst the large files containing the multimedia information are eventually transferred to optical storage.

These activities are labour intensive. This is partly because of the need to prepare the source material before capture - removing paper clips and staples from paper documents, for example. However, the greatest source of delay is the need to index items as they are captured. Performance in some applications, such as document imaging systems, can be improved through the use of recognition technologies to index documents automatically. Such technologies include optical character recognition (OCR), a technique by which characters printed in a standard typeface can be automatically read and encoded, and bar-codes - arrays of rectangular bars and spaces originally introduced in the early 1970s for retail use. Materials will often need to be *monitored* - by displaying a captured image on the screen, for example, in order to check its quality.

Once a data item has been checked and indexed, it may be transferred to some form of permanent storage. This may be a magnetic disk, but is increasingly likely to be one of the many forms of optical storage. In either case index information that identifies the location of every item will be held in a database and should be duplicated, on a separate system, in case the original index is corrupted.

The input data streams from the various sources are stored electronically as bits. Because the number of bits needed to represent any multimedia object is very large, the resulting binary file will take up too much storage. It will also be too large to transmit comfortably over a network. All this data must therefore be *compressed*, using one of a number of standard algorithms to eliminate as much unnecessary information as possible. The data will, of course, need to be decompressed in order to restore the missing information before it can be displayed or played back.

4.2.2   Development

The development of a multimedia application will generally be carried out using a variety of software tools. These tools, to be described in Chapter 6, allow the developer to carry out tasks such as creating scripts for presentations, building links between items (hypertext), editing, designing screens, overlaying video images with text and computer graphics and mixing audio input from different sources.

4.2.3   Output

Figure 4.4 shows the main output functions. These consist of the retrieval of data from store, final processing and recording of the completed application on some media for playback. Applications can be *recorded* in a standard format (composite or S-VHS for PAL or NTSC) on videotape for playback. Videotape may also be used to deliver the completed application to an optical disk company that will use it to set up a master disk from which to press copies for publication.

It is now possible to purchase a compact disk recorder that can be used to write a multimedia application to disk directly from the computer. This method can be used to generate small numbers of copies for use in house.

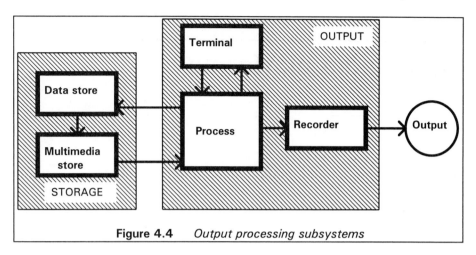

Figure 4.4   *Output processing subsystems*

Summary

Multimedia applications are complex to develop. Managers need to understand the basic functions and subsystems related to input, development and output that are common to all types of data. To achieve compatibility between the various software and hardware products involved, substantial planning and investigation will be required in each area before decisions are made. Data capture in particular is very labour intensive and expensive. Managers are advised to seek ways in which this task may be automated. Whilst the basic functions of capture, digitisation, compression, processing and storage are the same for all multimedia data types, there are major differences in the way in which these tasks are carried out for image, audio and video. Chapters 7, 8 and 9 will explore these differences further. First we will look at the range of platforms and tools currently available to support the development of multimedia applications.

CHAPTER 5

Multimedia platforms

This chapter starts by examining the limitations of the personal computer as a multimedia platform. It describes the impact of the Multimedia PC (MPC) specification, which has been introduced to encourage the adoption of a standard desktop platform for multimedia applications. Several widely available platforms now offer some support for multimedia, including IBM PCs, Apple Macintoshes, Sun SPARCstations and other Unix workstations. Enhancements to the operating system such as Video for Windows, Presentation Manager, QuickTime and Solaris Live! are outlined. New products for desktop videoconferencing are described. The chapter closes with a review of some developments in PC architecture that will improve support for multimedia.

5.1 Personal computers for multimedia today

The personal computer has gone through several stages in its short lifetime. Early standalone systems supported only alphanumeric data and employed a simple command line interface. The next generation extended support to text and simple graphics, which could be accessed via a menu-driven interface. The first multimedia systems were launched in the mid-1980s by two companies - Apple and Commodore. From its first appearance in 1984 the Apple Macintosh proved to be a major influence on the personal computer market. It popularised the graphical user interface (GUI) and supported text, graphics, animation and sound output - the first multimedia personal computer. In July 1985, when Commodore launched the Amiga, it too supported most of the things that are seen as multimedia today. Its features included two audio channels, speech synthesis, animation at 30 frames per second and video output compatible with the US television standards, all supported by a multitasking operating system.

These systems were readily adopted for applications such as videographics, presentations, interactive displays and computer-based training systems. However, they had certain disadvantages for general business use, most notably their non-conformance with the de facto standards that had emerged for personal computing. These were based on Intel's 80x86 family of processors, the IBM PC bus architecture and the MS-DOS operating system.

5.1.1   Limitations of the personal computer

The basic IBM PC-compatible machine was not a natural multimedia platform.It was weak on processing power and had no integral support for audio or video. All such facilities had to be provided via adapter boards. Extensions to the operating system were also required to control various pieces of external equipment including microphones, audiotapes, VCRs and video cameras. System software, such as Microsoft's Multimedia Extensions for Windows (now part of Windows 3.1) and Video for Windows, incorporated facilities to do this.

Audio and video adapters
Audio adapters supported the recording, digitising and playback of voice and music. Video adapters captured and processed still images and mixed them with the normal screen display. Originally they were designed to handle analogue video, which could then be overlaid with computer graphics and text. Later products were developed that could digitise the images as well. Other boards could capture, digitise, compress, decompress and play back motion video, using a dedicated video processor to handle the large volumes of data involved. At first these employed proprietary compression technology such as Intel's DVI (Digital Video Interactive). They are now more likely to implement one of the defined standards (JPEG for still image, MPEG for video and H.261 for real-time video) that Chapters 7 and 9 will describe in detail.

Bus architecture
Probably the weakest feature of the PC, in the context of multimedia, is its bus architecture. A *data bus* is an internal communication line that carries data from one part of the computer to another. The amount of information that a bus can carry - its *bandwidth* - is measured by its frequency range, which states how often regular waves or pulses occur in the circuit in terms of megahertz (MHz) or millions of cycles per second. The term 'bandwidth' is also used to refer to the amount of data - measured in kilobytes per second (KB/s) or megabytes per second (MB/s) - that can be transferred by the bus. Similar terms are used for external networks, such as Ethernet, where bandwidth is measured in kilobits per second (Kbit/s) or megabits per second (Mbit/s).

Existing bus architectures were designed to handle small packets of data, in bursts, with error checking. In contrast audio and video require the transmission of continuous data streams. New bus architectures, described in Section 5.4.2, may overcome this problem. In the meantime it is necessary to avoid moving motion video over the data bus.

Networking

Finally, if the PC application is to transmit multimedia information over a network, the separate voice, video and data streams have first to be merged (*multiplexed*) into a single stream in the computer. This stream then has to be demultiplexed by the machine that receives it. Implementation of multiplexing is a software function that requires additional processing in the computer and possible extensions to the operating system. Standards are needed for these functions to permit the interchange of data between multimedia applications based on technology from different suppliers.

5.1.2   The evolution of the Multimedia PC

As we have seen, a whole industry of adapter boards and related equipment for multimedia applications grew up around the IBM PC and its clones. In November 1990, in an attempt to create some order out of this chaos, Microsoft announced a minimum configuration for a personal computer to run multimedia applications. This specification, which included compatibility with Microsoft's multimedia extensions to Windows, was supported by a group of suppliers that included Creative Labs, Fujitsu, Philips Consumer Electronics, Tandy and Zenith Data Systems. The Multimedia PC (MPC) Marketing Council, a subsidiary of the Software Publishers Association, was established to promote the specification and to issue licences to products that conform to it.

MPC Level 1

The first specification (MPC Level 1) was intended to encourage the adoption of a standard computing platform as an extension of the personal computer. Systems that conform to it may carry the MPC trademark. Upgrade kits must meet the CD-ROM, audio subsystem and input/output (I/O) requirements of the specification. The Council licenses the systems and upgrade kits that pass its certification test suites. Because it charges fees for the use of its trademark, not all products that meet the specification carry the MPC mark.

Most of the early MPC products sold were upgrades for existing computers with Intel 386 or 486 processors. However, computer manufacturers such as Compaq are starting to ship machines with integrated CD-ROM drives. Recent market research indicates that about 13 million such drives had been installed by the end of 1993 (EMB 1994). As CD-ROM becomes popular as a medium for distributing software, such machines are likely to become commonplace.

MPC Level 2

The original MPC specification was criticised as being too limited, costing too much money for too little capability. A revised version (MPC Level 2) was introduced in May 1993 to establish a performance standard for enhanced multimedia computing. It was designed for software-based video and new applications such as Photo CD, a form of compact disk for the storage of photographic images developed by Kodak that requires data to be recorded in more than one session. As Table 5.1 shows, this new specification is backwardly compatible with MPC Level 1. Both specifications are intended to define minimum functionality rather than to act as a recommendation for a particular system configuration. An existing IBM PC-compatible machine can be upgraded by adding features such as a CD-ROM drive and support for audio input and output for as little as £300, though a full MPC Level 2 upgrade currently costs twice this amount.

The MPC is just the first step towards the fully fledged multimedia platform. From the point of view of the business user who is interested in multimedia, the MPC specification is unsatisfactory because of its concentration on audio. Within the audio specification, the emphasis is on music rather than business requirements for audio - a point emphasised by the need to conform to the Musical Instrument Digital Interface (MIDI) standard.

Table 5.1 Minimum configurations for MPCs

	Level 1	*Level 2*
Processor	16 MHz 386SX	25 MHz 486SX
Memory	2 MB	4 MB
Hard disk	30 MB	160 MB
Floppy disk	3.5-inch high density	
Video display	640 × 480, 16 colours	640 × 480, 65,536 colours
Sound	8-bit digital sound	16-bit digital sound
	8 note synthesiser	8 note synthesiser
	MIDI playback	MIDI playback
CD-ROM drive	150 KB/s sustained	300 KB/s sustained
	transfer rate	transfer rate
	max average seek time	max average seek time 400
	1 second	milliseconds
		CD-ROM XA ready,
		multisession capable
I/O devices	101 key keyboard	
	two-button mouse	
Ports	MIDI I/O	MIDI I/O
	joystick	joystick
Operating system	Windows 3.0 with	Windows 3.0 with
	multimedia extensions	multimedia extensions
	or Windows 3.1	or Windows 3.1

Source: The Multimedia PC (MPC) Marketing Council

5.2   Multimedia hardware

5.2.1   IBM

IBM itself sees multimedia as an important market and is providing an expanding range of multimedia machines, adapters and software tools. In October 1991 the company introduced a customised version of the IBM PS/2, under the brand name Ultimedia, the first model to have multimedia features as standard. The Ultimedia product range, which is expanding all the time, includes:

- a range of audio and video adapters for capture and playback;
- the PS/1, PS/2 and ValuePoint families of products and multimedia upgrade kits;
- a desktop conferencing package called Person-to-Person, whose facilities include file transfer, shared whiteboard, remote pointer and, optionally, a video window;
- a suite of kiosks, incorporating variations of the PS/2 and a touchscreen, with optional transactional features (telephone and credit card reader);
- a speech server series that analyses the spoken word.

These products are supported by system software and a variety of software tools, which are described in Sections 5.3.2 and 6.2 respectively.

In addition, multimedia capabilities can be integrated into IBM's mainframes (ES/9000), mid-range processors (AS/400), and personal workstations (RISC System 6000). In November 1992, IBM announced a framework for distributed multimedia computing, which is closely aligned with the OSI Reference Model (IBM 1992). This document outlines the steps that IBM intends to take to provide both new systems, enabled with multimedia, and enhancements to the traditional infrastructure for distributed computing. It is likely to prove essential reading for managers who intend to introduce multimedia into a new or existing IBM environment.

5.2.2   Apple

Like IBM, with whom it is co-operating in a number of joint ventures, Apple sees multimedia as an essential part of its present and future computing systems. Unlike IBM it has made support for a range of data types an integral part of all its products since the mid-1980s. All Macintoshes have built-in speakers to play digitised sound in stereo and can support grey scale or colour images and animations. Several have support for sound input or a built-in microphone and a video port through which to play back presentations. Video capture and hardware-assisted play back have been supported by boards from third party suppliers. The new range of Power Macs, based on the Power PC processor, includes support for telephony, voice recognition, sound generation, and improved handling of digital video.

Apple also sees CD-ROM as an important way to push the market forward and was one of the first companies to include an internal drive in its machines as a standard feature. A multimedia version of the Performa 600, for example, includes a double-speed multisession CD-ROM drive that can play Photo CDs.

Key software products, which are bundled with the hardware, include HyperCard, an authoring tool that can be used to organise information in a non-linear way, and QuickTime. The latter, described in more detail in Section 5.3.3, provides software support for sound, video and animation (which Apple describes as dynamic data), software compression and decompression, and standards for file formats and interfaces.

5.2.3   UNIX workstations

The UNIX workstation market currently lacks the impetus given to the personal computer market by the activities of the MPC group, described above. However, multimedia is a natural extension of many applications such as document image processing that currently run on these platforms. They are particularly suitable for applications that combine advanced 2D and 3D graphics with multimedia data types.

Sun

Sun was the first of the UNIX workstation vendors to exploit the opportunity offered by multimedia. Audio I/O has been available on the SPARCstation since its launch. Most of Sun's desktop systems currently support 16-bit audio I/O and a connection to the Integrated Services Digital Network (ISDN) - a system that can carry voice, image and data over two 64-Kbit/s telephone lines. A CD-ROM drive that supports the CD-ROM XA (Extended Architecture) and Photo CD specifications is available as an option. Support for still images, motion video and video communications is available in the form of adapters from Sun and third party suppliers. The SunVideo capture/compression card and video camera can be used with any SPARCstation. The systems run Solaris, Sun's operating system, which is based on Unix system V.4. A new version, Solaris Live!, which offers multimedia support, is described in Section 5.3.4.

Silicon Graphics

The Indy workstation, introduced by Silicon Graphics (SGI) in 1993, also provides hardware and software for capturing and communicating sound and image over a network or via an ISDN interface to a digital phone line. It comes with a small digital colour camera on top of the monitor, a microphone, internal speaker and stereo headphone. The Indy supports a wide range of I/O devices (including 3D stereo glasses) and can take analogue video from camcorder, videodisk player or video camera. The audio subsystem supports four-channel stereo input and output at 16-bit sampling rates. As with all SGI's systems, it offers high-performance 2D and 3D graphics on the X Window System. An ambitious user interface - called Indigo

Magic - is designed to incorporate voice recognition so that the microphone can be used to control the workstation. Facilities for desktop conferencing such as call set up and shared whiteboard are supported by SGI's InPerson software.

5.3   System software

5.3.1   Microsoft Windows

With more than 70,000 Windows NT Software Development Kits sold and over 5,000 commercial applications running under Windows, Microsoft justifiably sees its family of operating systems as the foundation of multimedia computing on the desktop. Support for multimedia within Windows is provided by a range of elements:

- Object Linking and Embedding (OLE) technology to let users insert multimedia elements into software programs.
- Media Command Interface (MCI) to allow Windows-compatible applications to control multimedia devices such as CD-ROM drives, audio and animation players. The Digital Video-MCI command set, designed in conjunction with Intel, supports digital video computing.
- Audio Video Interleaved (AVI), a file format for digital video under Windows, designed to be cross-platform compatible.

In addition Microsoft's Visual Basic programming system supports the use of multimedia data types, including digital video, in applications. Visual Basic and Microsoft C++ will be adapted to target new platforms, providing a range of tools for both the linear and interactive video markets.

Video for Windows
Video for Windows consists of a set of tools based on the AVI file format, together with an add-on module for Windows 3.1 and a CD-ROM. It is designed to enable developers to capture and digitise video sequences using an adapter board, edit them and use OLE to incorporate them in a wide range of applications. Users can play the same sequences back, using hardware codecs or runtime software decompression, on all versions of Windows, although the quality will depend upon the hardware. Three software codecs are included in the package: Microsoft's Video and RLE together with Indeo, Intel's video recording and playback technology based on DVI.

The Windows Telephony API
The Windows Telephony application programming interface (TAPI) was created by Intel and Microsoft as a standard interface for the integration of telephones and personal computers. It will allow applications programs to control basic telephony functions such as call set up, answering and termination, as well as supplementary

functions such as hold, transfer, conference and call park. It is independent of the underlying telephone network and equipment. A personal computer can be connected directly to the telephone network or through a telephone. Multiple personal computers can share telephone resources through a voice server. Alternatively a server can be connected through a switch-to-host link.

Multimedia Viewer Publishing Toolkit

The Multimedia Viewer is intended to meet the needs of multimedia publishers. Designed for use with an MPC or equivalent platform, it provides both authoring tools to enable publishers to create titles and runtime software to allow end users to play them back.

5.3.2 Multimedia Presentation Manager/2

To support its Ultimedia hardware, IBM provides a multimedia version of its graphical user interface, Presentation Manager. This extends the OS/2 operating system to allow applications to control a wide variety of devices in a standardised manner. Features include:

- a common interface for the control of logical and physical devices;
- services for reading, writing and manipulating multimedia data objects;
- support for a variety of formats for image and audio files;
- data streaming and synchronisation for the transfer of large amounts of data from one device to another;
- close captioning to provide a visual representation of spoken words;
- a series of mini programs called 'applets', each of which is designed to accomplish a single task such as playing an audio device.

The standard user interface conforms to IBM's Common User Access (CUA) specification. An optional toolkit contains sample programs and documentation together with C language bindings to assist the developer.

5.3.3 QuickTime

The main competitor to Video for Windows is Apple's QuickTime, an open software architecture that integrates dynamic data, such as sound, video and animation, for which Apple uses the term 'Movie'. Apple intends to make QuickTime available on a broad range of platforms. The first of these, QuickTime for Windows, is the same as QuickTime 1.0 on the Macintosh.

QuickTime introduces a new Movie file format that can be used to contain dynamic data. Within a Movie file, homogeneous data, such as video or sound, is grouped into tracks. QuickTime takes care of synchronisation of these tracks when the Movie file is played back. It has become part of Apple's system software, providing a standard platform for multimedia development.

The QuickTime architecture consists of system software, file formats, Apple compressors and human interface standards. There are three basic components to the system software:

- Movie Toolbox, a set of system software services, enables developers to incorporate support for sound, video and animation in their applications;
- Image Compression Manager (ICM) allows developers to take advantage of numerous compression schemes within their applications without having to make modifications;
- Component Manager registers the capabilities of external system resources such as digitiser cards and VCRs with the Macintosh system software so that any application can access these capabilities.

QuickTime supports two file formats. The Movie file format is a container for all dynamic data. This will provide developers of cross-platform applications with a standard way of exchanging dynamic data from one computing environment to another. The second format consists of extensions to PICT, Apple's standard file format for graphics information. These will support any image compression scheme registered with the Compression Manager. In addition previewing of small thumbnail versions of pictures makes it easier to browse still image libraries. There is a choice of three schemes for software compression and decompression of still images, animations and video.

Human interface standards are supported by guidelines for dynamic media that will ensure ease of use and consistency across applications. There are two main components. The standard movie controller provides users with a consistent way to control movies whilst the standard file dialogue box offers developers a preview option for still images and video.

The first version of QuickTime was released at the end of 1991. Version 1.5, announced in October 1992, includes a new compression algorithm called Compact Video, which was developed by SuperMac Technology, a closed-captioned text track to provide captions over movies, and software support for Photo CD. The software includes a slide show viewer and thumbnail browsers.

Apple has announced moves to integrate Avid Technology's Open Media Framework (OMF) Interchange with QuickTime in order to provide support for digital video editing. OMF Interchange, which has been endorsed by over 30 vendors, provides a standard for broadcast-quality digital video with accompanying audio over networks in a way that is independent of both device and system type (Avid 1993). It is designed to encapsulate all the information required to transport a variety of digital media as well as rules for combining and presenting the media. The OMF and Movie formats will eventually be integrated to form a single media integration standard.

5.3.4   Solaris Live!

Solaris Live! is a new multimedia environment for Sun's workstations that provides an umbrella definition for all multimedia software. Pulling together new and existing facilities, it includes:

- an imaging library and APIs to support the capture, display, compression, decompression, transformation, storage and retrieval of video and image data;
- libraries for 2D and 3D graphics applications;
- driver interfaces for capturing, manipulating and playing 8- and 16-bit audio data streams;
- tools to allow multimedia to be integrated into an application or sent over the network;
- tools to support the capture and playback of image and audio.

Future directions for Solaris include integration with telephone systems, whilst object-oriented extensions through Project DOE (Distributed Objects Everywhere) are intended to make the development and deployment of distributed multimedia easier.

5.4   Future directions

5.4.1   Personal computers for real-time communications

The first generation of platforms for multimedia were designed for standalone applications. In future multimedia information will be accessed over local or wide area networks in both stored and real-time applications. A new generation of products, which can support ad hoc communications between two or more people in the normal office environment, are coming onto the market.

Choice of system
These personal computers, designed to support real-time audio and video communications on the desktop, have to satisfy a number of technical requirements:

- they must support cameras and audio telephony equipment that have not been part of the traditional personal computer;
- they must be able to transmit real-time video and audio over wide area and (eventually) local area networks;
- they must be compatible with H.320 - the emerging international family of standards for audiovisual telephony;
- they must support data sharing and manipulation by two or more users.

They must also fit into the normal personal computer environment. For most businesses this is likely to be a combination of Intel 80x86 processors, with MS Windows and a network operating system such as Novell NetWare.

The new products, which I will call *video PCs*, are intended for ad hoc use in the normal office environment, in contrast to conventional videoconferencing equipment that is used in specially equipped studios or conference rooms that have to be booked in advance. Lower prices are reflected in reduced quality of video and audio and, in many cases, the absence of features such as control of background noise and echo cancellation. These machines differ from conventional videoconferencing systems in a variety of ways:

- they are not intended to be dedicated videoconferencing terminals; users will therefore have access to all the normal programs and features on their PCs;
- they are designed to run in the normal desktop environment (e.g. Microsoft Windows); users will thus use the keyboard and mouse to access software tools and to initiate calls;
- video output will appear within a window on a standard 14-inch monitor, in contrast to the large full-screen monitors (20-inch and above) provided with all standard videoconferencing systems;
- a telephone handset is usually provided for audio communications;
- prices are much lower than those for videoconferencing systems, typically £3,500 as opposed to £8-10,000 for an entry-level rollabout system.

Customers may purchase these video PCs either as an upgrade kit consisting of camera, one or more add-in boards and software, or as a complete system. For around £3,500 at the time of writing, a 486-based PC can be equipped with a video camera, a *codec* to code analogue audio or video information in digital form and decode digital data back into analogue form, and an ISDN connection.

These products should be assessed for quality as well as price. Quality may be measured in terms of the resolution of the screen in pixels and the rate at which it is refreshed. All managers are familiar with broadcast TV standards and may wish to assess new video products against this background. In Europe the TV standards specify a 625-line screen updated at 25 frames per second (fps). In contrast two formats have been adopted for the H.320 visual telephony standards: the Common Intermediate Format (CIF) which is 352 × 288 pixels and Quarter CIF (QCIF) which is 176 × 144 pixels. Frame rates on video PCs are generally between 10 and 15 fps, but may be slower if the network is heavily loaded.

The combination of QCIF resolution and a slow frame rate in a small window on a 14-inch PC may well prove unacceptable for sustained communications in the office environment. Other problems may arise where video PCs are linked to other videoconferencing equipment and low-resolution images are projected onto 27-inch monitors in conference rooms. Because of these limitations, users may find that the greatest benefit of video PCs is their ability to combine audio telephony with desktop computing facilities.

Suppliers

Video PCs are now available from an unusually disparate set of companies, ranging from traditional videoconferencing suppliers such as Compression Labs and PictureTel, through telephone operators such as BT and telephone equipment suppliers such as Northern Telecom, to PC manufacturers such as IBM, Olivetti and NCR, and microprocessor suppliers like Intel. All these companies see desktop communications as an important market.

During the first few years these video PCs will be sold mainly to value-added resellers (VARs) - who will use them to develop and sell specific applications such as kiosks linked to remote experts in the retail and banking sectors - and to a few large end users who need to be ahead of the market. To encourage these activities, many suppliers are providing toolkits to build applications. IBM and BT have also published the application programming interface for the video communication system they have developed (BT 1992).

Prices will remain comparatively high until processors become available in volume. Motorola, for example, is currently integrating BT's video coding technology into a multimedia communications processor set that will be capable of handling real-time video, still image and data. The planned availability of this processor set was mid-1994 at a cost of around $100 in volume. By 1995 it will be possible for personal computers to incorporate the processor set on the motherboard - like VGA processors today. As a result BT expects the price of its codec to fall by around one-third each year. However, the cost of other components, particularly cameras, is unlikely to fall by a similar rate so video personal computers are unlikely to become commonplace on the desktop until the end of the decade.

Compression Labs (CLI)

CLI's Cameo Personal Video System was the first to provide video telephony over standard ISDN lines to a desktop computer. Cameo Model 2001 is currently available on Macintosh IIci, IIfx and Quadra platforms, under System 7 with QuickTime, plus ISDN and video digitising cards. The system includes an external video processor and camera. One full 64-Kbit/s channel is devoted to voice, the second is used for video at frame rates up to 15 fps. The transfer of snapshots and data files is also supported at 128 Kbit/s.

PictureTel

The PictureTel Live! PCS 100 was introduced in July 1993. It is an upgrade kit, pre-packaged for 386- and 486-based PCs using the ISA bus and running MS Windows 3.1. The PCS 100 consists of two add-in boards containing the codec and ISDN terminal; software for file transfer, screen sharing and interactive collaboration; a video camera that can be rotated through 90 degrees to transmit document images and a speakerphone. The product supports the H.320 standard at full CIF resolution. In addition a proprietary audio algorithm may be used to optimise audio bandwidth when communicating with other PictureTel equipment.

BT

BT is playing an important role in the desktop market through the VC8000, a video codec that forms the basis of products from IBM and Olivetti. The codec is marketed as part of BT's Vision Technology. It combines an ISDN interface, video handling and a processor to compress and decompress video signals on one adapter board so that video never has to be moved over the main bus. The VC8000 conforms to the H.320 standards.

BT also sells a self-contained videophone unit - the VC7000 - that consists of a monitor, integral camera, dial keypad and codec. A PC can be connected to the VC7000 to allow the simultaneous transmission of voice, video and data.

IBM

In 1994 IBM introduced ScreenCall, the result of a joint project with BT known as CoCo. ScreenCall combines IBM software derived from its Person-to-Person conferencing product for local area networks (LANs) with BT's Vision Technology (the VC8000 codec, camera, audio unit and connection unit). The software supports audio and videotelephony and the ability to share and annotate materials in a window known as a Chalkboard.

Olivetti

The Personal Communications Computer (PCC) is also designed around BT's Vision Technology. It incorporates Olivetti's IM-Age software (one result of an ESPRIT project called MultiWorks) which supports audio and video telephone calls using a handset linked to the PC, real-time co-operative form filling on screen, exchange of text, sharing the contents of a window with mutual annotation, fast file exchange and the transmission of true-colour, high-definition images.

AT&T Global Information Solutions (GIS)

AT&T, like BT, has developed a video codec, the AVP 4000, which is used by AT&T Global Information Solutions (formerly NCR) in the TeleMedia family of products. The first of these, TeleMedia Connection, is an upgrade kit for personal computers consisting of two adapters and application software (TeleMedia Manager) for Microsoft Windows. A separate ISDN controller card is required. A video camera and external audio unit with microphone and speaker are available.

Northern Telecom

Northern Telecom has developed a set of products for a PC or Macintosh. Visit Voice is a software package that provides screen-based telephony, using personal call management features to control telephone and voice messaging from the PC. Visit Video is an upgrade kit for videoconferencing applications that consists of a video camera, codec, ISDN adapter and software for screen sharing and file exchange. It operates over a 64-Kbit/s ISDN line and, unlike the other products mentioned, over corporate networks using Northern Telecom's Meridian 1 PBX.

Intel

In January 1994 Intel announced its ProShare family of products for personal conferencing. This included two software packages and a video upgrade kit. The ProShare Standard Edition allows two remote users to share a common workspace, whilst the Premier Edition extends these facilities to include the sharing of applications. The ProShare Video System 200 consists of adapters, a video camera, hands-free headset with microphone and the Standard Edition software. Calls can be set up and controlled using a mouse and a graphical keypad.

Unlike the other video PCs described in this section, ProShare is based on a proprietary video compression system - Intel's Indeo technology. At the time of the announcement it was supported by more than 20 other companies. In practice this move is likely to be more significant for communications between users on local area networks, where adherence to international telephony standards is less important, than it is for external communications. It should be noted that Intel also has an agreement with VTEL to license its H.320 conferencing software for incorporation into Intel video system products.

5.4.2   PC bus developments

Within a personal computer, there are three basic types of bus. The control bus conveys control signals, whilst the address bus indicates the address of the data that is being written to or read from memory. The third bus is used to transfer data. This *data bus* normally consists of between 8 and 32 bi-directional lines depending on the capacity of the computer's memory in addressable bits.

In order to support multimedia applications, the requirements for any new data bus must include:

- increased speed;
- standardisation in order to encourage an active market for third party peripherals at low cost;
- compatibility with the existing market for adapter boards.

The original IBM XT had a limited 8-bit data bus. It was followed by the IBM AT with a 16-bit bus that evolved into the ISA (Industry Standard Architecture) bus. The ISA bus is limited to 8 MHz and transmits data at about 1 MB/s, which is adequate for data traffic under DOS but proves to be a bottleneck for graphical user interfaces such as Windows.

In 1987 IBM introduced the Micro Channel Architecture (MCA) for its high-end PS/2s. This was a proprietary architecture and was incompatible with ISA. As a result IBM's competitors announced the Extended ISA (EISA) bus. Both these options are capable of a higher performance than ISA. They have a 16- or 32-bit data path, and were aimed at improving data access to hard disks and LANs rather than graphics performance.

The majority of personal computers sold still have an ISA bus - inadequate for multimedia applications, which consequently need to by-pass the bus. Current video offerings do this either by having all the electronics on one card or by putting cards into adjacent slots with direct connections. However, such an approach may be limited by mundane issues such as the number of slots available for adapter boards. Too few slots may make it impossible for personal computers to be upgraded for video.

A more recent approach to handling high-bandwidth devices such as graphics is to introduce a local bus - a specialised local connection. Two such approaches have been proposed: VL-bus and PCI.

VL-bus

VL-bus is a standard developed by the Video Electronics Standards Association (VESA) and agreed by about 60 companies. In this scheme, peripherals such as graphics, hard disk controller and LAN are given a direct high-bandwidth connection to the central processing unit (CPU) and memory. On a typical 486-based machine this means that such peripherals can access the CPU at 33 MHz on a 32-bit bus. The specification provides for a 64-bit bus in future.

Peripheral Component Interconnect (PCI)

In contrast to VL-bus, which is an extension to the existing personal computer architecture, Intel has announced the Peripheral Component Interconnect (PCI) bus - a completely new kind of motherboard architecture (see Figure 5.1). A PCI-based computer could have expansion slots for ISA, EISA and VL-bus. All peripherals would run on the PCI bus, whilst an I/O bridge can be used to give access to the ISA, EISA or MCA buses for slower peripherals. This scheme would achieve improved data access whilst maintaining compatibility with existing products. A Special Interest Group for PCI was formed in June 1992. Other companies have announced their commitment to PCI - for example, Digital Equipment will use it for its Alpha AXP and Apple with its Power PC products.

PCI is intended to be an open standard, able to handle full-motion video images with sound at a peak bandwidth of 133 MB/s. It will provide 32-bit access at 33 MHz to support a data transfer rate around 67 MB/s.

QuickRing

A future development is QuickRing, Apple's local bus technology, said to be capable of up to three times the speed of VL-bus or PCI with a peak bandwidth of 350 MB/s. QuickRing is an auxiliary bus that uses high-speed circuits to connect the plug-in boards, which can thus access both Apple's NuBus and the higher speed QuickRing local bus. It can achieve data transfer rates of 180 MB/s. Its point-to-point topology will be suitable for applications such as digital video and multimedia. It can support external connections for peripherals and network connections in future.

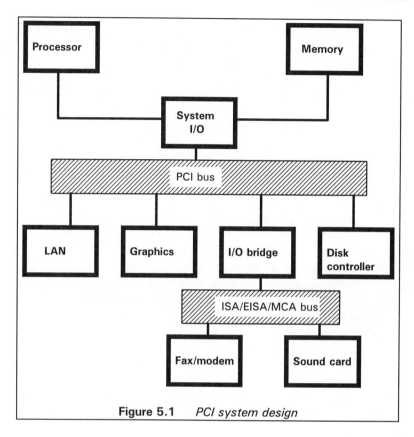

Figure 5.1   *PCI system design*

5.4.3   New standards for video connectors

The choice of a local bus on its own will not be sufficient to solve the problems of handling digital video on a PC. Further improvements can be achieved by redesigning the adapters that slot into these buses and that connect the various digital video and graphics devices. At present these products suffer from lack of bandwidth, leading to poor performance, and high costs as the result of the duplication of components. As with the local bus, solutions have been proposed by separate coalitions: two from VESA and one from Intel and ATI Technologies. Their activities will lead to the development of a new range of graphics boards and accelerated perfomancé for video and graphics applications.

VESA Advanced Features Connector (VAFC) and Media Channel (VMC)
VAFC and VMC were announced in November 1993. The VESA Advanced Features Connector (VAFC) is intended as a low-cost, short-term solution. By

supporting a 32-bit data path instead of the 8 bits currently provided by VGA connectors, it will enable video to be used at resolutions up to 1024 × 768 pixels with 256 colours at a 75-Hz refresh rate.

A more permanent solution is offered by the VESA Media Channel (VMC), which also provides a 32-bit data path. VMC defines a dedicated multimedia bus that provides an independent path for the simultaneous processing of up to 15 high-bandwidth video streams, allowing it to support applications such as videoconferencing with multiple video windows. The maximum transfer rate is 132 MB/s. Video and graphics will be integrated through a shared frame buffer. VMC adapters can be connected to one of the existing bus or local bus architectures - ISA, MCA, EISA, VL-bus or PCI.

Shared Frame Buffer Interconnect (SFBI)

SFBI was announced in August 1993. The Intel-ATI approach is that a single board should be used to connect all graphics and video devices. This will reduce the costs incurred by the duplication of memory and special components, such as digital to analogue converters, on separate adapters for special functions. SFBI will support a data transfer rate of about 100 MB/s in 32-bit mode or up to 200 MB/s for a 64-bit implementation.

Summary

Managers who want to develop multimedia applications are faced with a wide range of platforms for development and delivery. At present these are less than ideal for mainstream business purposes. Most have evolved from the need to develop customised training and retail applications, which were typically expensive standalone systems. Others are adapted to the needs of videographics and entertainment industries, with high levels of support for music and animation. However, recent developments indicate increasing interest amongst suppliers for providing support for multimedia - especially real-time video - in the business environment. Where possible managers should select hardware and software that offer support for recognised industry standards.

References

[Avid 1993] *OMF Interchange Specification: Version 1.0*, Avid Technology, May 18, 1993.

[BT 1992] *Project CoCo: Software API specification*, IBM UK Limited/British Telecommunications plc, July 1992.

[EMB 1994] 'Market report', *European Multimedia Bulletin*, vol. 4, no. 4, pp. 14-15.

[IBM 1992] *Multimedia distributed computing: IBM's directions for multimedia distributed systems*, November 10, 1992.

CHAPTER 6

Development tools

This chapter discusses the choice of tools for building applications and reviews some of the products that are available commercially. The importance of cross-platform compatibility is stressed. Hypertext and hypermedia - a way of representing information in a non-linear way - are introduced. The chapter closes with a review of the high-level standards required to cover the organisation of multimedia data, such as MHEG and HyTime for hypermedia and ODA for compound documents.

6.1 Developing applications

6.1.1 Types of development tool

In addition to all the hardware equipment and components described in the previous chapter, developers will also need software tools for building multimedia applications. These tools allow the developer to carry out tasks such as editing audio and video data from files. They can be used to build prototype applications. In some cases, they may be sufficient to create production versions.

Commercial products are available to suit a range of needs, from sales managers who want to create their own presentations on personal computers to professional developers who want to build major training or retail applications.

Presentation tools
Traditional business presentations make use of 35-mm slides or foils for the overhead projector. Presentation packages enhance or replace these aids, allowing

users who are not videographics professionals to create multimedia presentations on a PC. They will be able to capture video from a camcorder, combine it with computer-generated graphics and animations and output the result to videotape. Such packages may include a 'timeline' on the screen to enable the user to edit image and audio data into a time-dependent sequence. Dynamic presentation tools allow them to generate presentations that can be run on the computer from magnetic or optical disk. These packages are supported by disks containing clip media - collections of images, audio and video clips - supplied either with the presentation tools or by third party suppliers. Such products are intended to appeal to creative directors, sales and marketing executives, graphics artists and corporate designers.

Authoring tools

Authoring tools, in contrast, are designed for professional application developers, enabling them to create interactive multimedia applications such as courseware or point-of-information systems. They support features such as layout, graphic design, animation, control of branching and navigation - the manner in which the end user will be able to move through the application. This control may be based on a hypertext approach, described in more detail in Section 6.1.3, by which the user can choose to follow links that connect nodes, which contain a wide variety of data types - including animation, audio and video.

Authoring tools may also provide screen design tools to support the layout of text, images and 'hotspots' - places where user interaction is required. Libraries may support audiovisual and graphics functions and implement multitasking capabilities under different operating systems.

Scripting languages

A script is a set of commands written in a form that resembles a computer program. Such a set can be associated with an interactive element - a button, for example - on the screen. Commercial toolkits often have their own scripting languages, supported by script editors, interpreters and debuggers. MacroMedia's Director has Lingo, Asymetrix's Multimedia ToolBook has OpenScript, while Apple's HyperCard has HyperTalk, as we have already seen. The availability of a programming language such as C on many different platforms helps to ensure the portability of software written in that language. In the same way, a scripting language that is available on different platforms will make it possible to write a multimedia application that can be played on a variety of delivery machines. ScriptX, from Kaleida Labs, is intended to fill this role.

Iconic interfaces

Some authoring tools employ a form of visual programming, using icons, to create a two-dimensional graphic design that allows authors to visualise and edit applications. Individual screens are represented by elements in a flow chart. Authors create paths that the end user can follow by placing specific icon elements on the flow chart and linking them to other elements.

Tools for real-time video

Applications, such as remote consultations, that incorporate audiovisual telephony will require additional support. This may include directory services (to provide a name-based directory that includes the appropriate addresses for telephone, data and video) and a call set-up service to take the address and establish the appropriate network connections. Suppliers of the video PCs described in Section 5.4.1, such as PictureTel and Olivetti, sell software tools to allow developers to build real-time video applications.

Programming languages

Commercial authoring packages, though useful for building prototypes, have limitations for the development of production systems. Each package has its own 'look and feel' which it tends to impart to all the applications that it has been used to build. This may be unacceptable to companies who want to create applications that reflect their own house style. In addition, system overheads may be incurred, which prevent the application from achieving the sort of fast response times that are acceptable to users, who now have very high expectation levels. Developers may therefore find that they need to create their own tools to handle all or part of an application, using a third generation language such as C. An object-oriented language such as Smalltalk or C++ might also be used. In an object-oriented system, the data and its related procedures are packaged together as software objects, an approach that is well suited to the development of multimedia applications. Many of the authoring tools discussed in this chapter have adopted an object-oriented approach. In some cases libraries of standard objects (known as class libraries) are available. Chapter 18 provides an overview for readers who are not familiar with the technology.

6.1.2   Cross-platform compatibility

In practice many developers may wish to be able to develop an application that is capable of running on more than one delivery platform. Considerable savings in time and resources can be made, both in developing and in maintaining applications, if this can be achieved. There are several ways to do so:

- by using a commercial tool, such as MacroMedia Director, that provides run-time software to allow applications to be played back on both the Macintosh and the IBM PC;
- by choosing a scripting language, such as ScriptX, with cross-industry support which ensures that applications can be played back on all conforming platforms;
- by adopting an industry-approved or international standard, as these become available.

Support for standards in commercial products is still very limited. Industry standards are currently subject to approval by the IMA, as described below. International standards, mostly still under development, are covered in Section 6.4.

Interactive Multimedia Association (IMA)

Founded in 1988 the IMA is a professional trade association of companies, institutions and individuals involved in producing and using interactive multimedia technology. Its members include Apple, IBM, Intel, Philips and Sun. The IMA defines a multimedia platform as 'any hardware, operating environment and applications program interface (API) implementation that provides multimedia capability'. Different classes of platform will share basic characteristics and similar functionality.

Under its Compatibility Project, which is designed to ensure compatibility within a group of similar platforms, the IMA will develop or adopt specifications for each class covering an API and minimum hardware capabilities. The first such specification has already been published (IMA 1991). It defines a command set and interface specification to allow applications based on interactive video and DOS to run on different systems without modification. The US Department of Defense (DoD) has adopted this specification as a military standard, MilStd 1379/D, for all hardware and applications procurements from March 1991 onwards. The IMA is also working with the National Institute for Standards and Technology (NIST) to develop a family of Federal Information Processing Standards (FIPS) to cover multimedia procurements for the Federal Government. As the DoD and US Federal Government are the largest users of multimedia in the world, these moves towards standardisation are likely to have a major impact on the industry.

The IMA's Architecture Technical Working Group, formed in 1991, has decided upon an architectural model for cross-platform compatibility, whilst the Digital Audio Group has recommended an interchange format. Focus Groups have been formed to develop industry recommendations for data and file exchange, multimedia scripting languages and software services.

6.1.3 Hypertext and hypermedia

Hypertext or hypermedia provides a way of representing and managing information in a flexible and non-linear way that is appropriate for many multimedia applications. Instead of passively watching a program on mammals, for example, the user can choose his or her own route through the material provided. The user does this by following a series of links that lead to related pieces of text or other types of data.

Vannevar Bush, President Roosevelt's Science Adviser, is generally credited with the first description of a hypertext system. His proposed Memex was a machine for browsing and making notes in an extensive on-line text and graphics system. Its essential feature was the ability to tie two items together because 'the human mind

... operates by association. Man cannot hope fully to duplicate this mental process artificially, but he certainly ought to be able to learn from it' (Bush 1945). Bush's ideas were taken up and advanced by Douglas Engelbart at Stanford Research Institute (SRI) during the 1960s and by Ted Nelson who coined the term 'hypertext'.

Basic terminology

In a *hypertext* system objects in a database, called *nodes*, are connected to one another by machine-supported *links*. The user can follow these links from node to node in order to access the information they contain. The contents of a node (normally text) may be displayed in a *window* on a computer screen. Such a window can be moved, resized, closed and stored as a window icon. The contents of a node may be scrolled behind the window. Windows can contain any number of *link icons* (also called *targets* or *buttons*). These are words or phrases, usually highlighted, which represent pointers to other nodes in the database (see Figure 6.1). Clicking on the icon with the mouse activates the link and causes the system to open a new window to display the selected node. Users can create new nodes and add new links.

Hypertext systems can be accessed in any one of three ways: by selecting link icons and following the links from node to node, by searching the database for some keyword in the normal way, or by navigating the database using a *browser* that displays the network as a *graph*. The sequence of nodes that the user has accessed forms a *path* (Bergoray 1990).

In *hypermedia* systems a node may contain any information that can be controlled, presented and edited on a computer (e.g. text, graphics, animation, images, sound). The terms 'hypertext' and 'hypermedia' are frequently interchanged.

Types of hypermedia system

There are four broad types of system based on hypermedia technology (Conklin 1987):

1. General purpose systems are available today in commercial implementations.
2. Problem exploration tools are designed to support early unstructured thinking in problem solving or project design.
3. Browsing systems are intended for teaching, reference and public information where ease of use and ease of learning are crucial.
4. Macro literary systems are large-scale implementations that have been proposed to support large on-line libraries in which all links between documents are machine supported. They derive from the mostly hypothetical work of Bush, Engelbart and Nelson described above.

A number of early systems were designed to provide platforms for experimentation with hypertext in a range of applications. HyperCard remains the best known and most widely used commercial system, though many prototypes have been developed in academic or research groups.

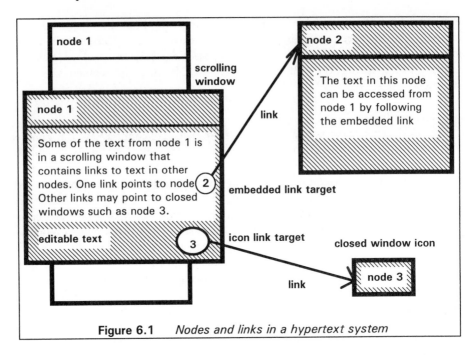

Figure 6.1   *Nodes and links in a hypertext system*

Interest in the use of hypermedia has been greatly increased by the success of the World Wide Web (WWW) project, a distributed hypermedia system started by CERN (the European Laboratory for Particle Physics). Information providers set up hypermedia servers on the Web, which can be accessed by browser programs over the Internet. The browser reads hypermedia documents and can fetch a related document from another source. If the server has search capabilities, the browsers will permit searches of documents and databases.

The Dexter Hypertext Reference Model

The variety of hypertext projects led to inconsistencies of approach and terminology. To remedy this, a workshop was organised at the Dexter Inn in New Hampshire in 1988 to achieve consensus on basic hypertext concepts. The result of this group's activities were later formalised in a paper first presented in 1990. The Dexter Hypertext Reference Model (Halasz 1994) provides a standard terminology with a formal model of the important abstractions found in a wide range of hypertext (and hypermedia) systems. It thus serves as a standard against which to compare the functionality of these systems. It also makes it possible to develop other standards for interchange and interoperability between different hypertext systems.

Dexter divides a hypertext system into three layers as shown in Figure 6.2:

- the *runtime* layer controls the user interface;
- the *storage* layer is a database containing a network of nodes (called

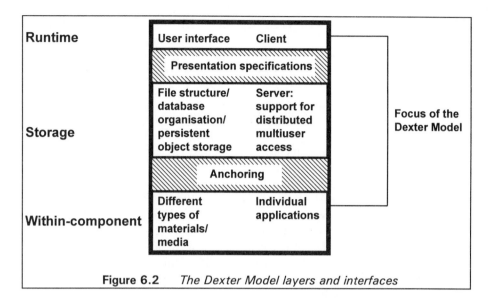

Figure 6.2   *The Dexter Model layers and interfaces*

components) connected by links;
- the *within-component* layer is the content structure inside the nodes.

The main focus of the model is on the storage layer, which consists of a set of components. The interface between storage and the runtime layers includes *presentation specifications* that determine how components are presented at runtime. These specifications might include information on screen location and the size of a window, for example. The within-component layer corresponds to individual applications. Its interface to the storage layer is via *anchors* that consist of an *identifier*, which can be referred to by links, and a *value* that picks out the anchored part of the material. The runtime layer is responsible for handling links, anchors and components at runtime.

Further work carried out in the DeVise hypermedia (DHM) project at Aarhus University in Denmark (Grønbæk 1994) extends the model in a number of ways. DeVise supports authoring as well as browsing. The project developed a set of tools and a prototype implementation. The Dexter Model provides a leading formal model for interconnecting textual data. It forms one basis for the HyTime standard, described in Section 6.3.1 (Bryan 1994).

6.2   Commercial tools

6.2.1   Authoring tools

Application development tools can be obtained from a variety of different suppliers.

Some hardware vendors provide such tools themselves to support development on their multimedia platforms. We have already seen some of these from IBM, Apple and Sun in the last chapter. In addition, companies such as VideoLogic and FAST that supply adapter boards also provide software development kits for their products.

Major systems software suppliers such as Microsoft and Novell are also interested in multimedia and supply (or plan to supply) packages to support it. Another group of software companies specialises in selling authoring tools and related packages such as clip art libraries. These include Asymetrix, MacroMedia (formed from MacroMind, Paracomp and Authorware) and AimTech. Table 6.1 presents a summary of the most popular tools.

In order to compete, these products need to provide high levels of added value - functionality well beyond the software tools that come with the hardware or system software. They come in a range of levels to suit different groups of users. For example, MacroMedia supplies four packages, of which Action! is designed for the general business presentation market and MediaMaker for desktop video publishing, whilst Director and Authorware Professional are intended for developers of professional multimedia applications.

Other tools are the result of research projects. One such project, MultiWorks, which was funded by the European Commission through its Esprit programme, led to the development of a number of hardware and software systems, including IM-Age from Olivetti. IM-Age, which is a system for authoring and delivering open interactive multimedia presentations for Windows, now forms part of the software that will be available to developers on Olivetti's video PC - the Personal Communications Computer.

Authorware Professional

Authorware Professional from MacroMedia is a cross-platform authoring package that allows the developer to edit presentations on either the Macintosh or Windows using a visual programming interface with a small number of icons.

Table 6.1   Authoring and presentation tools

Product	Platform	Supplier
Authorware Professional	Macintosh Windows	MacroMedia
Director	Macintosh Windows	MacroMedia
HyperCard	Macintosh	Apple
IconAuthor	Windows	AimTech Corp
LinkWay 2/LinkWay Live!	DOS	IBM
Multimedia ToolBook	Windows	Asymetrix Corp
Storyboard Live!	DOS	IBM
ToolBook	Windows	Asymetrix Corp

Director

MacroMedia also supplies Director, a tool for creating professional multimedia presentations, animations and interactive applications on the Macintosh. It provides an overview for the high-level design and assembly of the basic elements of the application, plus support for the detailed design of individual elements. It includes support for graphics and animation, timeline and an interactive scripting language called Lingo. Runtime support (called Players) is available for both Macintosh and PC platforms.

HyperCard

HyperCard, introduced in 1987, is a tool for the organisation of information in a non-linear way using a box of index cards as a model. The user stores information - a mixture of text, graphics, numbers and sound - on the cards, which can be displayed on the Macintosh screen. Groups of cards can be organised into 'stacks'. Specific tasks such as sorting, browsing, or printing a report are undertaken by clicking on buttons. Scripts to give directions to the buttons can be written in the HyperTalk language.

IconAuthor

IconAuthor from AimTech Corp uses a visual programming approach rather than a scripting language to define the interaction and flow of control. The set of icons corresponds closely to actions found in conventional programming languages, with additional icons for media-specific presentation and interaction.

LinkWay

IBM supplies two authoring packages for its personal computers under DOS, designed to work with its audio and video adapters. LinkWay can be used by teachers and courseware developers to create interactive hypermedia applications for training and education. Icons are used to provide links between screens.

Storyboard Live!

A second authoring package, called Storyboard Live!, from IBM is intended for use by presenters and design consultants who want to develop presentations and kiosk applications. It consists of five modules. The first of these, Electronic Presentation, creates the storyline for the presentation. Picture Maker is used to edit images and graphics, Story Editor to include video from a video camera or VCR, Picture Taker to capture and import screen images, and Story Teller to play back the presentation.

Multimedia ToolBook

ToolBook from Asymetrix is a visual programming system (Figure 6.3). MultimediaToolBook provides additional capabilities including animation and full-motion video editing. The user constructs a 'book' that consists of a series of pages. Each page may have one or more objects, such as buttons, graphics and text. Interactivity is provided by associating a script with an object that the user can

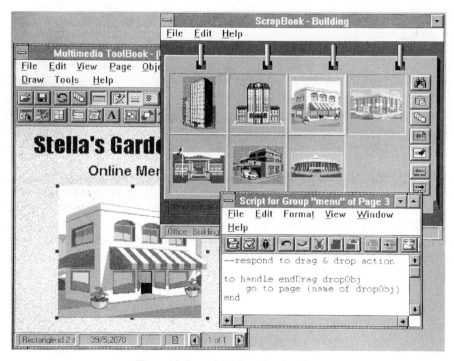

Figure 6.3   *Multimedia ToolBook*

select. ToolBook has a scripting language called OpenScript, through which scripts can be associated with a specific object and activated using message passing.

6.2.2   The role of ScriptX

Unlike the authoring packages described above, ScriptX was intended from the start as a solution to the problem of cross-platform compatibility. Kaleida Labs, a joint venture between Apple and IBM, was formed in mid-1992 to work on advanced multimedia programming and runtime technologies to be used in the next generation of interactive software across a broad range of hardware platforms.

The Kaleida Platform consists of the development framework and the Kaleida Media Player. ScriptX is an object-oriented development framework - a library with more than 250 core classes and a set of tools to use these classes to create applications (EMB 1994). If an author creates a ScriptX title on any of the supported authoring platforms, that title will be portable and may be played back from CD-ROM or over a network on any runtime system that has installed the Kaleida Media Player, a software package for handling interactive multimedia applications. Initially versions will be available for Apple Macintosh System 7 and Windows 3.1. Other delivery platforms are planned, including OS/2, UNIX, PowerPC and various set-top converters for use with a television set.

This cross-platform portability is achieved by saving the file in ScriptX format, rather as the PostScript format is currently used for files intended for desktop publishing. The title does not normally contain any platform-specific information - all the media and scripting commands are stored in a platform-independent manner in the title files. These files will be able to recognise the limitations of the playback system and adjust the title to play at an optimal speed on that machine. In addition libraries of ScriptX objects can be created and moved between applications. These objects may contain audio, video, behaviours and combinations of these data types. Other objects can be used to incorporate information about ownership of content and payment of licence fees. They can even hold authorisation codes that can be used to prevent children gaining access to unsuitable material, for example.

From the developer's point of view, ScriptX offers the possibility of significant cost savings and a reduction in risk, since the same application will run on several different platforms. A number of hardware vendors, including Apple, IBM, Hitachi, Mitsubishi and Toshiba, have endorsed ScriptX by joining the Kaleida Alliance. Content developers, publishers and other media creators can join the Kaleida Worldwide Developer Program, which provides training as well as early access to the software development kit. ScriptX has been submitted to the Interactive Multimedia Association for consideration as the IMA's Recommended Practice for Multimedia Scripting.

6.3   Standards

Standards are required at all levels of a multimedia system, from the physical requirements of the network to the design of the user interface. Current standards for multimedia can be classified as those related to the content of the material, which are discussed in the appropriate chapters under compression, and those which govern its structure. The latter include the activities described below on the structure of documents in general, such as SGML and ODA, and those that concern multimedia and hypermedia in particular, such as HyTime and MHEG.

At international level the relevant work is carried out mainly by two bodies, ISO and ITU-T. Standardisation of information technology is handled by a Joint Technical Committee (JTC1) of the International Organisation for Standardisation (ISO) and the International Electrotechnical Commission (IEC). JTC1 is organised into subcommittees (SC) and working groups (WG). The results of their discussions go through a series of drafts before being published as an international standard (IS). Standardisation of telecommunications is handled by the Telecommunication Standardisation Sector of the International Telecommunication Union (ITU-T), which publishes Recommendations. In some cases ISO and ITU have set up joint working groups under the JTC1 umbrella. Individual members of these working groups represent their respective nations.

Information on standards that are relevant to hypermedia and multimedia is available from Open Information Interchange (OII) in Luxembourg. OII is an initiative within the IMPACT programme of the Commission of the European Communities Directorate General (DG XIII B), whose objective is to promote awareness and use of media-independent coding standards for information interchange in the electronic information services market.

6.3.1   Standards for document architecture

The concept of a standard for electronic documents has evolved over a number of years. Two standards developed during the 1980s separate the logical structure of a document from its appearance. Neither SGML nor ODA was intended to deal specifically with multimedia. That is done by a new standard called HyTime.

Standard Generalised Markup Language (SGML)
SGML, a language for formally describing the structure and content of documents, is based on work done in the late 1960s. SGML is also the syntax used by the documents so described. It was published in 1986 by ISO as IS 8879. This standard covers the content of a document and its logical structure in terms of such things as headers and paragraphs. Activity on SGML continues in JTC1/SC18/WG8.

SGML is based on the concept of document type definitions (DTDs). These can be used to govern the creation of documents that conform to the definition. They are not limited to documents that can be printed and can thus be used for multimedia documents on compact disk, for example. Whilst SGML states how a DTD should be specified it does not control the DTDs themselves, which are created by individuals, companies or consortia. The Open Software Foundation, for example, has announced two DTDs, one for large technical books and one for reference pages.

SGML marked an important move in the direction of separating information from its presentation, thus making possible different presentations of the same information. It is now supported by an increasing number of products and services and by SGML Open, a non-profit international consortium of companies that provide them.

Open Document Architecture
The next steps were to include the layout of the document and to extend the scope of its content. These resulted in Open Document Architecture (ODA), a joint ISO/ITU activity (JTC1/SC18/WG3). ODA takes a similar approach to SGML but stresses blind interchange. It is intended for marking up certain classes of documents so that they can be transferred between systems from different computer companies without loss of structural information. In theory each company provides two document converters, between ODA and its own standard. If there are eight companies in the group, 16 converters are required. This is clearly much better than having to provide converters between all possible internal formats since, if there are n companies involved, $n*(n-1)$ converters will be required - 56 converters for a

group of eight companies. In practice the weakness of ODA has proved to be the lack of commercial support and the length of time required for the standards committees to establish new document application profiles.

ODA has been published by ISO as IS 8613 and by ITU-T as the T.410 Series Recommendations. These define three types of ODA document:

1. Processible documents interchange the logical structure (e.g. subordinate chapters, sections and paragraphs), allowing the person who receives the document to revise it.
2. Formatted documents interchange the layout structure as a sequence of pages, with positional information such as areas defined for character content, for example, and fonts. They are non-revisable and can merely be printed out.
3. Formatted processible documents allow both the logical and layout structure to be interchanged, making them more flexible. The receiver can print the image or edit it first.

ODA supports the markup of both layout and content. The document architecture is separate from the content structure. Table 6.2 shows the three content structures that have been defined so far.

Work is in progress on other types of content, including audio, on support for hypermedia (known as HyperODA) and for data in documents. Planned extensions include new content architectures for image and moving pictures and an interface to MHEG (described in the next section). There is also activity on functional profiles to reduce the scope of the standard for simple applications. The ITU-T T.501 Series Recommendations cover document application profiles for the interchange of different types of documents.

HyTime

The Hypermedia/Time-based Document Structuring Language, known as HyTime, (IS 10744), was published in November 1992. It seeks to standardise some of the facilities required by all hypermedia applications, in particular those concerned with the addressing of portions of hypermedia documents and their component multimedia information objects, including linking, alignment and synchronisation.

Table 6.2   ODA content formats

Content	Related ISO standards	Related ITU-T standards
Character	Coded character sets for text communication (IS 6937) 8-bit coded graphic character sets (IS 8859)	Character content architectures (T.416)
Geometric graphics	Computer Graphics Metafile (IS 8632)	Geometric graphics content architecture (T.418)
Raster graphics		Raster graphics content architectures (T.417)

It does not standardise data content notations, encoding of information objects or application processing. HyTime will allow a complete multimedia application - including its structure, hypermedia links, synchronisation and timing - to be encoded in a linear stream.

HyTime is built upon the Standard Generalised Markup Language (SGML) and will use Abstract Syntax Notation 1 (ASN.1) to allow bit string representation for interchange. It complements standards for individual multimedia objects such as JPEG for still images and MPEG for audiovisual material (Goldfarb 1991).

HyTime 'engines' must be able to separate HyTime attributes from other SGML attributes, validate them and associate certain actions with each HyTime element. Only one commercial product has been announced so far: TechnoTeacher, Inc. is developing a C++ class library called HyMinder, based on its MarkMinder product for SGML (Bryan 1994).

6.3.2   Standards for interaction

Another new set of standards covers the exchange of information and interaction between applications. These activities follow work undertaken in France during the 1980s by AFNOR, the French national standards body, which led to proposals on audiovisual scripts.

MHEG
The Multimedia and Hypermedia Information Coding Expert Group (MHEG) is a joint ISO/ITU activity (JTC1/SC29/WG12) that is working to define the representation and encoding of multimedia and hypermedia information objects that will be interchanged within or across applications or services (Colaitis 1993). Its aim is to enable bit stream specifications for multimedia and hypermedia applications on any platform. MHEG covers topics such as synchronisation, buffer memory, input objects - buttons or menus, for example - and interactive objects like prompts. It is designed to meet the requirements of multimedia applications running on workstations from different vendors and interchanging information in real time. Such applications include computer-supported co-operative work, electronic publishing and audiovisual systems for training and education. The MHEG standard is being developed in two parts: Part I covers ASN.1 notation and Part II deals with SGML-based notation. Both should become international standards (IS 13522) in 1994.

SMSL
The Standard Multimedia/Hypermedia Scripting Language (SMSL) is another joint ISO/ITU activity, which involves the SGML and MHEG working groups. It is concerned with the development of scripts that control user interaction with multimedia and hypermedia documents. Formerly known as Audiovisual Interactive Scripts, it has been renamed to avoid confusion with ITU-T work on AVI Services (AVIS). SMSL is intended to enable cross-platform compatibility and portability of

multimedia scripts.

The SGML group is interested in defining a data model, based on the HyTime and SGML standards, which could be used to define a set of services that could be implemented by various scripting language vendors. It is currently collecting contributions from interested parties and expected to launch a committee draft (CD) during 1994.

The MHEG group is studying appropriate coding methods, as an extension to the work already done. Members are currently involved in a study as to how existing scripting products could be integrated in the future standard (Fromont 1993).

6.3.3   Frameworks and reference models

As we have seen, multimedia affects many different areas of application development. No single reference model yet exists to pull these pieces together and specify how they should interface with one another. The OII initiated a preliminary study in this area (REFMOD 1993) which identified three existing reference models - ODP, the Berkom Reference Model and MHMF - that may contribute to a future model for information interchange. Further work in this area is planned. The consensus at present is that this should aim to help users rather than standards makers and should therefore take place outside the framework of the standards institutions.

Open Distributed Processing (ODP)
ODP is a joint ISO/ITU activity (JTC1/SC21/WG7) whose objective is to enable distributed system components to interwork in heterogeneous environments. The profiles and application standards that have been developed should be relevant to distributed multimedia applications.

The Berkom Reference Model
Berlin Communications System (Berkom) is an R&D activity initiated by Deutsche Bundespost to promote services for its future broadband optical fibre network. The Reference Model consist of three main platforms:

- an interworking platform that provides a network interface for multimedia end systems;
- a communications platform that provides the transport interface to multimedia teleservices;
- a generic applications platform that provides different applications with an interface based on generic multimedia teleservices.

It is intended to serve as a basis for a multimedia-specific application programming interface. This is considered to be critical for multimedia applications that are portable across different platforms and will also support integration of different media.

Multimedia/Hypermedia Model and Framework (MHMF)
MHMF, a JTC1/SC18 activity to provide a framework for current and future multimedia standardisation, is still at an early stage of its development.

Summary

Creating a multimedia system involves a substantial investment in time and money. Managers will wish to ensure that the resulting application is not dependent on a single supplier for support. Wherever possible components of the system should conform to existing standards for file formats, interchange, content and structure. Initiatives are under way that will encourage the development of cross-platform compatibility.

References

[Bergoray 1990] J.A. Bergoray, 'An introduction to hypermedia issues, systems and application areas', *International Journal of Man-Machine Studies*, vol. 33, pp. 121-147.

[Bryan 1994] M. Bryan, 'Why HyTime?', *OII Spectrum*, vol. 1, no. 6, pp. 19-26.

[Bush 1945] V. Bush, 'As we may think', *Atlantic Monthly*, vol. 176, no. 1, pp. 101-108. Reprinted in S. Lambert and S. Ropieque, eds, 'CD-ROM: The New Papyrus', Microsoft Press, 1986.

[Colaitis 1993] F. Colaitis, 'MHEG: the future international standard for multimedia and hypermedia objects', *OII Spectrum*, vol. 1, no. 3, 19-28.

[Conklin 1987] J. Conklin, 'Hypertext: an introduction and survey', *IEEE Computer*, vol. 2, no. 9, pp. 17-41.

[EMB 1994] 'The Kaleida Platform: a review of key benefits', a Kaleida White Paper, reprinted in *European Multimedia Bulletin*, vol. 4, no. 4, pp. 6-11.

[Fromont 1993] 'SMSL: standard multimedia/hypermedia scripting language', *OII Spectrum*, vol. 1, no. 2, pp. 24-31.

[Goldfarb 1991] C.F. Goldfarb, 'HyTime: a standard for structured hypermedia interchange', *IEEE Computer*, vol. 24, no. 8, pp. 81-84.

[Grønbæk 1994] K. Grønbæk and R. Trigg, 'Design issues for a Dexter-based hypermedia system', *Communications of the ACM*, vol. 37, no. 2, pp. 41-49.

[Halasz 1994] F. Halasz and M. Schwartz, 'The Dexter Hypertext Reference Model', *Communications of the ACM*, vol. 37, no. 2, pp. 30-39.

[IMA 1991] IMA Compatibility Committee, *Recommended practices for multimedia portability*, Version 1.1, Interactive Multimedia Association.

[REFMOD 1993] 'An open information interchange reference model - is it feasible?', *OII Spectrum*, vol. 1, no. 3, pp. 11-19.

CHAPTER 7

Image

This chapter outlines the many different types of image that modern computer applications may need to handle. It then describes the technology and components that are required to capture such images. Digitised images require a very large amount of storage space. All images should therefore be compressed, if possible, to reduce the amount of information that has to be stored or transmitted. The chapter closes with a review of the most important international standards that deal with image encoding and compression.

7.1   Images and applications

Computer applications are now required to handle many types of image in a wide variety of applications. Their needs will vary according to the type of image that has to be supported. *Bitonal* (black and white) images include text in business documents such as A4 letters and forms. These images are typically scanned and stored in electronic file folders for use in applications such as insurance claims and mortgage processing. Optical scanning and storage technology are also replacing microform in record management systems where documents such as patents, medical records, taxation forms and bank records need to be archived. Small items such as cheques and credit card vouchers are handled electronically in high-volume transaction processing systems.

A second type of bitonal image, known as line art, includes engineering drawings in computer-aided design (CAD) applications, diagrams in technical manuals for the aerospace and defence sector, charts, flow diagrams, circuit diagrams, maps and cartoons. Some business documents, such as forms, may consist of a mixture of lines, printed text and manuscript. A mixture of scanning and recognition technologies will be needed to handle such images.

Continuous tone images, which include photographs, halftones and single frames from a video, may be grey scale or colour. *Grey scale* images contain several shades of grey. They are used in applications such as page layouts and libraries of press clippings for newspapers and publishers or aerial photographs, satellite information and seismic data in scientific and technical applications. Typically these applications require much higher quality images than the document processing systems referred to earlier. Medical images from magnetic resonance imaging (MRI) and computer-aided tomography (CT) scans, for example, may be used for remote diagnosis by radiologists.

Colour (multispectral) images, such as old books and rare manuscripts for libraries or high-quality images of paintings and display items in art galleries and museums, may be required in some specialised applications. There is an increasing demand for colour photographs in everyday multimedia systems such as electronic catalogues in the retail sector. The range of applications is increasing all the time. For example, consumers as well as professionals can now have their 30-mm colour photographs processed and stored on Photo CDs for display on a TV or computer screen. Clip art libraries containing images can be purchased on floppy disks or CD-ROMs for use in business presentations.

Whilst images can be used to enhance existing applications, the combination of imaging with other technologies - knowledge-based systems or pattern matching algorithms, for example - is opening up promising new areas for investigation and development, such as fingerprints and photographs for identification purposes in security systems.

7.2   Image capture

Most of the types of image outlined above are normally captured using an optical scanner or camera, whose purpose is to convert the image into a rectangular array of points called picture elements (*pixels*). An optical scanning system consists of a light source, a document holder and a light detector. During scanning the light beam moves to and fro across the document. The reflected light from each pass is converted into electrical signals, which in turn are changed into digital form for processing and stored as an array of pixels (or *raster*). The size of this array depends on the type of image to be captured:

1. Bitonal images have only two intensity values and can therefore be held in 1 bit per pixel, with a value of 1 or 0.
2. Grey scale images have several shades of grey. They are held in n bits per pixel, where the number of levels of grey supported is $2^n - 1$ (for example, an image with 15 levels of grey plus white requires 4 bits per pixel to store it).
3. Colour images are characterised by the intensity of three primary colours and

grey. The number of colours simultaneously available that can be supported by n bits is $2^n - 1$ (for example, an image containing 255 colours plus white requires 8 bits per pixel to store it).

The size of the array also depends upon its density, described in terms of the number of pixels per inch in one direction. This is also used to described the resolution of the scan in terms of dots per inch (dpi). The choice of resolution is linked to the resolution required on the output device(s). For example, computer display screens need between 70 and 200 dpi, laser printers typically need 300 dpi, whilst offset printing needs up to 1,000 dpi.

The speed of capture varies from three A4 pages per minute (ppm) for desktop scanners designed for personal computers up to 30 ppm for high-speed scanners. Small items such as cheques and credit card vouchers can be captured by such scanners for use in transaction processing systems. High-resolution digitising cameras are used to capture the images of the items - two cameras may be used to capture the upper and lower halves of the document simultaneously in order to reach the required speed. Arrays of charge-coupled devices (CCDs) are used in such cameras.

Imaging cameras are available for the capture of high-resolution images (up to $2{,}200 \times 1{,}700$) for use in colour artwork. Still frames may also be captured from moving video sequences using a video digitiser or frame grabber - a topic that will be covered in Chapter 9. Specialist equipment is required to digitise MRI and CT scans that must be displayed on high-resolution screens ($2{,}500 \times 2{,}000$ pixels by 256 levels of grey) for diagnosis.

7.3   Compression

7.3.1   Why compress?

The number of bytes needed to represent an uncompressed image is very large. Consider a single A4 sheet of paper. The scanner may capture this as bitonal, grey scale or colour data as described above. The raster data is then held in temporary storage, usually on magnetic disk. Table 7.1 shows the space taken up by this document when it has been scanned at 200, 300 and 400 dpi.

In order to reduce the amount of storage space required for a document, the image must be converted into a different, and smaller, form by removing surplus information. There are three main ways of converting image data. Text in document images may be converted from raster to ASCII, a standard set of 7-bit codes for the digital representation of letters, numbers and special control characters. Line art can be vectorised, using mathematical formulae. Bitonal and continuous tone still images can be digitised and encoded using a variety of established algorithms. Reductions of the order of between 2:1 and 50:1 can be achieved for images using current international standards. The actual figure achieved for an individual image depends

Table 7.1 Storage requirements for uncompressed A4 sheet

Resolution (dpi)	Bitonal (MB)	Grey scale (MB)	Colour (MB)
200	0.48	1.9-7.7	15-61
300	1.09	4.4-17.4	35-140
400	1.93	7.7-30.9	62-247

Notes: An A4 sheet is 210 × 297 mm or 8.27 × 11.69 inches.
Bitonal images require 1 bit/pixel.
Grey scale images are assumed to require 4-6 bits/pixel.
Colour images are assumed to require 32-128 bits/pixel.

upon its content and the quality required when the image is restored. These requirements must be set against limitations on storage space.

7.3.2   Text conversion

Raster to ASCII conversion is carried out using some form of recognition technology. Character recognition techniques have been commercially available for nearly 40 years, starting with the use of magnetic ink character recognition (MICR) on cheques in 1956. Optical character recognition (OCR) was introduced in the 1960s for fixed-pitch fonts. It was based on matching the scanned characters to standards held in memory. A standard was required for each font so that as the number of fonts grew, the size of the library increased and so did the time required to select the correct font and match the characters.

In contrast omnifont OCR is based on the use of techniques from artificial intelligence and is therefore also known as intelligent character recognition (ICR). Each character is identified by the presence or absence of sets of particular features that are independent of typeface and font size (feature recognition). Early versions had to be trained to recognise a specific font, but recent technology can handle any font, including mixed fonts in the same document. ICR systems can handle proportional spacing, tables, graphics and, in some cases, hand-printed characters.

Special techniques are needed to handle forms, based on mark recognition - a technology originally introduced to handle examination papers with multiple choice questions. Forms recognition enables the system to switch to the correct application software, which can then be used to detect signatures, incorrectly completed forms, and so forth.

Conversion is carried out on the raster data by isolating individual characters, identifying the characters, validating the data and transferring to a file. Considerable savings can be made in storage requirements by converting images to ASCII text files - a reduction of between one-fifth and one-tenth of the uncompressed image. In addition there is the benefit of being able to access the contents of the original document. There is therefore a growing interest in the benefits of using recognition technologies in combination with image processing to capture information for full-text searching, along with the original image, in industries such as chemicals and pharmaceuticals.

7.3.3   Vectorisation

Vector data treats an image as a series of points and mathematical functions that describe geometric figures such as lines, circles or arcs. The process of converting raster data into vector data is known as vectorisation. It is suitable for images containing alphanumeric characters and line drawings such as forms, organisation charts, flow diagrams, circuit diagrams, maps and cartoons. The vector representation of an image can be very much smaller than the raster data, especially for rectilinear information such as forms, which can be reduced to as much as 1/200th of the uncompressed size at 300 dpi. Text can be removed and converted separately to ASCII. However, very complex images that are difficult to describe in mathematical terms may actually increase in size when vectorised.

7.3.4   Image compression

Images that are not suitable for conversion to text or vectorisation (in other words complex line art and continuous tone images) are compressed using standard algorithms to eliminate as much unnecessary information as possible. Images currently have to be decompressed in order to restore the missing information before they can be displayed or printed (although prototype systems exist that can manipulate compressed images). Individual still images may be compressed by spatial redundancy techniques. These remove the repetition of patterns within each frame (intra-frame compression). I will illustrate this idea by means of a simple example. Figure 7.1 shows a simple image enlarged so that each square represents one pixel.

If white pixels are represented by a 0 and black pixels by a 1, a simple way to compress this is to record just the number of consecutive '0's and '1's in each line. The result of applying this one-dimensional run-length algorithm is shown in Table 7.2. If the same sequence is repeated on more than one line, this information can be used to compress the data still further using a two-dimensional run-length algorithm, as shown in Table 7.3.

In this trivial example the original data can be recovered without loss - a method known as *lossless* compression. Greater compression can be achieved by using more sophisticated methods in which sampling techniques are used to represent areas of the image. In some of these methods - known as *lossy* methods - the data is not exactly recoverable.

In practice compression standards such as JPEG (described in Section 7.4.2) and MPEG and H.261 (discussed in Chapter 9) use a mixture of techniques. A typical sequence would be:

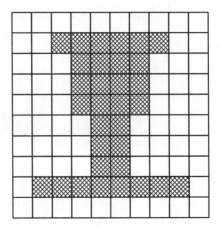

Figure 7.1 *Image prior to encoding*

- preparation including analogue to digital conversion;
- processing using an algorithm such as the discrete cosine transform (DCT) to transform the data into a different mathematical domain that is more easily compressed;
- quantisation to reduce the precision at which the output is stored (e.g. by reducing the number of bits per pixel);
- entropy encoding (e.g. run-length) to remove any redundant information in the resulting data stream.

These steps are reversed by the decompression process (Steinmetz 1994). Compression may be either *symmetric* - if decompression is a step-by-step reversal of compression - or *asymmetric*. Asymmetric compression typically takes much longer than decompression and needs a much more powerful computer.

Table 7.2 One-dimensional run-length encoding

10 '0'		
2 '0'	6 '1'	2 '0'
3 '0'	4 '1'	3 '0'
3 '0'	4 '1'	3 '0'
3 '0'	4 '1'	3 '0'
4 '0'	2 '1'	4 '0'
4 '0'	2 '1'	4 '0'
4 '0'	2 '1'	4 '0'
1 '0'	8 '0'	1 '0'
10 '0'		

Table 7.3 Two-dimensional
run-length encoding

10 '0'		
2 '0'	6 '1'	2 '0'
3 '0'	4 '1'	3 '0'
again		
3 '0'	4 '1'	3 '0'
4 '0'	2 '1'	4 '0'
again		
again		
1 '0'	8 '0'	1 '0'
10 '0'		

7.4   Standards

7.4.1   Standards for encoding images

As we have seen, all image data has to be encoded and compressed in some way for storage. Standards are required to ensure that this data can be transferred between applications - an area that is of particular interest to the CEC's Open Information Interchange (OII) initiative (Stephenson 1993).

Text
A range of standards exists for character coding. The basic 7-bit set usually known as ASCII is standardised as IS 646. This set, which covers the English alphabet and is consistent with the 7-bit sections used in many network developments, is limited to a total of 128 characters. Extensions, including 8-bit codes, exist but are not universally recognised.

There are current attempts to develop a 4-byte universal coded character set that can be used for non-alphabetic characters and for languages other than English. In ISO this activity (draft standard 10646) is carried out by JTC1/SC2. A group of major vendors has produced an alternative version, called Unicode. Under a recent merger agreement, these two versions now seem to be moving towards a genuinely universal set that will support 34,168 characters representing 22 different subsets of characters and symbols (Adams 1994).

Graphics
ISO has developed the Computer Graphics Metafile (CGM) standard (IS 8632) for the capture, storage and transfer of graphical information. CGM is used for the content structure of geometric graphics in ODA, as described in Chapter 6. The transfer of engineering product data between different systems is covered by the Initial Graphics Exchange Specification (IGES) format. IGES level 3 has been

adopted by the US Government as part of its Computer-aided Acquisition Logistics System (CALS) directive.

Image

TIFF (Tagged Image File Format), developed and controlled by Aldus and Microsoft, is widely used as a format for the exchange of image data. TIFF consists of a set of images, with a header that contains options that determine the coding of the images. Several standards groups are currently working in this area, including an ISO technical committee (TC 130) which is looking at a set of Digital Data Exchange Standards (DDES) for the exchange of colour image data between electronic pre-press systems. The TIFF header format is included as a work item in this activity.

Images must also be compressed in order to reduce storage space and to make it easier to transfer them over networks. International standards exist for the compression of different types of still image, as described in the next section.

7.4.2   Standards for compressing bitonal images

The compression and decompression of bitonal still images are currently covered by the Group 3 and Group 4 standards for document transmission via fax, published by ITU-T as Recommendations T.4 and T.6. The original Group 1 standard (T.2) was a bitmap standard that involved transmitting each pixel. Group 2 (T.3) adopted a one-dimensional run-length method of coding. Group 3 is a two-dimensional version of the run-length code for bitonal image compression, whilst Group 4 is a more efficient version for high-speed digital data transmission.

JBIG

A new international standard for bitonal images is currently under development. The Joint Bi-level Image Coding Expert Group (JBIG) is a collaboration between ITU-T and ISO/IEC to develop a compression standard for the lossless encoding of bitonal still images. JBIG is currently a draft international standard (DIS 11544).

JBIG will provide better compression than the existing Group 3 and Group 4 fax standards and can also be used for grey scales or colours with limited bits per pixel (up to about 6). Its main advantage is that it provides progressive coding to build up the whole image rather than the line-by-line approach of the fax standards. This will make it better for browsing on low to medium rate communication links.

7.4.3   JPEG

Continuous tone still images are covered by the Joint Photographic Experts Group (JPEG) - a collaboration between ITU-T and ISO to develop a general purpose compression standard for both grey scale and colour images. This standard, finalised in 1991 as Draft International Standard (DIS) 10918-1 and 10918-2, is designed for use in a wide range of applications including image storage and retrieval, publishing, graphic arts, colour facsimile, printers and scanners and medical imaging.

An amendment known as 'JPEG-2' extends the specification to include a number of features such as adaptive quantisation. The official designation will be 'Enhancements to JPEG'. The current target is November 1994 for the standard, which will be CD 10918-3.

JPEG does not refer to a specific image file format. Two file formats that are currently in use - though not standardised - are JFIF (JPEG File Interchange Format), a low-end format that transports pixels, and TIFF 6.0, an extension of the TIFF format, which will record much more detail about an image.

Applications

JPEG is designed to exploit the known limitations of the human eye, which is less sensitive to small changes in colour than in light and shade. It therefore works well on photographs and naturalistic artwork, but is less successful with line art. In general the more complex and subtly rendered the image, the more likely it is that JPEG will do well on it. Conversely it will do badly with images that have very sharp edges, which tend to come out blurred unless a very high-quality setting is chosen. Such sharp edges are rare in scanned photographs, but are fairly common in borders or overlaid text. It follows that JPEG is particularly unsuitable for bitonal images. It is also not very useful for grey scale images with fewer than 16 levels of grey. Furthermore because it is intended for compressing images that will be looked at by humans, it may give rise to unacceptable errors in images that are to be analysed by machine.

Technology

Because of the scope and variety of target products a three-part algorithm has been defined: a baseline system, an extended system and a special function used to provide lossless compression (Wallace 1991). The baseline system, which is mandatory, is a lossy technique based on the discrete cosine transform (DCT), a relative of the fast Fourier transform, followed by variable word length encoding. The extended system adds features such as more sophisticated coding, lossless transmission and progressive build up.

An important requirement was that the standard should support a wide range of image quality ratings. The user or application should be able to adjust the compression parameters in order to determine the trade-off between the amount of compression (and thus the size of the compressed file) and the quality of the resulting image. JPEG is capable of reducing the size of an image by a factor between 10:1 and 20:1 without visible loss. Greater compression (in the range 30:1 to 50:1) is possible if some reduction in quality is acceptable. Very small files can be used for applications like indexing image archives where quality is not important. For such applications, 100:1 compression is quite feasible. In contrast the lossless compression mode typically gives about 2:1 compression.

Products

To achieve this variety of options, there are four modes of operation. For each mode, one or more coder/decoders (*codecs*) are specified by the standard. Within a mode, codecs differ according to the precision of source image samples or the coding method used. JPEG should thus be regarded not as a single standard, but as a toolkit to span a wide range of applications. Individual implementations from particular manufacturers will not cover the entire range of possible options. The standard was designed to be open so that it can be implemented either in software on a range of CPUs or in hardware for high-performance applications. Available systems include processors for compression and decompression, add-in boards for PCs, development kits and software tools. Most currently available JPEG hardware and software handles only the baseline mode.

7.4.4   Fractals for compression

Whilst the international standards for still image and video are based on the discrete cosine transform, a proprietary technology called Fractal Image Compression has been developed by Iterated Systems. The fractal transform was invented by Michael Barnsley, a co-founder of the company. It can be used to generate fractal equations for still or moving images. During compression the image is searched for fractal transform codes. The least important ones are discarded and the remaining equations are structured to form a highly compact Fractal Image Format (FIF).

The algorithm is said to give three distinct advantages over DCT: high compression efficiency, resolution independence and software decompression. It is claimed that it can maintain image integrity at compression ratios of up to 100:1, enabling a 640 × 400 24-bit true colour image to be held in 10 KB. The representation of the image is independent of the resolution of the display so that scale, aspect ratio and colour depth can be changed at decompression. Images can thus be displayed at any resolution - including the use of a form of interpolation to create one that is higher than the original - without file conversion.

Some wild claims have been made for the use of the fractal transform, which have aroused a degree of scepticism amongst researchers. Because the technique is proprietary it is difficult to obtain an independent assessment. In practice it appears to perform as well as other methods like DCT or vector quantisation (VQ), a method of identifing patterns from a predefined table, which it resembles. The results of tests are said to indicate that JPEG is better for low compression ratios, while for high compression ratios (above 50:1) fractal encoding is better. However, at high compression ratios images may be so severely distorted that they are not worth using.

As fractal image compression is inherently an asymmetrical technique, a compression board is normally used to encode images - the image above would take up to 12 minutes to compress on a 33-MHz 486-based personal computer. Decompression by software is, in contrast, very fast. The same computer can decompress and display a sequence of 256 × 116 24-bit colour images at 30 frames per second - the equivalent of full-motion video. This is making fractals attractive to software developers who can bundle software decompression modules with their applications and sell them to users to run on standard PCs. For example, Microsoft has used fractal image compression in Encarta, its multimedia encyclopaedia, which includes 7,000 high-quality photographs stored on a CD-ROM.

Summary

The use of still images in computer applications, though currently rather overshadowed by the excitement of recent advances in desktop video, is well established in document imaging and geographic information systems. Hardware and software to support these applications are readily available and international standards have been established for image compression. A number of major computer suppliers, including Digital Equipment and IBM, provide support for image data types in their system software. Consequently this is a significant area for the developer who is considering the introduction of multimedia. Chapter 15, which describes some current applications, examines the impact of the introduction of imaging systems on existing business practices, especially those concerned with supervision and control.

References

[Adams 1994] G. Adams and H. M. Ross, 'Fundamentals of the universal character set', *OII Spectrum*, vol. 1, no. 4, pp. 1-14.

[Steinmetz 1994] R. Steinmetz, 'Data compression in multimedia computing - principles and techniques', *Multimedia Systems*, vol. 1, no. 4, pp. 166-172.

[Stephenson 1993] G. Stephenson, 'Information interchange - providing the right framework', *OII Spectrum*, vol. 1, no. 1, pp. 15-23.

[Wallace 1991] G. K. Wallace, 'The JPEG still picture compression standard', *Communications of the ACM*, vol. 34, no. 4, pp. 31-44.

CHAPTER 8

Audio

This chapter outlines some of the uses of audio in multimedia applications. It then describes the requirements for music and speech, together with an explanation of the methods used to capture and encode audio. The chapter closes with a review of the international standards that are relevant to audio telephony and audiovisual applications.

8.1   Audio applications

The audio side of multimedia has attracted relatively little attention in the computer industry. This is partly because of the massive publicity devoted to video. It may also be because the use of audio in business information systems is not clear. As we saw in Chapter 5, the existing multimedia platforms that support audio seemed designed for the entertainment market.

Despite this neglect, audio clearly has an important role in multimedia applications. Special effects, such as music and voice, can be added to applications, especially training and point-of-sale or point-of-information systems. A voice commentary can be used to narrate what is happening on-screen or to highlight and reinforce key concepts. Combined with still pictures or animations, it can be used to explain an idea or a process to the user in a more effective way than text or graphics alone. Music can be used to attract customer attention or to create a particular mood.

A huge volume of audio material already exists on records, tapes and compact disks. However, almost all of this will require copyright clearance before it can be used. Existing legislation such as that covering performing rights for music that is played in public areas may be unsuitable for new multimedia applications. A point-of-sale system, for example, might contain a large number of short musical extracts. It would be difficult and very costly to identify when each extract was played and make the requisite royalty payments. Libraries of sound clips can be purchased, free of copyright, for such applications. However, application developers may prefer to generate their own audio material.

In some specialised areas audio on its own may form the core of a multimedia application. One such example is the provision of systems to help visually handicapped people. A recent project involved the downloading of a daily newspaper to a special terminal in the user's home. Here he or she could choose to listen to a speech processing system read selected articles aloud or have them displayed in a large typeface on the monitor.

As costs come down and the technology improves, interest in using speech processing and recognition in more general business applications will increase. It is already possible to use simple commands to control a computer as part of the user interface.

8.2   Audio capture

A sound digitiser is used to capture and digitise analogue sound from audiotape, cassettes, records, CD-ROM and the original audio version of compact disk known as CD-DA (compact disk-digital audio). Alternatively original music can be recorded using a microphone or composed on instruments that are attached to the computer through a MIDI interface.

Once captured, audio is then stored on hard disk or optical media and can be edited and played back through speakers connected to the computer or through a headset. Many computers are now equipped with built-in sound processors and speakers. However, externally powered speakers will provide higher sound clarity and volume. They will be needed if the audio source is a separate compact disk drive that needs to be attached to speakers, as shown in Figure 8.1, and cannot play through the computer (Apple 1990).

8.2.1   Music on the computer

A variety of tools are available to support musicians who want to compose and edit music using a multimedia system. These include sequencers, which record MIDI information rather than sound. This information can then be edited and sent back to the MIDI instruments for playback.

MIDI

Musical Instrument Digital Interface (MIDI) is an industry-standard connection for computer and digital control of musical instruments. It provides a way to record,

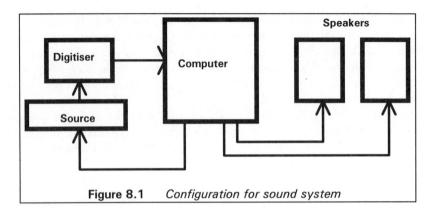

Figure 8.1   *Configuration for sound system*

play back and synchronise the settings needed to control sound-producing devices. MIDI coding is also used in some multimedia editing and control systems.

MIDI includes standards for the hardware itself (for example, the cables and connectors) as well as for the electronic information in the form of MIDI messages that are sent from one device to another. A computer with a MIDI interface can be used to control other MIDI-compatible devices through a MIDI port - a five-pin connection socket built into a device for connecting MIDI cables. There are three types of port: MIDI In receives data, MIDI Out sends data and MIDI Thru relays data without reading the message. The device also requires a microprocessor that is able to send and receive MIDI messages. These communicate musical events such as note-on/note-off or the pitch bend of a note.

The Multimedia PC specification, described in Chapter 5, emphasises the use of MIDI. All systems must have at least one MIDI port with MIDI In, Out and Thru.

8.2.2   Voice on the computer

The use of voice is likely to be far more important than music to most managers who want to develop multimedia information systems. Until recently this was not well catered for by suppliers. Suitable adapters and software are now available from several suppliers including Apple, Microsoft and Creative Labs. The Windows Sound System, for example, consists of a 16-bit audio card, microphone, headphones and a software application that is designed to support business audio. It includes voice recognition (so that the user can teach it to recognise commands), voice synthesis, and support for importing sound clips into applications that make use of OLE. It also allows users to synchronise audio with digital video.

Speech recognition technology, once used mainly by people who were unable to type due to physical disabilities, is now closer to being of practical use in the office. IBM has started to ship its Personal Dictation System for OS/2. In addition to supporting dictation at around 70 to 100 words per minute for text input, the system can be used to control the functions of the computer system and its applications. It can be trained to recognise the voice of an individual speaker uttering simple commands such as 'save file' and 'close window'.

If speech recognition is to be used in business applications, then good acoustic conditions will be required to reduce ambient noise. Success rates are also affected by factors such as the size and composition of the vocabulary used, the attitude and speaking style of the user, and the type and placement of the microphone. Suitable applications are those that require relatively limited vocabularies in a quiet environment. They include inspections, sorting and visual monitoring where hands-free operation is required (Schmandt 1990).

A quiet environment will also be required for the use of video PCs in the office. Traditional videoconferencing equipment supports full duplex audio without echo. PictureTel's IDEC technology, for example, adjusts the audio to maintain maximum sound quality without recalibration, allowing participants to move around the room. An enhanced version is provided in the company's video PCs, designed to suppress unwanted background noise from air conditioning or fans in PCs.

8.3   Compression

As human beings are more sensitive to variations in the quality of sound than in the quality of image, multimedia systems will be required to support high standards for audio. Techniques to encode audio information are already well developed.

Sound consists of pressure differences in the air. A microphone picks up these differences and feeds them through an amplifier. This analogue signal is first digitised using an analogue to digital converter (ADC). The computer *samples* the input waveform at regular intervals and converts the amplitude to a binary code, using pulse code modulation (PCM).

For speech the audio signal is sampled at 8 kHz (i.e. 8,000 times per second) and 8 bits - representing 256 different amplitude values - are used to code each sample. The technique of limiting the number of values in this way is known as *quantisation*. This method of encoding will generate a stream of 64,000 bits per second (written as 64 Kbit/s), which needs to be put into packets for transmission over a network. For music of the quality provided by compact disk, the signal is sampled at 44.1 kHz (i.e. 44,100 times per second) and 16 bits are used to code each sample. In stereo this will generate a stream of 1.4 million bits per second (Mbit/s). Further compression can be achieved by suppressing silences or by better methods of coding:

1. Non-linear PCM assigns the amplitude value points non-linearly. For example, a logarithmic scale can be used to assign codes more sparsely at the maximum amplitudes and more densely near the zero-crossing point.
2. Differential PCM (DPCM) encodes the differential of the signal instead of the signal itself. The range of differentials is usually smaller than the range of amplitudes.

Table 8.1 Sound quality and level of digitisation

Sampling frequency (kHz)	Quantisation (bits)	Format	Quality	CD quality
44.1	16	PCM	HiFi music	CD-DA
37.8	8	ADPCM	HiFi music	CD-I level
37.8	8	ADPCM	FM broadcast (music)	CD-I level B
18.9	4	ADPCM	AM broadcast (speech)	CD-I level
8	8	PCM	Telephone	N/A

3. Adaptive DPCM (ADPCM) dynamically adjusts the range of amplitude values to match the expected range of amplitudes in the input data stream.

Apart from CD-DA, other compact disk formats that are commonly used in multimedia applications have specific requirements for audio. Compact disk interactive (CD-I) is a self-contained multimedia system, described in more detail in Chapter 10. It is possible to store up to 72 minutes of high-quality audio on a compact disk to the CD-DA standards. However, no other data can then be stored on the disk. For most CD-I applications, therefore, audio is encoded using fewer bits and lower sampling rates, as shown in Table 8.1. CD-ROM XA, designed as a link between the workstation environment supported by CD-ROM and the consumer environment, uses the same sound formats as CD-I.

Multimedia PC audio requirements
The minimum audio requirements for the Multimedia PC specification include:

- a CD-ROM drive with CD-DA outputs and volume control;
- Digital to audio (DAC) and analogue to digital (ADC) converters with linear PCM sampling and support for microphone input;
- an internal music synthesiser;
- internal analogue audio mixing capabilities that can combine input from three sources into a single stereo signal.

For MPC Level 1 the mandatory requirements are for 8 bits to be used to encode samples taken at 22.05 kHz (i.e. 22,050 times a second) for the DAC and 11.025 kHz for both the DAC and ADC. At Level 2 these are increased to 16 bits to be used to encode samples taken at 44.1, 22.05 and 11.025 kHz for both the DAC and ADC.

8.4   Standards

So far we have considered audio on its own, or overlaid on top of text, graphics or still image. New developments make it possible to combine audio with visual data in two kinds of applications - real-time audiovisual telephony and applications that use stored audiovisual material such as film clips. These have different requirements. However, in each case facilities are required for the audio, for the video elements and for system requirements that are needed to synchronise the two data types together. There are separate standards activities for real-time and stored audiovisual applications, which the next chapter will discuss in more detail. Each of these activities contains an audio component, which is outlined below.

8.4.1   Audiovisual telephony

The H.320 family of standards for audiovisual telephony forms the basis for communication between equipment from different manufacturers. Most, if not all, the video PCs now being developed will support these standards, which include the three ITU-T G series recommendations shown in Table 8.2.

8.4.2   Audiovisual applications

The Moving Picture Experts Group (MPEG), an ISO/IEC working group (JTC1/SC29/WG11), has been developing standards for video and associated audio since 1988. The standard for the first phase (known as MPEG-1) defined a bit stream for compressed video and audio optimised to fit into a bandwidth of 1.5 Mbit/s - the data rate of optical media such as CD-ROM. The standard consists of five parts, of which the audio part (11172-3) addresses the audio compression techniques required. The remaining parts, which deal with synchronisation, video, compliance testing and software coding, will be covered in Chapter 9.

MPEG-1 Audio

MPEG-1 allows for two audio channels. These can be either single (mono), dual (two mono channels), normal stereo (in which one channel carries the left audio signal and one channel carries the right audio signal) or joint stereo (in which one channel carries the sum of the signals and the other their difference). The standard uses 16 bits to encode samples at three frequencies: 44.1 kHz (as for CD-DA), 48 kHz (as for digital audiotape) and 32 kHz (Steinmetz 1994).

The MPEG committee chose to recommend three different coding schemes

Table 8.2   Standards for speech encoding

Standard	Description
G.711	Pulse code modulation (PCM) of voice frequencies
G.722	Audio coding at 7 kHz within 64 Kbit/s (ADPCM)
G.728	Coding of speech at 16 Kbit/s using low delay code excited linear prediction (LD-CELP)

(known as layers) for different target applications, in which increasing complexity and decreasing target data rates make more demands on processing power. The minimum bit rate for all layers is 32 Kbit/s, but the maximum rates vary as follows:

- Layer 1, a simplified version of Layer 2 for low complexity, has a maximum bit rate of 448 Kbit/s. The target rate is 192 Kbit/s per channel.
- Layer 2, which is identical with Philips' Musicam system, has a maximum rate of 385 Kbit/s and a target rate of 128 Kbit/s per channel. It has been designed as a trade-off between sound quality per bit rate and encoder complexity. Layer 2 has been proposed for the future Digital Audio Broadcasting network.
- Layer 3 has a maximum rate of 320 Kbit/s and a target rate of 64 Kbit/s per channel, in line with ISDN Basic Rate Access. Its format specifies a set of advanced features that are designed to preserve as much sound quality as possible even at rather low bit rates.

The layers are downwardly compatible - in other words a Layer 3 decoder must be able to decode any Layer 1, 2 or 3 MPEG Audio stream whilst a Layer 2 decoder must be able to decode Layer 1 and Layer 2 streams. In practice most activity has focused on Layer 2.

MPEG-2 Audio

The second phase (MPEG-2), currently under development, is designed for transmission of digital television and video telephony over fibre, satellite, cable, ISDN and other networks. It defines a bit stream for video and audio coded at around 3 to 10 Mbit/s. There are three parts to the standard, of which the audio part (IS 13818-3) has attained DIS (Draft International Standard).

MPEG-2 Audio is designed to maintain compatibility with MPEG-1, while adding discrete surround-sound channels to the original MPEG-1 limit of two channels. MPEG-2 Audio coding will supply up to five full-bandwidth channels, an additional low-frequency enhancement channel and/or up to seven channels for commentary or multilingual requirements. The main channels (Left, Right) in MPEG-2 Audio will remain backwards compatible with MPEG-1, whereas new coding methods and syntax will be used for the additional surround channels. The MPEG-2 Audio standard will also extend the stereo and mono coding of the MPEG-1 Audio standard (using additional sampling rates of 16, 22.05 and 24 kHz) to provide improved quality for bit rates at or below 64 Kbit/s per channel.

The MPEG group has carried out a set of subjective tests to validate the current performance of the MPEG-2 multichannel audio coding standard. More than 20 listeners took part at each test site. The programme material was selected from 64 items provided internationally for these tests. The results showed that at the bit rates (320 and 384 Kbit/s) selected for the tests, the average performance of most codecs was satisfactory, but all codecs showed deviations from transparency for some of the items. Higher bit rates may therefore be needed in order to reach the desired quality level. As a result, it was agreed that MPEG-2 will have an audio extension which is not backwards compatible with MPEG-1. Schemes that are being considered include Dolby AC-3.

Summary

Audio is the Cinderella of multimedia technology. While standards for encoding audio in telephony and digital music are well established, the use of audio - particularly voice - in business applications remains neglected by both suppliers and users. Much work has gone into the development of compression techniques for moving video, in both real-time and stored applications. The synchronisation of audio with video in these applications is a difficult task. Managers should be aware of the need to achieve acceptable levels of voice synchronisation in desktop audiovisual applications - a point often obscured in demonstrations by suppliers.

References

[Apple 1990] *The Apple guide to multimedia development tools*, Apple Computer UK Limited, June 1990.

[Schmandt 1990] C. Schmandt, M. S. Ackerman and D. Hindus, 'Augmenting a window system with speech input', *Communications of the ACM*, vol. 23, no. 8, pp. 50-56.

[Steinmetz 1994] R. Steinmetz, 'Data compression in multimedia computing - standards and systems', *Multimedia Systems*, vol. 1, no. 5, pp. 187-204.

CHAPTER 9

Video

This chapter starts by outlining the real and potential uses of video. Current use is largely confined to audiovisual material stored on analogue videodisk and played back as part of training or POI/POS applications. In future real-time video communications will be available on personal computers. The chapter then goes on to describe the technology and components that are required to capture and compress video images, including conversion to and from broadcast TV standards. It closes with a review of the most important international standards: the H.320 family for audiovisual telephony and MPEG for stored audiovisual applications. Proprietary techniques such as DVI are also included.

9.1　Video applications

The launch of audiovisual applications on personal computers has attracted much attention. The use to which this technology will be put in the future is rather less clear, although some early experiments point the way. We can think of video applications in two groups: playback of stored audiovisual material and real-time audiovisual communications.

The first group is well established. Training applications based on interactive videodisk have incorporated analogue video sequences as a standard technique. Public information systems also incorporated video clips, often as a way of attracting the attention of the user. The use of digital video in networked systems is still restricted by the technical problems of transferring large volumes of time-dependent data. Possible applications include the use of servers to hold libraries of video clips (for use in advertising, for example).

Audiovisual communications may be one-to-one, as for example in a meeting between two people, each of whom has a videophone or video camera mounted on a personal computer. Compared to conventional videoconferencing equipment, these personal video systems seem rather limited. The combination of a small image (a window on a 14-inch monitor), low resolution and relatively slow frame rate means that current products are unlikely to satisfy users' requirements for lengthy face-to-face 'meetings' such as recruitment interviews where eye contact and body language are important. They could, however, be successfully used in situations where the discussion involves other forms of interaction. For example, a sales director might wish to contact sales executives in different cities. Each executive could display the latest forecasts on the computer, using a shared workspace. The quality of the video links is of secondary importance in this case.

Real-time video communications may also be one-to-many. In this case only one person has a video camera; everyone else receives the video on their computers, as in a live broadcast. This latter approach is suitable for internal company communications - the company President's Christmas message, for example. More importantly it can form a part of a distance learning project. For example, in a university programme for US high schools that use personal computers for teaching the fine arts, the instructor can talk to students on remote locations via a real-time video link, as well as showing them still images of paintings.

9.2 Video capture

9.2.1 Converting video for the computer

Conventional broadcast TV, audio and video signals are analogue, whilst computers handle digital information. Multimedia systems need to be able to handle information in both analogue and digital forms, because:

1. Analogue video and audio signals may need to be converted into digital form so that they can be manipulated more easily.
2. Applications developed on computers may need to be converted back into analogue form for playback - from videotape, for example.
3. Analogue and digital forms may be combined in one application, as when a live television broadcast is run in a window on a computer screen, for example.

Conversion between analogue and digital video presents a number of technical difficulties. The situation is complicated by the different and incompatible standards that have been adopted by the different industries involved.

A TV screen may look superficially like a computer screen but it differs in a number of important ways. Most computers and some video systems use a *component signal* made up of three basic colours - red-green-blue (RGB) - that are individually controllable. Broadcast TV and most video systems use a *composite signal* in which luminance (brightness) and chrominance (colour), together with synchronisation information, are combined into a single signal. A decoder is needed to change a composite signal from a video source into an RGB signal for display on a computer screen.

A complete image in a sequence of moving film or video is called a *frame*. In most broadcast video, the screen is *interlaced*. Two sets of alternating lines are broadcast. Even-numbered lines are drawn at one pass, odd-numbered lines are in a second pass. This allows an image to be broadcast at comparatively low frame rates (25-30 fps) without excessive flicker. The eye averages similar values so the image remains clear. Computer screens, in contrast, are *non-interlaced* - video lines are presented sequentially. To compensate for this, frame rates are faster - 66.7 frames per second (fps) for the Macintosh, for example.

Video resolution varies between broadcast standards - 625 lines for the US standard (NTSC) or 525 lines in Europe for the PAL and SECAM standards. In contrast, a computer with a VGA screen has a resolution of 640 × 480 pixels, with a 256-colour palette. On a television set the picture is extended to fill the entire screen, known as *overscan*, so that part of the picture at the edges is lost. Computer screens use *underscan*, in which the entire picture is visible, surrounded by a black border.

So conversion from analogue to digital video requires a decoder to convert a composite video signal to an RGB signal and a scan converter to accelerate interlaced video for a non-interlaced computer screen. In addition if computer graphics are to be combined with the video signal, a synchronisation generator lock (genlock) will be required to combine the two. This allows the system to set its timing to match the timing of the video signal.

9.2.2   Creating videos on the desktop

The market for video adapters and related equipment has evolved rapidly. Each generation of products is swiftly overtaken by the next, as compression methods are improved, whilst at the same time proprietary techniques give way to developing international standards.

Video overlay boards
The first generation of adapter boards provided overlay and genlock facilities - the ability to combine broadcast quality analogue video with computer-generated text and graphics. They were designed for use with videodisk players. It was possible to mask part of the video image on-screen, so that the remaining part appeared to be playing in a window, surrounded by text. However, the image itself could not be manipulated - its size and position thus remained constant.

Digitisers

These were followed by a range of digital video capture devices (digitisers or frame grabbers) that could be used to accept PAL or NTSC signals from a videodisk player, video cassette recorder or video camera, and digitise them. Single frames could be 'grabbed' and stored as still images (Figure 9.1). Some of these adapters could provide real-time manipulation of the video image, including the ability to change its size, position, brightness, saturation, contrast sharpness and hue. A full screen of video could be scaled to any size and placed anywhere on the screen, within a window if desired.

Compression boards

In 1989 Intel introduced a new proprietary compression technology for audiovisual applications called DVI. Intel itself supplied both processors and adapter boards for real-time compression and decompression. These compressors can take a data stream from a digitiser board, compress it and store it on hard disk in real time. Other suppliers brought out adapters of their own, using Intel's processor set.

More recent products support the emerging international standards for image compression, JPEG and MPEG. Although JPEG is essentially a standard for still images, in practice it has proved to be popular for compressing motion video. This is because each frame is compressed separately, thus making frame-by-frame editing much simpler. Several suppliers sell adapters that support motion video to the JPEG standard (known as Motion JPEG) with synchronous audio.

The MPEG standard, in contrast, is designed specifically for audiovisual

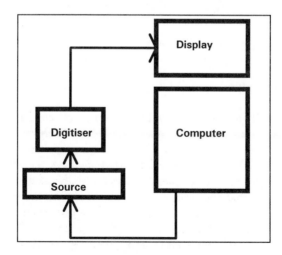

Figure 9.1 *Configuration for video system*

applications stored on digital media such as CD-ROM. MPEG adapter boards are now available that can play back stored video from compact disks.

Creating video applications

Business applications such as presentations and desktop video publishing can now be created using a simple approach. The equipment consists of a personal computer, an adapter board, a video source such as a professional camcorder and a software package such as MediaMaker from MacroMedia. The latest adapters support compression to the MPEG audio and video standards.

Video editing

Post-production work on video material, such as editing, adding titles and mixing sound tracks, used to be carried out on videotape. It is now frequently performed using dedicated software running on a personal computer or workstation. Professional on-line systems for the non-linear editing of digital material are attracting the attention of the computer industry - Microsoft has just acquired SoftImage, for example.

Simpler systems are also available that enable users to edit video on the desktop. These are essentially small desktop studios for creating presentations. They allow the user to take an input signal from a variety of analogue video sources, which can be controlled by the computer, such as videodisk players, videotape players and video cameras. This signal may be either composite or a component signal such as S-VHS. It is then digitised. Frames from separate sources can be synchronised and mixed with audio. Digital effects can be added, together with graphics, text and titles. The final version can then be output as a composite or component signal in either NTSC or PAL format. Presentations can thus be recorded on videotape in a range of formats for playback.

9.2.3   Real-time video

The new video PCs are designed to support a different set of standards - those for audiovisual telephony described in Section 9.4.1 below. Each PC is equipped with a small digital CCD camera, which may be either built in or free-standing. Although the latter may seem rather more precarious, they do have the advantage that they can be freely moved by the user to point at different parts of the room. Some come with a small stand so that they can double as a document camera. In either case, some form of lens cover is desirable so that users can ensure their privacy.

The camera will be accompanied by at least one adapter board to support a variety of functions, including coding and decoding, an ISDN interface, audio telephony interface and system requirements such as synchronisation. As Chapter 5 pointed out, it is necessary to avoid using the PC bus to move audio and video information. If more than one board is required, these should be in adjacent slots with direct links between them.

9.3 Television

9.3.1 Broadcast TV and video standards

There are three incompatible international standards for broadcast TV and videotape:

1. National Television Standards Committee (NTSC) is the colour standard used in the USA, Canada and Japan. It specifies a screen with 525 horizontal scan lines updated at 59.94 Hz - a rate just under 30 frames per second (fps).
2. Phase Alternation Line (PAL) is the colour standard developed in Germany and used in the UK, most of Europe, Africa, Australasia and South America. It specifies a 625-line screen at 50 Hz or 25 fps.
3. Système Électronique Couleur avec Mémoire (SECAM) is the French colour standard used in eastern Europe and the (former) USSR, parts of the Middle East and Africa. It also specifies a 625-line screen at 25 fps.

Each standard handles colour in a different way. In each case the *aspect ratio* (the ratio of the horizontal to vertical dimension of the screen) is 4:3. Media such as videotape and videodisk are designed to support one standard and are not generally interchangeable, though some videodisk players will play disks in either PAL or NTSC format.

9.3.2 High-definition television (HDTV)

Improvements to these standards have been the aim of much research work over the past 20 years. This work has concentrated on higher resolution and changes to the aspect ratio to provide a wider screen, with dimensions similar to those used in the cinema.

Hi-Vision
The Japanese standard for analogue HDTV, Hi-Vision, defines an interlaced screen with 1,125 scan lines and an aspect ratio of 16:9, updated at 60 Hz - rather than 59.94 Hz, which would have made it compatible with NTSC. The Japanese Government has promoted Hi-Vision through several projects at a number of locations during the late 1980s and early 1990s.

Grand Alliance
Work in the USA started in earnest in July 1986 when the Society of Motion Picture and Television Engineers (SMPTE) began standardisation procedures for HDTV. Its adaptation of Japanese work on the 1125/60 specification became known as SMPTE 240M. A further series of proposals were submitted to the FCC for approval to become the US standard for HDTV.

In a radical move, the FCC asked the companies concerned to work together on a single proposal. This 'Grand Alliance' - AT&T, David Sarnoff Research Center, General Instrument, MIT, Philips Consumer Electronics, Thomson Consumer Electronics and Zenith Electronics - has now agreed on most of the components for a digital HDTV standard. The FCC Advisory Committee on Advanced Television Service (ACATS) has approved all the subsystems which include a system for packeted data transport, MPEG-2 for video encoding, Dolby AC-3 - which beat Philips' Musicam in the listening tests - for audio encoding, modulation technology from Zenith and a set of scanning formats varying from 720 progressive scan lines at 24 fps to 1,080 interlaced lines at 30 fps.

Field testing of these subsystems began in April 1994. The Alliance is expected to deliver a prototype system for testing late in 1994, to be followed by an ACATS recommendation to the FCC in the spring of 1995 that it should be adopted as the US HDTV broadcast standard. Sets are expected to come to market in 1997.

European Launching Group for Digital Video Broadcasting (ELGDVB)
In Europe, under the direction of the European Commission, products and services for advanced television were concentrated on the MAC (Multiplexed Analogue Components) family of transmission standards. The Commission has now accepted that digital television will arrive much sooner than originally expected.

A new directive, intended to encourage a market based on common digital standards for transmission by cable, satellite and terrestrial means, specifies:

- a 16:9 aspect ratio is to be adopted for all widescreen services;
- widescreen formats in 625 lines that are not entirely digital must use the D2-MAC transmission system or one that is entirely compatible with PAL or SECAM;
- high-definition formats that are not entirely digital must be transmitted in HD-MAC.

A group of 85 companies has formed the European Launching Group for Digital Video Broadcasting (ELGDVB) to develop technology for the European market, expected to be based on MPEG-2. A separate initiative in Sweden, Denmark, Finland and Norway is developing the HD-Divine terrestrial digital TV system, also expected to be based on MPEG-2 Video.

9.4   Compression

The development of compression standards is essential to the future of multimedia. The need for compression is greatest with video. Without compression, each frame of colour video will require a storage space of 7.4 Mbit. Thus only about 22 seconds of full-screen, full-motion (FSFM) video could be stored on a 600-MB optical disk. To play it back would require a transfer rate of 221 Mbit/s, which far exceeds the available rate of 1.5 Mbit/s. Compression is the key to resolving the discrepancies between requirements and reality - and ever increasing processing power is required to drive sophisticated compression algorithms.

As Chapter 7 explained, individual still images are compressed by spatial redundancy techniques. These remove the repetition of patterns within each frame (*intra-frame compression*). For motion video, in addition, temporal redundancy techniques are necessary to remove repetition between frames (*inter-frame compression*). At the heart of the main image compression techniques lies the discrete cosine transform (DCT), which is used to transform the data into a different mathematical domain that is more easily compressed.

Coding of real-time video is carried out in a series of steps:

1. The codec first creates a frame consisting of thousands of pixels by sampling the analogue signal from the camera.
2. It divides the frame into blocks consisting of 16 × 16 pixels of luminance (brightness) and 8 × 8 pixels for each of two chrominance (colour) channels.
3. It then analyses the blocks to determine what data should be sent in order to avoid sending data that has not changed since the previous frame.
4. If major changes have taken place, it uses intra-frame coding to send entirely new data.
5. If there are only small differences, it uses inter-frame coding to add to the information already available.
6. If there are no changes, it repaints the block.
7. If there is a good match for the block that is being sent near its original position in the previous frame, the codec uses motion compensation to move the block as a whole.
8. It then uses the DCT algorithm to reorganise the pixel information within each block into a more compact form by generating a series of mathematical coefficients that represent some combination of pixel values.
9. It uses quantisation to scale and round the coefficients in order to produce good approximations that can be sent in fewer bits.
10. Finally it uses two-dimensional and run-length encoding to reduce the lengthy strings of zeros produced by quantisation (Richardson 1992).

There is thus a common core of techniques that can be carried out by programmable digital signal processors (DSPs), whilst other features such as pre- and post-processing, motion compensation and audio enhancements remain proprietary. Pre-processing includes filtering to remove temporal redundancy (where something does not change much between frames) and spatial redundancy (where detailed information in a pattern, for example, is spread over a number of frames). Post-processing can be used to remove unwanted picture elements (artefacts) and restore missing data (e.g. lines dropped from a frame).

Compression based on DCT can give rise to a number of problems. For example, it may degrade crudely, producing a 'block' effect on the display. More importantly, it is believed to be near its theoretical limit. Researchers are therefore looking to new techniques for the new generation of algorithms. These include fractals, described in Chapter 7, and wavelets.

The theory of wavelets derives from work in mathematics and signal processing. It provides a set of concepts, methods and algorithms that are suitable for non-stationary signals and for numerical signal processing. Stationary signals (such as white noise) can be decomposed into linear combinations of sines and cosines, which can be studied and processed using the methods based on the Fourier transform. In contrast signals that are not stationary - where transient events occur that cannot be predicted even with statistical knowledge of past behaviour - can be composed into linear combinations of wavelets. Work on the application of wavelets to image compression is currently under way in a number of research establishments.

9.5   Standards

9.5.1   Audiovisual telephony

H.200 Recommendations
The first recommendations for visual telephone systems were adopted by the CCITT in 1984 and widely used in Europe. These defined the compression algorithm and the number of frames per second that could be processed. They permitted codecs to operate at speeds of 768 Kbit/s or 2 Mbit/s. By the mid-1980s it was clear that a standard for lower bit rate video was needed. Work commenced on an $N \times 384$ standard. This was soon overtaken by advances in technology and in 1988 work began on a $p \times 64$ standard. This led to the new series of ITU-T Recommendations for the infrastructure of audiovisual services, shown in Table 9.1.

There is currently no formal activity on an H.200 option for still frame graphics, which require a higher resolution than motion video, or for the transmission of non-video data such as spreadsheets or word processing documents during a conference.

Recommendation H.261 describes the video coding and decoding methods for the moving picture component of audiovisual services at the rate of $p \times 64$ Kbit/s, where p is in the range 1 to 30. It describes the video source coder, the video multiplex coder and the transmission coder.

The ITU-T has adopted two formats for video telephony:

1. Common Intermediate Format (CIF) defines a picture of 352 pixels by 288 lines.
2. Quarter-CIF (QCIF) defines a picture of 176 pixels by 144 lines, with lower luminance and chrominance, giving a poorer quality image.

All H.261 codecs must be able to operate with QCIF, whilst CIF is optional. Two main applications were envisaged. For low values of p (1, 2), the standard is suitable for desktop video using the QCIF format. The current range of video PCs using

Table 9.1   H.200 Recommendations for audiovisual services

Standard	Description
H.200	Framework for Recommendations for audiovisual services
H.221	Frame structure for a 64 to 1,920 Kbit/s channel in audiovisual teleservices
H.230	Frame-synchronous control and indication signals for audiovisual systems
H.231	Multipoint control units for audiovisual systems using digital channels up to 2 Mbit/s
H.233	Confidentiality system for audiovisual services
H.242	System for establishing communication between audiovisual terminals using digital channels up to 2 Mbit/s
H.243	Procedures for establishing communication between three or more audiovisual terminals using digital channels up to 2 Mbit/s
H.261	Video codec for audiovisual services at $p \times 64$ Kbit/s

ISDN fit this profile. For values of p greater than or equal to six, the standard is suitable for videoconferencing using the CIF format. Videoconferencing equipment accessing 384 Kbit/s lines matches this profile (Liou 1991).

H.320 Recommendations

A further series of recommendations now covers systems and terminal equipment for audiovisual services. Recommendation H.320 covers the technical requirements for narrowband visual telephone services where channel rates do not exceed 1,920 Kbit/s. Recommendation H.331 covers broadcasting type multipoint systems and terminal equipment. The H.320 family of standards for audiovisual telephony forms the basis for communication between equipment from different manufacturers. It is anticipated that Recommendation H.320 will be extended to a number of Recommendations each of which would cover a single videoconferencing or videophone service (narrowband, broadband, etc.).

Most video PCs will support the mandatory requirements of the H.320 family of standards: H.261 for video coding at QCIF resolution and 7.5 fps, G.722 and G.711 for audio coding and H.221 for channel control. In addition they may choose to support H.320 conformant options that include full CIF resolution and increased frame rates up to 15 fps. Individual suppliers may also provide their own enhancements to the standards, as well as extensions that consist of proprietary algorithms. The latter are necessary to ensure compatibility with products already in the field. These options, enhancements and extensions to the standard leave plenty of scope for suppliers to gain a competitive edge and confuse the customers.

9.5.2   Audiovisual applications

The Moving Picture Experts Group (MPEG) is an ISO/IEC working group, which began in 1988 to develop a standard for video and associated audio on digital storage media. Unlike JPEG and H.261, MPEG is an asymmetrical technique - encoding takes 10 times as long as decoding. It is therefore essentially an algorithm for delivery platforms. MPEG-1 products are already available and MPEG-2 products are under development, even though the standard has not yet been finalised.

MPEG-1
The standard for the first phase (known as MPEG-1) defines a bit stream for compressed video and audio optimised to fit into a bandwidth of 1.5 Mbit/s - the data rate of optical media such as CD-ROM, digital audiotape (DAT), write-once read-many (WORM) and magneto-optic (MO) disks as well as communications channels such as ISDN and LANs (Le Gall 1991). The standard consists of five parts:

- the system part (11172-1) deals with synchronisation and multiplexing of audiovisual information;
- the video part (11172-2) addresses the video compression techniques;
- the audio part (11172-3) addresses the audio compression techniques;
- conformance testing (11172-4) is designed to provide a basis for methodologies for testing bit streams and decoders for conformance with parts 1, 2 and 3;
- software coding (11172-5) is a response to the ever increasing processing capability of computers that will make possible software implementation of the first three parts of the standard.

The video part defines a compressed bit stream, which ensures compatibility between the encoder and the decoder. However, the compression algorithms used are up to the individual manufacturers, who can thus obtain (or claim) a proprietary advantage whilst operating within the scope of an international standard. There is no mandatory picture format or bit rate. The specification allows images up to 4,095 × 4,095 by 60 fps in resolution and bit rates up to 100 Mbit/s. In practice a subset known as the Constrained Parameters Bitstream (CPB) has been widely used. This limits the resolution to a source input format (SIF) of 352 pixels × 240 lines by 25 fps or 352 × 288 by 30 fps (slightly better than VHS quality) and the bit rate to 1.862 Mbit/s. In practice, the latter is often increased up to 6 Mbit/s.

The MPEG-1 standard has been adopted by a number of vendors, including Philips which has incorporated it in the 'White Book' specification for video on compact disk-interactive (CD-I). Some early video-on-demand products are based on it. However, vendors have taken advantage of the open nature of the specification to add proprietary extensions and enhancements, which are now starting to appear under descriptions such as MPEG-1.5 or MPEG-1++. These can operate at 2 Mbit/s and above, making them just adequate for transmitting VHS quality video.

MPEG-2

The second phase (known as MPEG-2) is currently under development. There are three parts to the standard, whose definition was completed in July 1993, each handled by a separate subcommittee:

- the systems part (13818-1) specifies coding formats for multiplexing audio, video, and other data into a form suitable for transmission or storage;
- the video part (13818-2), a superset of MPEG-1 Video, specifies the coded bit stream for high-quality digital video;
- the audio part (13818-3) specifies low bit rate coding of multichannel audio.

All parts are expected to reach IS (International Standard) status by the end of 1994. Another key MPEG-2 extension is Digital Storage Media Command and Control (DSM-CC), a protocol intended to provide support for interaction between set-top terminals and video servers, interaction with business video databases, CD-based MPEG video games, and a number of others. This is expected to reach working draft level by the end of 1994 and to achieve IS status in July 1996.

MPEG-2 Video builds on the completed MPEG-1 Video standard by supporting interlaced video formats and a number of other advanced features, including support for HDTV. It is designed to be backwards compatible with MPEG-1. In particular video encoded at MPEG-2 can be played back as an MPEG-1 bit stream. MPEG-2 is defined in terms of extensible profiles - each of which will support the features needed by an important class of applications - and levels, which limit parameters such as sample rates, frame dimensions and bit rates.

MPEG-2 Main Profile, shown in Table 9.2, was defined to support digital video transmission over cable, satellite and other broadcast channels, as well as for digital storage media and other communications applications. MPEG-2 Video Main Level, which will play the same role as CPB in MPEG-1, matches the sampling limits for CCIR 601 - an ITU recommendation for digital video. Between them, Main Profile and Main Level can support a range of applications within the limitations of current technology.

MPEG-2 is destined to play a significant role in the future of television. As we

Table 9.2   MPEG-2 Main Profile

Level	Samples	Lines	Frames (fps)	Bit rate (Mbit/s)	Quality
Low	352	288	30	4	CIF format, VHS videotape
Main	720	576	30	15	CCIR 601, studio quality
High-1440	1440	1152	60	60	4 × CCIR 601, HDTV quality
High	1920	1152	60	80	SMPTE production quality

Note: Numbers given are the upper limit in each case.

have seen, it forms the basis of the new European digital TV broadcasting standard, whilst in the USA the video and systems parts have been adopted by the Grand Alliance for the new digital HDTV standard. The acceptability of MPEG-2 audio and video quality is therefore of critical importance. A series of subjective tests of the Main Profile have been carried out in collaboration with the European Broadcasting Union (EBU), the ITU Radiocommunication Sector and the SMPTE. These involved a variety of test materials, encoded by a large number of software encoders. The pictures produced were subjectively assessed by over 250 observers from three continents. The results showed that for all test materials:

- 9 Mbit/s coding provides near transparent quality;
- at 6 Mbit/s the achieved quality for all test materials equals or exceeds that of conventional TV systems;
- at lower bit rates, such as 4 Mbit/s, high-quality pictures will be obtained on most picture material.

These results suggest that MPEG-2 video compression over a network that is capable of carrying between 3 and 6 Mbit/s should be adequate for most television services.

The MPEG-2 Systems standard defines two data stream formats: the Transport Stream, which can carry multiple programs simultaneously, and which is optimised for use in applications where data loss may be likely, and the Program Stream, which is optimised for multimedia applications, for performing systems processing in software, and for MPEG-1 compatibility. Both streams are intended to support a large number of known and anticipated applications. The Transport Stream is designed for the transmission of digital television and video telephony over fibre, satellite, cable, ISDN, asynchronous transfer mode (ATM) and other networks, and also for storage on digital videotape and other devices. The Program Stream is similar to the MPEG-1 Systems standard, with extensions to support new and future applications.

MPEG-4

Work on a new MPEG initiative for very low bit rate coding of audiovisual programs began officially in September 1993. This activity is known as MPEG-4 - the work on high-definition TV originally scheduled for MPEG-3 has now been absorbed into MPEG-2 High-1440 and High Levels. It will cover the coding of audiovisual programmes for transmission over very low bit rate channels (i.e. up to $176 \times 144 \times 10$ Hz with bit rates up to 64 Kbit/s) or storage within a reduced capacity.

A first draft of the Requirements document has been produced, which will form the basis of the technical work on the development of compression algorithms. MPEG-4 is scheduled to result in a draft specification in 1997, which will require the development of fundamentally new algorithmic techniques. When completed, the MPEG-4 standard will enable a whole spectrum of new applications, including interactive mobile multimedia communications.

9.6   Proprietary compression

9.6.1   Digital Video Interactive (DVI)

DVI technology originated at the David Sarnoff Research Laboratory at Princeton in 1983 and is now owned by Intel, which supplies a video processor, delivery and capture boards. These currently support two levels of compression for full-screen, full-motion video:

1. Real Time Video (RTV) can be compressed and decompressed in real time, thus allowing developers to edit their work interactively.
2. Presentation Level Video (PLV) is an asymmetric technique for high-quality video. Digitisation and compression are done by a large computer at a DVI compression facility.

DVI is a proprietary algorithm based on the discrete cosine transform. Products that support DVI are available from other suppliers, including IBM and Microsoft. Intel provides software decompression, under the Indeo trademark.

9.6.2   Other proprietary techniques

Fractal Image Compression
Fractal Image Compression was described in Chapter 7. Iterated Systems also offers a version called VideoBox that supports full-motion video. This is claimed to support software decompression at 30 fps in a 320 × 200 window with 15 bits of colour, using a 33-MHz 486 computer. The storage requirement is about 4 MB for 1 minute of near-VHS quality video. Other companies are believed to be developing proprietary video compression technology that will also be based on fractals.

QuickTime
Apple's QuickTime, which is available on both Macintosh and Windows platforms, includes several schemes for software compression and decompression including the Video compressor. This uses a proprietary method that can achieve ratios of between 5:1 and 25:1. It allows digitised video sequences to be played back from hard disk or CD-ROM at 15 fps in a 160 × 120 pixel video window. The most recent version (available only on the Macintosh at present) includes a new compression algorithm called Compact Video developed by SuperMac Technology. Playback rates of 10 to 15 fps in a 320 × 240 video window or 20 to 30 fps in a 160 × 120 window can be achieved with software decompression.

Video for Windows
Like QuickTime, Microsoft's Video for Windows also incorporates a choice of software decompression. Two of these, Video and RLE, are Microsoft's own

products. The third is Indeo, Intel's video recording and playback technology based on DVI.

Summary

Desktop video communications are currently seen by some suppliers as the next 'killer' application that will enable them to sell more personal computers. In practice this is most unlikely to be true. Managers should be aware of the technical limitations of these systems. Most assessments to date are based on what users say they will do with the equipment, rather than what they will actually do in practice. For example, it is far from clear that many people will really want to share and edit documents in real time over remote links. The need to use stored audiovisual material in business applications, other than its conventional use in training and POI/POS systems, is also unresolved.

References

[Apple 1990] *The Apple guide to multimedia development tools*, Apple Computer UK Limited.

[Le Gall 1991] D. Le Gall, 'MPEG: A video compression standard for multimedia applications', *Communications of the ACM*, vol. 34, no. 4, pp. 46-58.

[Liou 1991] M. Liou, 'Overview of the px64 kbit/s video coding standard', *Communications of the ACM*, vol. 34, no. 4, pp. 59-63.

[Richardson 1992] S. Richardson, 'Videoconferencing: the bigger (and better) picture', *Data Communications*, June, pp. 103-111.

CHAPTER 10

Storage for multimedia

This chapter reviews the role of traditional magnetic storage media before describing the new optical media. Access to magnetic storage is still essential for on-line processing and for applications such as video on demand that require high-speed transfer rates. Optical storage is already making a major impact on the multimedia market as a result of the benefits that it offers in terms of capacity, life span and cost. The different types of optical media reviewed include analogue videodisk, compact disk, and the use of writeable storage media such as WORM and magneto-optic (MO) disks. Finally the growing series of specifications for different forms of compact disk (CD-DA, CD-ROM, CD-ROM XA, CD-I, Photo CD and Video CD) are described.

10.1   Choice of storage

Despite optimistic predictions the paperless office has not materialised - instead the mountain of paper continues to grow relentlessly. Faced with the cost of storing all this paper, businesses are looking for other means of holding information. Micrographics has been available for archival and records management for the past half century and its use continues to grow, if slowly. It is not, however, suitable for the storage and retrieval of information that requires processing by computer. Magnetic media have also been available for many years and, in contrast to micrographics, are suitable for dynamic applications. However, the cost/capacity ratio of magnetic storage and its limited life span make it unsuitable for the bulk storage of business documents. Thus managers have already started to turn to optical media to handle their storage and retrieval needs.

It is difficult for most people to picture the huge increases in storage capacity that have become available. A typical four-drawer filing cabinet may contain 68 files, each holding 344 pages. If scanned at a resolution of 200 dpi and compressed as described in Chapter 7, this file would take up 9.65 MB of storage. Thus the total capacity of the filing cabinet is equivalent to 656 MB (IMAT 1988). In comparison, a single CD-ROM can hold 550 MB of data - almost as much as the filing cabinet.

Nevertheless, as we have seen, multimedia data can exhaust even this capacity. The same CD-ROM can contain no more than about 30 minutes of full-screen, full-motion (FSFM) video, even after compression.

The factors influencing the choice of a suitable storage system for multimedia will vary according to the user's circumstances. They include:

- the quantity of data to be stored, required access time and acceptable transfer rate;
- the type of information to be stored: alphanumeric data, text, line art, halftones or grey scale, colour, audio, video;
- the stability of the data, the rates at which it is acquired and changed, its expected life span and any legal requirements;
- how many copies of the data are to be made, the distribution of such copies, whether hard copies of documents are required, whether the system must be portable between sites;
- the cost of data preparation, capture, storage media and other related equipment;
- the number of users, their skills, experience and likely training needs;
- interfaces required to any existing systems, standards, backup requirements, security;
- conversion of existing data such as the transfer of archives from microfiche to optical disk.

Thus the selection of a storage system is potentially a very complex process. Other non-technical factors must also be taken into account such as the long-term stability of the suppliers and standards involved.

10.2   Magnetic media

Magnetic storage is suitable for dynamic data that requires frequent change. In image applications Winchester disks may be used as temporary storage for data after it has been captured and before it is indexed and allocated to permanent storage on optical disk. They are also used as a cache to hold data that must be accessed quickly and for index information held in databases. Data may be kept on-line in magnetic storage during processing and then archived to optical media. Magnetic media are also well suited to applications such as video on demand where large amounts of time-dependent information must be transferred at high bit rates. Data held on-line on magnetic storage is easily accessible. Performance, as measured in terms of average access times and data transfer rates, is approximately three times better than for optical media.

RAID

The use of random arrays of inexpensive disks (RAID) for data storage is a concept developed at the University of California in 1987 as an alternative to the single, large, expensive disks (SLED) used in traditional mainframe systems. Data is stripped across several physical drives (the RAIDset). Three factors influence the choice of configuration of these drives - performance, availability and cost. There are several levels of RAID, which seek to optimise any two of these factors, by trading off the third one as follows:

- RAID 0 (stripping) improves request rate or data rate via variable data chunk sizes. It provides no redundancy and is suited to applications that require high performance for non-critical data.
- RAID 1 (shadowing) provides two complete sets of all user data. It can also improve the read request performance, because the controller can read from whichever drive is closest to the required data. Write performance on the other hand will be degraded because the system must write to both members of the shadow set. The redundancy inherent in RAID 1 makes it ideal for system drives and/or critical files.
- RAID 0+1 combines stripping and shadowing, thus providing the same performance as RAID 0 with the reliability of RAID 1.
- RAID 3 offers improved bandwidth. With chunk sizes smaller than the average request rate, a single request spans all disks and the data rate is maximised. Because the request rate is limited to that of a single drive, there is no improvement in simultaneous data output capability.
- RAID 5 offers improved read bandwidth and improved I/O throughout. Chunk sizes are larger than the average request size, allowing a single request to each disk, boosting the request rate.
- RAID 6 offers similar performance to RAID 5; write performance is slightly worse, but it can survive any two disk failures.

RAID has attracted attention as a storage technology for the new media servers that will be used for applications such as video on demand. For example, Digital Equipment's Video Interactive Information Server (VIIS) takes advantage of RAID 5 technology. The disks in the array are mounted in exchangeable plug-in units that can be hot-swapped even when the system is in operation.

Not everyone agrees that RAID is the best technology for video. Microsoft claims that it is expensive, because it is manufactured in small quantities, and is also not optimal for video. In Microsoft's new server technology, codenamed Tiger, audio and video can be stored on hard disks with a small computer systems interface (SCSI) at a fraction of the cost of other storage media.

10.3   Optical media

Because of its high storage capacity and potentially long life span, optical storage has played a significant role in the development of multimedia. Although optical videodisk was invented by Friebus in 1929, modern optical technology using a laser to record and read information from a replicated disk dates from 1972 when prototype systems were demonstrated by Philips and MCA.

This was followed by the introduction of the compact disk (CD), the (trademarked) name for the digital audio disk developed jointly by Philips and Sony. Compact disks for use in audio systems became available in the early 1980s. The use of the CD format for the storage of digital text and images came with the introduction of the compact disk read-only memory (CD-ROM). Further extensions were to follow. Section 10.4 reviews the various CD formats and their role in the commercial marketplace.

The types of optical storage described so far take the form of read-only media, designed for the mass distribution of information. This information is pre-recorded and stored either in analogue form on videodisk or in digital form on compact disk. In each case a master disk has to be prepared, from which a large number of copies can be made. In contrast, other types of optical storage are now manufactured and distributed as blank media on which users can record their own data in digital form.

Optical disks can be classified according to a wide range of different factors, such as the type of substrate or the method of construction. These factors affect the cost and durability of a disk. Several different techniques have been developed for recording data on the disks, some of which are reversible and are used for erasable disks, whilst others are irreversible and used for write-once disks. Both disks and drives are available in a variety of sizes and formats. Disks may be single or double sided. The amount of information stored on a disk varies depending on the recording technique.

This wide variation in the optical products available is a source of confusion for both users and suppliers. Progress on standards for optical storage media has been very slow. The main considerations are the physical layout of the media, logical file formats, drive mechanisms, interfaces, controllers and device drivers.

10.3.1   Analogue media

Videodisk is the general term for disks that are used to store video information in analogue form. Most early systems were *linear* - users played back information in the order in which it was recorded on the disk. These systems were superseded by *interactive videodisk (IV)*, which gives the user far more flexibility by allowing access to individual frames of video. The standard videodisk format is LaserVision, a system developed by Philips and supported under licence by other manufacturers including Sony, Pioneer and Hitachi who sell disks and drives. It has been commercially available since 1978. Disks, available in 8-inch and 12-inch sizes, support analogue video with stereo analogue sound. Several other videodisk formats are now available, some of which support digital sound.

Up to 54,000 frames of FSFM video can be stored on one side of such a disk, together with two audio tracks that may be recorded separately. Full motion in this context means that the video can be played back at 25 or 30 fps. There are two ways of recording this information, whose characteristics are summarised in Table 10.1: constant linear velocity (CLV) and constant angular velocity (CAV). In the former case, the length of track used to store one frame is always the same - the speed of rotation is varied to keep the same length of track passing the head. It is difficult to retrieve a single frame accurately, so CLV is best suited for linear recordings that are usually played back through a TV monitor.

In contrast, on a CAV disk each frame is stored in one revolution of the disk (the track length differs), whilst the disk rotates at a constant rate. Each frame may be identified and coded, to allow for the random access that is essential for interactive video. CAV players can be linked to a computer through an RS232 interface.

Five levels of interactivity - known as the Nebraska scale - have been established for videodisk systems:

- level 0 supports linear playback only;
- level 1 supports only direct controls such as start and stop, search, freeze frame, backward and forward motion;
- level 2 supports some interaction through an internal processor with limited branching, but cannot record responses;
- level 3 supports interactive use, controlled by an external computer, and the recording of user responses;
- level 4 supports the use of other optical media such as compact disk.

A typical level 3 delivery system will consist of a LaserVision player linked to a PC or Apple Macintosh through an RS232 interface, a monitor, overlay board and keyboard together with options such as a keypad, tracker ball, mouse or touchscreen.

The overlay board is a key part of the system. It allows two or more video signals to be combined. Computer-generated graphics may be placed over a sequence from the videodisk, using a genlock facility to combine the signals. Analogue boards can

Table 10.1   Comparison of interactive videodisks

	CLV	CAV
Configuration	spiral	concentric
Speed	variable	constant
Access	linear	random
Access time	10 s max	< 3 s/frame
Continuous playing time	60 min/side	36 min/side
Interactive use	no	yes

overlay part of the display so that the video appears in a window, but the image cannot be reduced or modified. Some overlay boards now digitise video information so that it can be manipulated.

Videodisks support one of the broadcast TV standards - NTSC or PAL - which are not compatible, though some players are capable of handling both formats. They are available as pre-recorded disks for the consumer market, customised training packages and generic courseware sold off the shelf. Although the main commercial use of interactive video has been in training, systems are also in use as point-of-information in museums and art galleries, and point-of-sale in shops.

Interactive video suffers from a number of limitations:

1. The information cannot be manipulated because it is stored in analogue form.
2. There is no support for networking.
3. The disks are expensive to produce.

Despite these problems, IV is appropriate for use in applications where there is a need for high-quality FSFM video in standalone systems.

10.3.2   Digital media

The disadvantages of videodisk have been largely overcome by the appearance of digital optical storage media. The first of these, the familiar audio compact disk, was launched by Philips and Sony in 1982. In 1985 the basic technology was extended to support up to 550 MB of pre-recorded digital data with the announcement of a specification for a data storage disk. The main problems with the use of this format - known as CD-ROM - for multimedia applications are its storage capacity, which is inadequate for motion video, and a data transfer rate that is limited to 1.5 Mbit/s.

Further announcements in 1986 and 1987 introduced CD-ROM XA and CD-I, developments that supported a mixture of text, still image, audio and - eventually - FSFM video.

The types of optical storage described so far take the form of read-only media, designed for the mass distribution of information. This information is pre-recorded and stored either in analogue form on videodisk or in digital form on compact disk. In each case a master disk has to be prepared, from which a large number of copies can be made.

In contrast, other types of optical storage are now manufactured and distributed as blank media on which users can record their own data in digital form. These include write-once read-many (WORM), magneto-optic (MO) and CD Recordable disks. Information on WORM disks can be recorded once and read back many times. As WORM disks cannot be modified or erased, they are suitable for storing large volumes of static data. In contrast information on MO disks can be erased either in bulk or in spots, and the media reused. Such erasable disks provide low-cost storage for non-static data. CD Recordable is a recent development that allows users to create their own compact disks in house in small quantities.

Drives for optical disks are available in three different configurations:

1. Standalone drives containing a single disk, which is inserted manually. These may be built into a computer or packaged separately.
2. Rack- or cabinet-mounted drives, containing several disks, each of which is inserted manually.
3. Jukeboxes - storage and retrieval units that can support several drives and up to 100 disks. The disks are stored in racks within the cabinet, retrieved automatically by a robotic arm and inserted into a drive. After reading has been completed, the disk is removed from the drive and returned to the rack automatically.

Drives may be available with or without software, controllers and interfaces. The SCSI interface has proved to be popular for both WORM and erasable disk drives.

10.3.3   Advantages and limitations of optical storage

All forms of optical disks provide:

- high storage capacity;
- random access to data;
- a guaranteed life span of between 30 and 40 years;
- the ability to handle new data types;
- removability and portability.

In addition WORM disks provide security of information, which cannot be erased or modified, and the ability to maintain an audit trail. These disks are suitable for archiving static data and providing remote access to large volumes stored at a local site. Erasable disks, on the other hand, provide low-cost, low access rate, non-static data storage. They are suitable for file and directory creation and general workspace.

Pioneer and other companies now supply dual function disk drives that can handle both WORM and MO disks. It will thus be possible to use MO disks for development and then move to WORM disks for distribution as alternative to CD.

As Table 10.2 shows, access speeds and data transfer rates for optical disks are still low in comparison to magnetic media, giving only about 25 per cent of the performance. However, average seek time has been steadily reduced. Moreover, costs are coming down, so in a few years MO drives will cost the same as hard disk drives. The PC of the future may be able to use MO as an alternative to the hard disk.

Table 10.2	Comparison of optical and magnetic media		
	5.25 hard disk	*5.25 WORM*	*5.25 MO*
Capacity	300 MB	325 MB/side	325 MB/side
Sustained transfer rate	32 Mbit/s	3.9 Mbit/s	7.4 Mbit/s
Average seek time	16 ms	53 ms	65 ms
Life span	5 years	30-40 years	> 10 years
Removable	No	Yes	Yes
Erasable	Yes	No	Yes

Whilst CD is an excellent publishing and distribution platform, it is too slow for the satisfactory playback of high-quality motion video. The main reason for this is that all disks are pre-recorded in CLV mode. As we saw earlier, on a CLV disk the length of track used to store one frame is always the same - the speed of rotation is varied to keep the same length of track passing the head. This is not a problem when playing music, but when trying to do random access to a CD-ROM, the need to accelerate and decelerate the disk is the biggest obstacle to making it faster. In contrast most magnetic disks spin at a constant angular velocity, so that the data density decreases towards the outside of the disk, but seeks are faster. In addition optical disk heads tend to be heavier than magnetic disk heads, so they have more inertia, and take longer to stabilise onto a new track. Many CD-ROMs also contain too much data to make effective use of RAM caches. This lack of speed will be noticeable in the use of CD-ROM for large random-access databases, or any kind of interactive multimedia application.

10.4   Compact disk specifications

As Table 10.3 shows, the term 'compact disk' (CD) now covers a variety of products, all of which are based on the original optical disk format developed by Philips and Sony.

10.4.1   Compact disk-digital audio (CD-DA)

In 1982 Philips and Sony launched *CD-DA*. This standard, known as the Red Book, covers the specification of a 12-cm diameter optical disk that can store up to 72 minutes of high-quality sound encoded using 16-bit linear PCM at a 44.1-kHz sampling rate.

CD-DA has proved to be a very successful consumer product. Players are available from Philips, Sony and others who guarantee that any disk that conforms to the standard - identifiable by the words 'digital audio' printed below the logo - can be played on any of their players anywhere in the world. The success of this approach was seen by Philips as the pattern for the launch of multimedia consumer products.

Table 10.3   Comparison of compact disk formats

Type of disk	Type of information	Specification
CD-DA	music	Red Book
CD+G	music, graphics	
CD-ROM Mode 1	text	Yellow Book
CD-ROM Mode 2	text, graphics, still image and audio (non-interleaved)	Yellow Book
CD-MO	recordable	Orange Book Part I
CD-WO	recordable	Orange Book Part II
Photo CD	photographs	Orange Book Part II, hybrid disks
CD-ROM XA	interleaved text, still image, audio and video	Yellow Book supplement
CD-1	text, graphics, audio, some video	Green Book
Karaoke CD	text, graphics, audio, FSFM video	
Video CD	text, graphics, audio, FSFM video	White Book

A variant on the format called CD+Graphics (CD+G), which allows a music producer to add still graphics to a CD-DA disk, has been used to a limited degree, most commonly in the Japanese marketplace.

10.4.2   Compact disk-read-only memory (CD-ROM)

CD-ROM is an extension of the CD-DA technology that can support up to 550 MB of pre-recorded digital data. A standard for CD-ROM - known as the Yellow Book - was announced by Philips and Sony in 1985. Mode 1 is for computer data. Mode 2 is for compressed audio data, image and video data. CD-ROMs (identifiable by the words 'data storage' beneath the logo) are best suited for the storage of text, but can support still image, graphics and audio if these are used separately - it is not possible to have commentary over pictures, for example.

CD-ROM is operating system dependent - different versions are required for MS-DOS and the Macintosh, for example. The directory format is covered by an ISO standard (IS 9660) - formerly known as the High Sierra standard. Level One is similar to an MS-DOS file system, with restrictions on filenames and directory names. Level Two allows longer filenames, up to 32 characters, whilst retaining many of the other restrictions. Level Two disks are not usable on some systems, particularly MS-DOS. Most CD-ROMs intended for the Macintosh are created in the Hierarchical Filing System (HFS) format, which is unrelated to High Sierra and IS 9660 formats.

CD-ROM is an economic medium for the publication and distribution of information. CD-ROMs are usually made by specialist companies who will make a master and then use that to duplicate the disks.

10.4.3   Recordable compact disk

The specification for recordable compact disks - known as the Orange Book - is in two parts: Part I covers *CD-MO* (Magneto Optic) disks whilst Part II covers *CD-WO* (Write Once) disks. It also defines a second type of CD-WO disk called a 'hybrid disk', of which Photo CD is an example.

A hybrid disk consists of a pre-recorded area and a recordable area. The pre-recorded area, which is read only, is used for the information that is manufactured into the disk in accordance with the Red, Yellow and Green Book specifications and that can be played on any CD player. The recordable area is where additional recordings can be made by the user in one or more sessions. Only the first session on the disk is readable by current CD players - additional software will be needed to read the additional sessions.

Several companies have recently launched recorders that can be used for single-copy 'one-offs', or low-volume CD production, including JVC, Philips, Sony, Yamaha and Pinnacle. The blank disks for CD recorders are not the same as a normal CD. The metal data surface is gold instead of aluminium. The recorder uses a high-powered laser to modify a dye layer that is between the gold and the plastic. Special authoring software, available from companies such as Dataware Technologies, is required to create the application.

A volume and file format standard (ECMA 168) for CD-WO and CD-ROM was approved as a European standard by the General Assembly of the European Computer Manufacturers Association (ECMA) in June 1992. This will allow CD-WO to be used more as a general purpose storage peripheral than is possible using IS 9660.

Photo CD

Photo CD is a technology developed by Kodak by which images on 35-mm film can be captured by an image scanner and written to compact disks in accordance with Part II of the Orange Book Hybrid Disk specifications. This makes it possible to write photographs to the disk in several different sessions. Those written in the first session will use the IS 9660 format and can be read by existing CD-ROM XA players connected to a computer running new software written for the Photo CD picture structure. Additionally, the photographs can be displayed on CD-I players and Photo CD players connected to a TV set. Photographs written to disk after the first session can be displayed on CD-I players and Photo CD players that have multisession drives - ones that can look for multiple index areas. New software and/or firmware will be needed to read these additional photographs with existing CD-ROM XA players.

10.4.4   CD-ROM extended architecture (CD-ROM XA)

Announced in 1986, *CD-ROM XA* is an interim development supported by

Microsoft, Philips and Sony. It supports simultaneous text, still image and audio together with some motion video - partial screen, 15 fps. A supplement to the Yellow Book published in 1991 defines the CD-ROM XA standard, including a new kind of track that may interleave Mode 2 compressed audio and Mode 2 data sectors. Additional hardware is needed to separate these when playing the disk. The hardware is programmed to separate the audio from the data, decompress the audio and play it out through the audio jacks. At the same time, the hardware passes the data to the computer. It requires a Mode 2 CD-ROM drive and upgrade card.

CD-ROM XA is the link between the workstation environment supported by CD-ROM and the consumer environment. It uses the same sound formats as CD-I (ADPCM levels B and C), but different graphics formats and operating systems.

A special kind of CD-ROM XA bridge disk - *Karaoke CD* - was developed jointly by Philips and JVC. These disks can be played on a dedicated Karaoke CD player or on a CD-I player equipped with a Digital Video cartridge. This concept was developed further in the White Book specification for *Video CD*, another CD-ROM XA bridge disk. These disks, typically containing films or music videos, can be played on a dedicated Video CD player, on a CD-I player equipped with a Digital Video cartridge or on a computer equipped with the appropriate hardware and software. The Video CD standard is supported by Philips, JVC, Sony and Matsushita. Both Karaoke CD and Video CD support FSFM video with CD-quality audio, using the MPEG-1 compression standard.

10.4.5   Compact disk-interactive (CD-I)

In June 1987 Philips, Sony and Matsushita published a new standard, the Green Book, for *CD-I* - a self-contained multimedia system based on compact disk and compatible with existing CD audio technology. At its launch CD-I supported text, graphics, four levels of audio including CD-DA, still video and partial screen video. Support for FSFM video to the White Book specification can now be provided by equipping the CD-I player with a Digital Video cartridge.

CD-I is a self-contained computer system, with its own processor unit based on the Motorola 68020, with specific video, audio and control hardware and a CD drive. It runs a real-time, multitasking operating system called CD-RTOS, based on the OS-9 operating system from Microware. A standard TV display is used for output. CD-I is a consumer product, aimed at repeating the success of CD-DA, so a CD-I disk will play on any CD-I player anywhere in the world. All CD-I players can play CD-DA disks and CD-I disks can contain CD-DA tracks.

A variety of players, designed for different markets, are available from Philips and Sony. These include:

- consumer players such as the CD-I 220 are intended for home use and are sold through retail outlets;
- professional players such as the CD-I 360 have specific features, such as

connectivity, a floppy disk drive or portability, and are more expensive than the consumer player; they are sold in the professional market for applications such as point-of-sale presentations;

- development players such as the CD-I 605 are designed for professional applications and for software development; they have features that enable title development, such as debugging tools and the ability to connect to an emulator.

Other companies also manufacture CD-I players, including Sony, Samsung, Matsushita, Sanyo and Kyocera. Manufacturers of players and disks require a licence from Philips. Content developers for CD-I do not need a licence. However, the specification for CD-I (and those for other coloured books) can only be obtained from Philips by signing a non-disclosure agreement and paying a fee.

As with the other multimedia platforms discussed in Chapter 5, applications can be developed for CD-I players by using an authoring system or by programming in a language such as C. Authoring tools for Macintosh and IBM PC platforms will not run on CD-I. It is necessary to buy tools and specialised software libraries that have been developed specially for the platform, such as MediaMogul and the Balboa Run-Time System, both available from OptImage, a Microware-Philips joint venture.

10.4.6   Other formats

In addition to the compact disk specifications developed by Philips and covered in the coloured books, many other companies have introduced their own formats. Table 10.4 lists some of the platforms available. These typically consists of specific hardware and software for audio, video and user input, a computer system and a CD-ROM drive. All will play CD-DA disks. Some may play other formats such as CD+G, CD-ROM XA and Photo CD.

Because these systems have different characteristics and features, they are generally incompatible. A title that has been developed for any of these systems cannot be played on any of the other platforms unless special steps have been taken by the developer of the title to ensure cross-platform compatibility. This incompatibility, which presents challenges for both users and developers, has been a major factor in delaying the growth of the market for compact disk titles.

Table 10.4   Commercial CD platforms

Platform	Supplier
3DO Multiplayer	Panasonic
CD32	Commodore
Jaguar	Atari
SegaCD	Sega
VIS	Tandy

3DO

The company seen as the major competitor to Philips is 3DO, a start-up which is promoting a technology that it wants others to adopt. The 3DO Multiplayer will play CD-DA, Photo CDs, digital video, interactive games and support virtual reality. The first machine to meet the 3DO Multiplayer specification is manufactured by Panasonic. Hardware licences have been granted to several other companies including Matsushita, AT&T, Sanyo, Goldstar, Samsung and Toshiba.

Summary

The choice of suitable storage media for multimedia applications is a difficult one to make. The available media have multiplied rapidly over the last 10 years. Specifications for compact disk continue to evolve and are not readily available. Many computers have been fitted with single-session CD-ROM drives that will be unsuitable for applications developed to the CD-ROM XA or Photo CD specifications. International standards have been slow to appear. Interactive videodisk should still be the first choice for any system that requires high-quality moving video.

References

[IMAT 1988] 'One optical disc: think of it as three filing cabinets', *Information Media & Technology*, vol. 21, no. 6.

CHAPTER 11

Communications

This chapter shows why multimedia puts additional pressure on communications systems. Local area networks are currently optimised to support data transfer in small packets. Several different development programmes are required in order to restructure these networks to handle continuous, time-dependent data streams. The development of appropriate services for wide area networks is outlined, with the likely impact of narrowband and broadband ISDN. The chapter closes with an outline of the likely impact of the digitisation of television on multimedia services.

11.1   Building multimedia networks

At present most multimedia applications still run on single-user systems, usually based on standalone personal computers. The problems encountered when developing multimedia applications are exacerbated when it comes to putting such applications onto networks. As we have seen multimedia data types require large amounts of bandwidth, even after compression. In addition audio and video change continually over time, so that any interruptions in transmission will be very apparent, especially in real-time applications such as conferencing. Where audio and video data are related, as they are in videoconferencing or the playback of video clips, they must be synchronised.

All networks for multimedia applications must therefore provide high-bandwidth capacity, synchronise different types of traffic and support different types of information flow. In addition, because users will not want to pay for the continuous availability of a high bit rate connection, tariffs for wide area networks must also reflect variations in demand.

Bandwidth

High-bandwidth capacity is required to support the transfer of large files (for example, in computer-aided design), high-definition image applications (for example, in medicine and publishing) and the development of video telephony and videoconferencing. Up to 140 Mbit/s may be required, though the development of better compression algorithms is likely to reduce the demand for this level of bandwidth. However, support for high bit rates is not just a question of capacity - optical fibre networks are capable of carrying gigabits per second - the technology for switching and processing must also be available.

Synchronisation

Co-ordination is required to preserve the synchronisation between video, sound and data transmitted over the network. The decentralisation of operations means that work groups are often distributed over a wide area. This in turn is leading to the development of applications such as computer-supported co-operative work (CSCW). These applications require high-speed interconnections and real-time support for group activities with very low transit delays and high throughput.

Different types of information flow

Multimedia networks must support two types of information flow. The first type, *isochronous* flow, is continuous and steady. It allows an exchange of information to take place in real time between message producer and consumer. Such dialogues may contain text, voice or image information. Isochronous information flow is already established on circuit switching networks for applications such as telephony and dedicated videoconferencing.

In contrast *asynchronous* flow is *bursty* - the data does not flow in a steady stream. Sometimes there is very little data, at other times it flows in a torrent. Typically a message is invoked and then processed or stored before being consumed. Such a message can contain text, voice or visual images. Most signals tend to be bursty in practice. As we saw in Chapter 9, compression techniques for video can lead to variable bit rates, as the amount of information transmitted depends on the nature of the content, the speed at which the image is changing and the image quality required. Asynchronous flow takes place in established services such as data communications on packet switching networks, where the data is divided into *packets* before being sent.

Both types of information flow will be required in mixed mode communications: for example, in remote medical consultations, processing of multimedia documents and distributed project management and production. A high-speed switched communications infrastructure is therefore required that can carry isochronous and asynchronous flow simultaneously. It should support circuit switching for fixed rate data like voice and uncompressed video and packet switching to allow dynamically allocated bandwidth for bursty traffic such as compressed digital video.

Variable demand

Demand for bandwidth is not constant. It may be low whilst users are exchanging text, but peak when video information is exchanged. Users will not want to pay for the continuous availability of a circuit that is capable of the sustained carriage of high bit rates. A wide area network infrastructure is needed that can provide exactly the bandwidth required at the instant it is required and subject to the appropriate tariff - bandwidth on demand with flexible billing.

11.2   Local area networks

In a local area network (LAN) each PC is equipped with an interface that is connected to the cable. The PCs, together with a file server and associated peripherals such as printers, form *nodes* on the network. Over the last few years personal computers have been networked in increasing numbers. It has been estimated that some 40 per cent of all business users were on a LAN in 1994. At the same time the average number of users per LAN was set to increase, thus further reducing the bandwidth per user.

The most popular types of LAN at present are Ethernet and Token Ring. These networks are designed to run conventional applications, transferring files of alphanumeric data in packets, which limit the amount of data that can be sent at one time. Furthermore because several nodes will be trying to access the network at the same time, packets sent by one node will be interspersed with data from other nodes.

Conventional files may typically be no more than 20 KB in size. In contrast a single image may be more than 1 MB. Files that contain audio and video data are larger still. Transmitting large data items such as images will slow down access to the network for all users. Real-time audiovisual communications present the most intractable problems for networks, which must be able to manage many live streams of time-dependent data.

11.2.1   Ethernet

Ethernet is a standard for physical layer access that began life at Xerox PARC in 1973. The key standard, agreed by the IEEE 802.3 committee in 1982, defined a 10-Mbit/s data rate using an access method called Carrier Sense Multiple Access with Collision Detection (CSMA/CD) in a bus-based network over a coaxial cable with about a 0.5-inch diameter. In a *bus network* all devices are logically connected in a line to a single cable (Figure 11.1).

Ethernet is a connectionless, contention-based scheme. Before a node sends out data, it listens to the network. If the network is quiet, it transmits data. Only the node for which the data is intended can pick it up. If more than one node transmits at the same time, there is a collision. The node will then wait for a random time

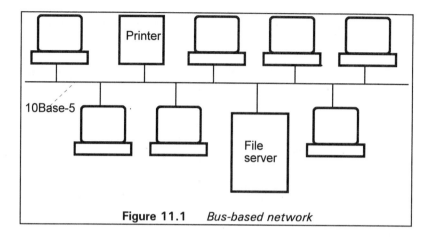

Figure 11.1   *Bus-based network*

before retransmitting data. As more nodes are added to the network there are more collisions, reducing the bandwidth still further - perhaps to as low as 2.5 Mbit/s. Such a scheme is obviously unsuitable for multimedia applications that require the transmission of large amounts of time-dependent data like video in a continuous stream.

The original standard, 10Base-5, was suitable for networks that consist of a small number of expensive workstations and peripherals. The maximum length of a segment was 500 metres and the maximum diameter of a network of segments connected by repeaters was about 2,500 metres. Further developments in cabling have made Ethernet suitable for the world of large networks of inexpensive PCs.

The arrival of 10Base-T in 1990, running on unshielded twisted pair (UTP) - a standard cable installed in most business premises - was particularly important. It was accompanied by a change in topology from bus to *star*, each node being connected to a central *hub*. 10Base-T is now the best-selling LAN infrastructure and one that must be accommodated in any new set of proposals for multimedia networks. Table 11.1 lists the available Ethernet options. The first figure in each case

Table 11.1   Ethernet options

Cable	Bit rate (Mbit/s)	Standard
Thick coaxial	10	10Base-5
Thin coaxial	10	10Base-2
Broadband coaxial	10	10Broad-36
Optical fibre	10	10Base-F
UTP	10	10Base-T
UTP	1	1Base-5
UTP	100	100Base-T
UTP (voice grade)	100	100Base-VG

is the data rate, and the second is usually the maximum distance in hundreds of metres. Thus 10Base-5 indicates baseband with a data rate of 10 Mbit/s over 500 metres.

Isochronous Ethernet (IsoENET) is the (trademarked) name for a single wiring scheme developed by National Semiconductor and IBM as a way of adding isochronous services to established Ethernet LANs. It allocates a 6-Mbit/s service that can be divided into standard 64-Kbit/s channels to support real-time interactive multimedia connections.

In contrast to the changes in cabling, the capacity of Ethernet LANs has not altered since their introduction. The bandwidth currently available is inadequate to support the concurrent use of multimedia data. The main point of dispute is how to improve this whilst maintaining compatibility with the existing infrastructure. Two proposals that would increase bandwidth to 100 Mbit/s have been presented to the IEEE committee for consideration.

100Base-T

100Base-T is compatible with CSMA/CD. It will run at 100 Mbit/s over UTP in segments up to 100 metres in length in a star-shaped configuration with a central repeater or hub, with a maximum network diameter of about 250 metres. Fast Ethernet is supported by a proposal from 3Com and a consortium of 16 vendors including Sun Microsystems and Intel. This proposal, under consideration by the IEEE 802.3 sub-committee, is based on the view that moving to fast Ethernet must not involve wholesale changes for users with existing Ethernet investment. Fast Ethernet should therefore be compatible with CSMA/CD and run on existing cables. 3Com favours two-pair Category 3 voice-grade cabling, though some others prefer single pair Category 5.

100Base-VG

A competing proposal, called 100Base-VG or AnyLAN, has been put forward by Hewlett-Packard and AT&T, supported by Novell and Microsoft. It is likely to be ratified by the IEEE 802.12 subcommittee during 1994. This sacrifices direct compatibility with the existing standard but adds security and dedicated bandwidth. 100Base-VG will run on voice-grade (hence the VG) UTP cabling (Category 3). It uses a non-broadcast isochronous approach that adds security and dedicated bandwidth. In doing this it sacrifices direct compatibility with the existing standard, using a new Demand Priority Protocol instead of the CSMA/CD access method in order to support time-dependent technologies such as multimedia and video. It also uses Quartet Signalling to enable it to transmit and receive on all four wires, rather than using one pair to transmit and one to receive. Although this increases capacity, it has implications for applications such as real-time videoconferencing that requires two-way communications.

11.2.2   Token Ring

Token Ring is based on technology developed in the 1960s that led to several proprietary implementations. The current IBM Token Ring implementation, introduced in 1985, is the basis for the IEEE 802.5 specification. This defines a ring architecture, in which the network takes the form of a closed loop with all the devices attached to the ring. It operates on the basis of a token, which is passed around the ring of nodes. If a node wants to transmit data, it waits till the token comes round, then grabs it, thus obtaining access to the entire bandwidth of the network for as long as it is required. When the node has finished transmitting, the token is released for the next user. This approach ensures that there are fewer data collisions than on Ethernet - which makes it a little more suitable for multimedia - and enhanced security.

Originally only 4 Mbit/s, Token Ring is now capable of carrying up to 16 Mbit/s. As more suppliers enter the market, the cost of Token Ring networks is coming down. Moreover, since UTP is now supported, cabling costs have also been reduced. IBM has committed itself to adding multimedia support to its implementation of Token Ring.

11.2.3   Fibre Distributed Data Interface (FDDI)

FDDI is an ISO standard for high-speed data networking using fibre optics. It is capable of carrying up to 100 Mbit/s over a distance of 40 km and is compatible with IEEE 802, the standard for local area networks. The first major products, which became available in 1988, were designed to interconnect to IEEE 802.3 LANs.

The topology is a dual-attached, counter-rotating Token Ring. Bandwidth is divided into synchronous and asynchronous traffic. Each station is guaranteed a certain portion of time for the transmission of synchronous traffic. Asynchronous traffic may have to wait for several tokens to pass if loading is high. However, this facility is optional and was not included in early implementations. A further disadvantage is that FDDI does not prioritise time-dependent traffic and so is unsuitable for voice and video traffic on busy networks. A second phase, FDDI 2, sets aside a portion of bandwidth dedicated to isochronous traffic.

Since installing fibre is twice as expensive as using copper, a further standards effort is looking at using the same technology over UTP. A draft standard is expected from the ANSI X3T9.5 TP-PMD committee, which has already endorsed 100 Mbit/s over UTP. One version, Copper Distributed Data Interface (CDDI) from Crescendo, is already supported by products from around 13 vendors.

11.3   New options for multimedia LANs

As multimedia PCs and workstations become available at acceptable cost, how should the local area network (LAN) be adapted to cope with the new demands that will be placed upon it? As we have seen, increased bandwidth on its own will not be enough to equip LANs to handle multimedia applications. As long as LANs continue to use a shared medium, they will continue to degrade under loading making them unsuitable for time-dependent applications such as video.

There are several possible ways of approaching this problem, which may be adopted on their own or in combination:

1. Provide a dedicated connection for each workstation using a switched hub.
2. Connect each workstation to a PBX that can handle audio and video.
3. Introduce Asynchronous Transmission Mode (ATM), a new technology that can overcome the limitations of packet switching.

Given the heavy investment that many users have made in existing LAN technology, the most likely strategy will be an approach that combines several of the above developments. Networks will evolve in a series of incremental steps over the next four or five years to support the increasing demands of new applications with a wide range of data types.

11.3.1   Dedicated connections with switched hubs

The arrival of the 10Base-T version of Ethernet in 1990 made it possible for each node to have its own segment of cable, providing a full-bandwidth 10-Mbit/s link to the server or hub (Figure 11.2). The overall performance of the network now depends upon the performance of the hub, which has to be capable of handling the total throughput. This will increase as additional workstations and segments are added. Proprietary switching technology may be used in the hub to enhance performance. These networks provide the infrastructure for a new range of products that support the transmission of video over LANs.

These new products are based on a *switched hub* from companies such as Kalpana and Lannet. The hub supports a *video server* that establishes continuous streams of

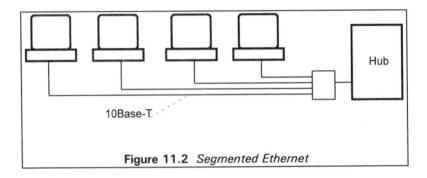

Figure 11.2 *Segmented Ethernet*

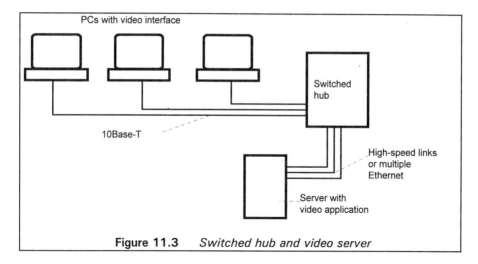

Figure 11.3 *Switched hub and video server*

video data (Figure 11.3). These streams are given priority over other transmissions by the hub, which must implement an isochronous channel within itself that can guarantee the transfer of video between two or more workstations regardless of the load arriving from other workstations.

Special software is required to allow full-motion digital video and audio files to be stored on the server and played back by multiple users on PC clients. Current video networking software packages include StarWorks from Starlight Networks and VideoComm from Protocomm. A third package, FluentLinks, was acquired by Novell as part of its plans to add multimedia capabilities to NetWare. The first phase, NetWare Video 1.0, enables users to store, manage and play back video- and audio-based multimedia applications within NetWare environments. It supports PC clients running DOS, Microsoft Windows and Video for Windows.

11.3.2   PBXs

An alternative approach to the provision of video is to use a circuit switching network based on a PBX rather than a hub. However, bandwidth on such networks is currently limited to 19.2 Kbit/s for asynchronous traffic and 64 Kbit/s synchronous traffic - much lower than the 10 Mbit/s available on Ethernet.

Suppliers of telecommunications equipment are currently very interested in getting into this market and have developed various strategies to tackle the existing limitations:

1. By carrying video over LAN connections supported by hybrid PBXs that can handle both circuit switching for telephony and packet switching for data. Ericsson's MD 110 BP, for example, is a combined PBX/LAN hub that can

handle both Ethernet and Token Ring networks. Fibre optic connections between PBXs can carry voice, video and data traffic at 100 Mbit/s.

2. By using one channel in the PBX for voice and video and another 64-Kbit/s channel for data as Northern Telecom has done, for example, using a data module in its Meridian 1 PBX. The company's video PC, Visit, can be connected to Meridian for corporate networking.

3. By using the PBX to switch video and voice whilst data is transmitted between PCs over a separate Ethernet. The two streams can then be integrated on the desktop as AT&T has done in its Personal Video System, for example. AT&T's Definity PBX also includes a data module that can switch data at up to 1.92 Mbit/s by aggregating channels.

Multimedia applications that run on these new PBX networks must be able to communicate with other applications running on data networks - in order to access data stored in a server on a LAN, for example. Two recent standards activities support this interworking by defining application layer protocols that allow an application running on a data network to work with one running on a PBX. The first is Computer Supported Telephony Applications (CSTA) from the European Computer Manufacturers Association (ECMA) based in Geneva, which most PBX vendors plan to support. Switched Computer Application Interface (SCAI), an ANSI standard, is designed to play a similar role but appears to have little vendor support at present.

Extensions to PBX equipment to support ISDN are also technically possible. Most PBX manufacturers plan to support Euro-ISDN basic access.

11.3.3   ATM

The long-term solution to support for multimedia applications on local area networks is the development of a new infrastructure that will overcome all the limitations of existing systems. The technology that is currently favourite to achieve this and to provide the basis for the next generation of networks, in both the local and wide areas, is asynchronous transfer mode (ATM).

ATM provides a high-speed, low delay service offering only the bandwidth required by the network user. It has developed from work on fast packet switching, combined with asynchronous time division switching. Unlike the conventional shared media networks described above, ATM provides:

- fixed cell length;
- dedicated media connection;
- connection-orientation.

In ATM digital information is transferred as a continuous stream of fixed length cells. These cells can contain any type of data - text, image, voice or audio. Because the cells are fixed length, hardware switching can be used, allowing it to emulate the dedicated circuits required for real-time audio and video. Because the cells are small packets, they can be used to handle the bursty data characteristic of conventional networks.

Each user is supplied with a dedicated media connection to a switch, which allows many connections to run in parallel. The application is given as much bandwidth as it requires - up to 155 Mbit/s today, scalable to 622 Mbit/s in future.

Developed as an infrastructure for broadband ISDN, ATM technology is being used by LAN vendors in small switched hubs. Current products include adapter cards for workstation interfaces, hubs with an ATM back plane and full ATM switches. These can be combined with the segmented Ethernet LANs described above. The networking topology could then evolve into tiers, with switched Ethernet or Token Ring at departmental level, supporting between 1 and 2 Mbit/s, and ATM in the backbone that connects the segments (Figure 11.4). This backbone must support multiple 1- or 2-Mbit/s flows between departments. It must provide continuous low latency services and scalable bandwidth. Eventually ATM could be used at departmental level, replacing the Ethernet and Token Ring segments, to provide 25 Mbit/s all the way to the desktop. Such a deployment of ATM on a wide scale throughout the enterprise would have the advantage of interconnecting naturally with public networks that will also be based on ATM technology.

11.4   Wide area networks

At present wide area communications for PCs can be provided either by connection to narrowband public service networks (PSTN or ISDN) or through a connection to an expensive private leased circuit. In contrast new networking technology based on

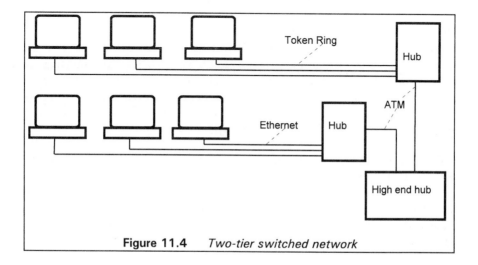

Figure 11.4   *Two-tier switched network*

Table 11.2   Capacity of wide area
communications services in Europe

Service	Bit rate
PSTN	14 Kbit/s
ISDN basic rate	2 × 64-Kbit/s channels
ISDN primary rate	30 × 64-Kbit/s channels
Frame relay	up to 2,048 Kbit/s
SMDS	up to 34 Mbit/s
Leased circuits	up to 45 Mbit/s
ATM	up to 155 Mbit/s

ATM can support user access at rates of up to 155 Mbit/s. Table 11.2 summarises the available services.

11.4.1   PSTN

Although digital technology is now widely used for trunk lines and switches, the public service telephone networks (PSTN) are currently restricted by the existing transmission equipment that is used to connect the customer's premises to the switches via the *local loop*. The cost of upgrading this equipment is the main factor which restricts the deployment of multimedia to the home and office.

Where improvements in the quality of the lines have enabled the use of high-speed modems, up to 64 Kbit/s may be available. These will provide a limited amount of support for multimedia applications, including videoconferencing on PCs. Poorer quality lines fall back to 14 Kbit/s. This is barely sufficient to support videotelephony using equipment such as the GEC Marconi analogue videophone marketed in the UK by BT. These products have limited functionality. The target is 10 fps on a 4-inch screen, but this is rarely achievable in practice.

ADSL

The telephone operators want to exploit their existing copper networks by using asymmetric digital subscriber line (ADSL) - a new technology for transmitting video down telephone lines. ADSL, which originated at Bellcore in the USA, is based on an extension of the signal processing techniques developed for ISDN. As the name suggests it provides an asymmetric link consisting of a high-speed channel from the switch to a subscriber and a low-speed telephony and control channel from the subscriber to the switch.

BT has attracted much attention recently with its plans to offer a video-on-demand (VOD) service to customers using ADSL. Technological limitations - and the reluctance of the respective governments to allow the telephone operators to offer entertainment services in competition with the cable companies - will restrict the use of ADSL. The theoretical limit on the distance from the telephone exchange to the customer is 5.5 km, which will be satisfactory in Europe where the average distance is less than 1.8 km. Over this distance ADSL-1 will support only about 2 Mbit/s, just sufficient for VCR quality video. An enhanced version will operate at 6 Mbit/s and will be able to carry four VCR channels or one broadcast TV quality channel. However, its distance will be limited to 3.5 km.

11.4.2   ISDN

The new Integrated Services Digital Network (ISDN), based on ITU-T recommendations for the transmission of voice and data down the same digital line, provides increased capacity on public networks. Two access services are available in narrowband ISDN:

1. Basic access (BA) provides 2 × 64-Kbit/s channels over telephone lines to businesses. These may be joined to provide the use of 128 Kbit/s.
2. Primary access (PA) provides 30 × 64-Kbit/s channels for large corporate users. These channels may be joined for high-bandwidth applications.

As we saw in Chapter 5, video PCs provide interfaces to basic rate ISDN. In the UK companies are already using the service to transmit multimedia data.

Euro-ISDN

A national network for multimedia services will be insufficient to meet users' requirements. Implementations of ISDN have differed between countries. Euro-ISDN is the result of a major pan-European effort to provide a common implementation, covering both the basic and primary access services. Its functionality is limited to five of the supplementary services:

- calling line identification presentation (CLIP), which enables the calling party to be identified;
- calling line identification restriction (CLIR), which enables the calling party to prevent his or her number being disclosed;
- direct dialling in (DDI), which enables a user on the public network to dial directly into a private ISDN network (e.g. via a private ISDN PBX);
- multiple subscriber number (MSN), which makes it possible to assign multiple ISDN numbers to a single physical interface;
- terminal portability (TP), which allows a user to move equipment from one socket to another, on a single-access installation, during a call.

All the European telephone operators, except Greece, have a programme for meeting the goal of availability of Euro-ISDN from 50 per cent of the country's telephone lines by the middle of 1995. By September 1993 there were 350,000 basic rate accesses and 38,000 primary rate accesses in Europe. However, as Table 11.3 shows, most of these were in Germany.

Table 11.3   Status of ISDN in Europe

Country	Euro-ISDN basic rate	Euro-ISDN primary rate	National basic rate	National primary rate
Austria	300			
Belgium			920	8
Denmark	2,200	76		
Finland	270	80		
France			88,000	11,500
Germany			230,000	16,000
Italy	2,000	50		
Luxembourg			24	
Netherlands	500	30	500	30
Norway			1,000	350
Portugal	250	50		
Spain	219	14		
Sweden	2,500	90		
Switzerland	4,750	270		
UK	12,500			9,500

Note: Number of connections on 1 September 1993.
Source: *Eurie '93 Handbook*

Broadband ISDN (B-ISDN)

Broadband ISDN (B-ISDN) will provide 140-Mbit/s access by the second half of the 1990s. It requires support from two key technologies: synchronous transmission and ATM switching. Equipment to support this combination is not likely to be available commercially until 1994. Synchronous digital transmission (SDT) enables individual channels within a multiplexed signal to be retrieved without de-multiplexing the whole signal. The relevant European standard, Synchronous Digital Hierarchy (SDH), is covered by the ITU-T G.700 series of recommendations. ATM will provide the infrastructure to support B-ISDN under ITU-T Recommendations accepted in November 1990. In future multiplexed ATM traffic could be carried by synchronous transmission links conforming to SDH recommendations at a maximum transfer rate of 135 Mbit/s.

11.4.3   Broadband networking

Broadband networking services will support data transfer rates beyond 2.048 Mbit/s. The first services - SMDS and frame relay - are aimed at the LAN interconnect market and cannot support isochronous traffic such as voice and video. As a consequence, broadband multimedia applications will not start until services based on ATM are available in the public networks in the late 1990s. Even then only large companies will have access to these services.

Frame relay
Frame relay is a technology developed primarily for data interconnect applications. Frames of data from LANs are carried, unaltered, across defined virtual circuits. The technology currently deployed in public services does not support voice or video information. Frame relay traffic can also be carried over ATM (and vice versa).

SMDS
Switched Multimegabit Data Services (SMDS), and its European counterpart CBDS, is a commercial switched broadband service intended for data applications. Current SMDS services are available at bit rates up to 34 Mbit/s in the USA and up to 25 Mbit/s in Europe. SMDS traffic can be carried in an ATM network (and vice versa). The delivery technology for SMDS is based on technology defined in the IEEE 802.6 standard, which is capable of carrying isochronous traffic as well as data. It is possible that SMDS will be extended to voice and video capability.

ATM
As we have seen ATM is suitable for bursty traffic and can cope with variations in bandwidth. In addition it can also offer users the facility to pay for the actual usage made of wide area circuits. This would enable a trade-off to be made between the quality of video needed by an application, for example, and its cost.

ATM's approach to network control also makes it an ideal candidate for providing a network infrastructure to a large number of service operators. Several major companies have adopted ATM for the trials of interactive television services that they are carrying out. In a trial with Viacom in Castro Valley, California, AT&T is using ATM technology to transmit video material over fibre optics to a television set-top box that will include an ATM device. The server has a Sonet (the USA version of SDH) interface to allow programming material to be transmitted to the system head-end from other parts of the network using the existing AT&T transmission systems.

ATM will also provide the backbone of Microsoft's new software-based solution designed for audio, video and other continuous media store-and-forward servers. The system, codenamed Tiger, is based on Windows NT Advanced Server. The Tiger server will provide a stream of continuous media bits to ATM switches, which will send the stream though multiplexers and modulators either to fibre/coax cable or to the public ATM network. These networks will transmit the media to set-top boxes or PCs in the home or in offices.

ATM Forum
The ATM Forum is a supplier organisation whose aim is to speed the implementation of ATM. The Forum has over 300 contributing and auditing companies, some of which also participate in ANSI T1S1 and other standards activities. It is divided into principal members, who create the technical documents, and auditing members, who see the drafts but cannot change them. The Forum has developed a series of specifications including the ATM User-Network Interface

(UNI) Specification and the B-ISDN Inter Carrier Interface (B-ICI) Specification.

11.5   Cable and broadcast communications

The television infrastructure provides an alternative to the telephone networks, especially for multimedia applications in the home. Most television signals are still transmitted in analogue form. Until very recently it was widely believed that digital transmission was still far in the future. However, as we saw in Chapter 9, activity in Europe and the USA is now concentrated on standards for digital television. Even in the traditional stronghold of terrestrial broadcasting, the move to digital television is under way. In the UK, for example, the Government underestimated the development of digital TV as well as the impact of satellite broadcasting. The 1990 Broadcasting Act therefore required the Independent Television Commission (ITC) to create an analogue Channel Five in order to increase terrestrial competition. The ITV companies and the BBC argue that there are insufficient frequencies for both analogue and digital channels and that effort should now be concentrated on a digital terrestrial channel.

The main advantages of digitisation are:

- the reduction of the bandwidth required for the transmission of programmes, which enables the number of channels to be increased;
- the increase in the number of channels means that a wider range of services can be supported;
- improvements in audio, equivalent to compact disk quality;
- the use of a common format for data that can be used in a wide variety of applications throughout the industry;
- the change from a linear medium to one that supports random access.

In the early stages consumers will be able to receive digital signals only if they have set-top boxes that can convert such signals into analogue form to display them on their existing TV sets. At a later stage they will be able to purchase new sets that can receive and display digital signals. In the short to medium term it will be necessary to transmit programmes in both analogue and digital form.

11.5.1   Cable TV

Community antenna television (CATV) was introduced in the USA during the 1950s as a way to avoid having everyone in a community spend a lot of money just to get good reception. Instead one very good antenna was installed with coaxial cable for distribution. The new CATV systems now being installed use a fibre trunk and limit the use of coax to the final stage of delivery to the customer's premises. They provide high bandwidth and can support a large number of analogue channels (up to

40) without compression. If digital compression is used, several hundred channels can be supported.

CATV was limited by its 'tree and branch' topology in which every customer receives the same set of signals. Subscription services (Pay-TV) over cable, which started in the USA in 1975, quickly led to the need to scramble the signals to prevent unauthorised reception. These signals were descrambled by a special converter connected to the television set in the customer's home. The introduction of individually addressable converters in the early 1980s provided the technology for pay-per-view (PPV) services - a form of subscription television in which the customer places a phone call to a special number to order an individual item such as a movie or a major sports event. Technological improvements now allow the customer to order these items 'on impulse' by pushing a button on a remote control or cable converter keypad to select a programme just before or whilst it is transmitted - a variation known as Impulse PPV.

Some interactivity can be provided with the existing system by allocating several channels to the programme and allowing the viewer to switch between them - to choose a different angle in a sports event, for example. The additional channels that digital compression make available can be used for a near video-on-demand (NVOD) service, in which a video is started at fixed intervals which may be as little as every 10 minutes.

The limitations of the tree and branch system can be further overcome by using optical fibre instead of coax to carry services into the customer premises. This will provide an individual path with a very high bandwidth but will be very expensive to install.

11.5.2 Terrestrial broadcast

For many years the transmission of television programmes was mostly by terrestrial broadcast, with an aerial for every house. This method provides widespread availability, but limited bandwidth. The signal is broadcast in analogue form and usually fed directly into the TV set. Digital transmission is now under consideration. This would increase the number of channels available, but would mean that customers would have to buy new set-top equipment. In the UK the transition from VHF 405-line to UHF 625-line television took between 15 and 20 years. The lifetime of television sets is currently around 10 to 15 years, so the change to a digital broadcast service is likely to take a similar amount of time.

11.5.3 Satellite broadcast

The first public demonstration of a satellite broadcast took place at the Tokyo Olympics in 1964. Large-dish systems for TV Receive Only (TVRO) broadcasts are used in the USA, mostly in areas where cable distribution is not economic.

Analogue services for direct broadcast to home by satellite (DBS) using small dishes have been operating commercially in Europe since the late 1980s. Digital DBS services started in the USA during 1994.

Most satellites currently transmit an analogue signal and have limited bandwidth. Moving to a digitally compressed signal will increase the number of channels available. In April 1994 Eutelsat demonstrated Europe's first high-performance simulcast of digital and analogue television in a single 36-MHz transponder. The demonstration uses MPEG compression technology from NTL and a single Eutelsat 2F1 transponder. The organisation used 27 MHz to carry one analogue TV channel and the associated subcarriers whilst using the remaining 9 MHz to carry the corresponding digital channel with audio and data.

Because a satellite sends the same signal to every customer, it can be used for applications such as news services, distance learning and more recently for updating distributed information services.

Summary

The introduction of multimedia into everyday business applications is strongly dependent upon improvements to networking infrastructure. Managers will need to be aware of the potential impact on company networks. In the wide area ISDN seems set to dominate for business applications. In the UK, where cable companies are permitted to provide telecommunications as well as entertainment services, improved compression techniques could stimulate them to provide a range of multimedia applications to consumers.

References

[Eurie 1993] *Eurie '93 Handbook: a User's Guide to Euro-ISDN*, Fischer & Lorentz and Ovum, 1993.

Part III

Applications

Multimedia is often said to be a solution in search of a problem. This attitude is a reaction to the view of multimedia as a separate technology in its own right, endowed with almost magical properties. As I have shown in previous chapters, multimedia is just a convenient term to summarise a whole series of changes in the infrastructure of modern computing and telecommunications. These changes will enable us to use a much wider range of data types in our systems. Part III describes their impact on existing and future applications.

Interactive videodisk has been used since the 1980s for computer-based training systems. Although these systems proved to be cost-effective, they have remained insulated from mainstream computing. They used analogue technology in standalone systems that were usually developed by training departments. More recently point-of-information and point-of-sale systems have been developed by marketing groups using similar equipment.

Digitisation has brought a number of changes that will lead to reduced costs and will increase the assimilation of multimedia with IT. Some applications such as document image processing already run on local area networks. Others will be supported in future. The advent of the Multimedia PC and MS Windows 3.1 makes it possible to incorporate audio and animation in desktop applications such as business presentations. Help facilities in word processing and spreadsheet packages can be augmented with images and audio messages. These features will familiarise users with multimedia and will raise expectations for office automation.

The appearance of video PCs with ISDN interfaces that can support audio and videoconferencing forms the basis for another set of applications that will include multimedia mail and computer-supported co-operative work.

CHAPTER 12

Multimedia in the real world

The early use of multimedia was largely for off-line training and education using interactive videodisk and standalone players. The introduction of digital media has made it easier to integrate multimedia into applications that run on desktop computers. The next and most important change is for these applications to become available over networks. Improvements in video technology and reductions in cost should present new opportunities for the use of interactive multimedia both in the office and at home.

12.1   Multimedia and the single user

Until recently the use of multimedia was largely confined to standalone implementations of two kinds of commercial application, computer-based training (CBT) and kiosks - a short-hand way of referring to point-of-information (POI) and point-of-sale (POS) systems. The earliest versions of these applications were customised systems, built around the use of interactive videodisk (IV).

Recent interest has centred on the use of CD-ROM with new digital technology such as Intel's DVI. This trend towards digital media should increase as more personal computers are shipped with integrated CD-ROM drives and system software that provides support for multimedia. Customised software is expensive to develop and maintain. The reduction in the cost of delivery platforms should encourage businesses to look for software packages that can be purchased off-the-shelf. In addition to courseware, such software will include new versions of existing products, such as spreadsheets, that have been enhanced to allow the inclusion of multimedia data types. It is also likely to include new applications such as tools that allow business users to develop multimedia presentations on their own desktop computers.

12.1.1   Computer-based training

Multimedia has been used for some years to enhance CBT systems for off-line training - the system whereby users leave their jobs for a day or a week in order to train on a dedicated system. American Airlines, for example, has used a multimedia system to train its flight attendants at Fort Worth, Texas. Typically the trainees would spend five weeks at the training centre learning how to handle the service of food, medical and emergency procedures. Forty per cent of that training was carried out by CBT using multimedia applications based on a Wicat system with a laserdisk player. The system, which incorporates audio and video, is also used for student tests.

More recently there has been much interest in the use of multimedia for just-in-time (JIT) training - flexible training that can be accessed by the user at any time. Bethlehem Steel, for example, has created an on-line help desk based on DVI technology for its large mainframe systems. The system allows the operators to interrupt their mainframe sessions and access the help desk when faced with a problem.

12.1.2   Kiosks

Multimedia kiosks, which provide details of products and services, have already been installed in shops, museums and public concourses. Typically they combine text and graphics; some also provide image, audio, animation and video. Information can be accessed by touchscreen (the most popular method), mouse or keyboard. Most incorporate some element of hypermedia to enable the user to move around the system.

Three examples will suffice to illustrate the range of applications already available. Home, a leading Danish real-estate chain, has developed a successful information kiosk to provide potential property buyers with 'candidate' information, based on the criteria set by the buyers. Florsheim Shoes in the USA uses a multimedia POS to promote and sell shoes in shops and department stores. Customers can order direct from the system, with delivery to their homes within hours. In the UK a public information system called Micro Gallery provides visitors with information about each painting. Based on Apple Macintoshes with touch-screens, this uses text, image and graphics to describe every painting in the gallery, as well as a wide range of other information by topic. Users can plan a tour and print off a map at the end of the session before they enter the main gallery.

Kiosks for point-of-sale and point-of-information systems have similar requirements for development and deliver platforms to those for CBT systems.

There is, however, no scope for package software - all systems are custom built - so the cost of development limits their use to large retail chains and public authorities. The use of digital media is particularly attractive in POS applications as it makes it easier to integrate such systems with the rest of the organisation's computerised systems over a network - to build up sales and marketing databases or update customer accounts, for example.

12.1.3   Multimedia on the desktop

Increased support for multimedia on standard platforms has encouraged sales of packaged software, making multimedia a feasible option for large-scale business use. As a result the emphasis is starting to shift from customised software for training to the development of software packages that incorporate multimedia for sale to the general business market

Business presentation packages

Business presentations currently use 35-mm slides or foils for the overhead projector. Suppliers are bringing to market a number of packages that they hope will replace these aids. Desktop video editing tools such as MacroMedia's MediaMaker allow users who are not videographics professionals to create presentations and output them to videotape from a personal computer. Dynamic presentation tools such as Action! (also from MacroMedia) will allow them to generate presentations that can be run on the computer from magnetic or optical disk. These tools will be supported by disks containing pre-packaged images, sounds and motion video - collectively known as clip media.

Such products are intended to appeal to creative directors, sales and marketing executives, graphics artists and corporate designers. They will be able to capture video from a camcorder on a personal computer, combine it with computer-generated graphics and animations and output the result to a VCR. Using video, music, graphics and animation improves the impact and effectiveness of a sales presentation, makes it more professional and helps to present a consistent image - qualities that are especially important at major conferences and exhibitions.

Information access

Users will be able to access information that is stored in multimedia databases on optical disks. Already an increasing number of companies are using CD-ROM as a distribution medium for software. Some also use it to distribute information. Apple, for example, uses it as a means of keeping its staff informed, whilst Sun has put its entire third party software catalogue onto disks, including demonstration versions of some of the packages. This in turn will ensure that CD-ROM drives are bundled with new PCs. By the end of the decade most desktops will have access to such a drive, either locally or over the network.

Most CD-ROMs for business use are still mainly text. However, just as printed publications may contain illustrations, so increasingly will electronic ones. For example, CID Publishing has produced a directory, aimed at the corporate travel and entertainment market, which contains details on 5,000 venues in the UK. Each venue has a text entry at no cost. Those that are willing to pay can have photographic images of their rooms and grounds included on the disk.

New user interfaces

As operating systems such as Microsoft Windows are extended to support a wider range of data types, a new generation of multimedia user interfaces (MUIs) will evolve naturally from today's graphical user interfaces (GUIs). These will allow the user to communicate with the computer in new ways - using speech or even gestures to issue commands, for example. IBM claims that users of its Personal Dictation System can dictate text straight into applications such as Lotus Notes or Word-Perfect, whilst at the same time using speech to control both the application and the operating system.

12.2   Multimedia on networks

No sooner have we adjusted to the idea of developing multimedia applications on CD-ROM instead of interactive video than the available technology seems ready to take another leap forward. In future applications will run over networks, just as other business applications already do. As we have seen, existing local area networks require substantial enhancements to handle multimedia in a satisfactory manner. Advances in wide area networking, especially broadband technologies and ISDN, will already support some business applications such as image transfer and videoconferencing. In the home a range of new interactive applications are being developed to run over cable or even telephony services.

12.2.1   Just-in-time training

Standalone training applications usually require staff to be absent from their desks for long periods. Once CBT courses have been transferred from interactive videodisk to CD-ROM, the natural step to consider is whether these courses need to be on standalone systems. Andersen Consulting, for example, developed a four-day self-study course on CD-ROMs for its staff that is presently offered off-site. The development team now plans to network its training courses, so that in future such courses can be used in the office as part of a move towards short interactive training periods.

As multimedia becomes an integral part of personal computers, business users will be able to receive audio instructions, pictures and animations that explain how to carry out a complex command. Embedded help screens have long been provided as part of standard spreadsheet or word processing packages. JIT training will enhance these existing help facilities with photographs, audio and video clips. Lotus already provides a system called Multimedia SmartHelp for 1-2-3 for Windows. This enables users of personal computers on LANs to access an animated help screen in order to learn how to use specific features of the spreadsheet.

12.2.2   New retail applications

Existing standalone POI and POS applications are difficult to maintain. Updating such systems by issuing new versions of the database on disk is a tedious procedure - one that retailers will increasingly find can be replaced by the use of networked services such as ISDN. At the same time the use of automated systems enables them to present a consistent sales message. When combined with the use of smart cards, business can be closed at the kiosk without the need for trained staff.

For banks in particular the automation of customer service facilities allows them to eliminate jobs, thus achieving annual cost savings. The back office space that is no longer needed for staff can be converted to customer use. The overheads associated with branch locations can be eliminated. Banks want to reduce the amount of staff time that is spent processing routine account transactions or answering basic product queries. New hardware already allows automatic teller machines, for example, to be combined with information services. Several banks have already employed these in trial systems to give their customers access to both account transactions and product transactions. Future systems could combine this with videoconferencing equipment to provide remote access to financial advisors.

12.2.3   Broadband applications

Some highly specialised networked multimedia applications have already been developed as part of broadband trials. SuperJANET, a project worth £18 million over four years, is a high-speed fibre optic network. Designed to link higher education and research institutions throughout the UK, SuperJANET uses the latest broadband technologies that can transmit data at up to 140 Mbit/s. In the first instance much of this data is high-quality images - images of brain structure obtained using magnetic resonance imaging (MRI), weather satellite data and images of rare documents, for example.

The first applications fell into a number of core areas including distance learning, group collaboration, remote access to information and visualisation of supercomputer data. Supercomputers generate huge data sets in calculations for computational fluid dynamics or global atmospheric modelling, for example. Scientists can often only understand and interpret this data if they can visualise it on a workstation. In one SuperJANET project 3D images of molecular models are being transmitted between the chemistry departments at Imperial College and Cambridge University, allowing different research groups to pool their areas of expertise. These images, generated by visualisation packages, can now be transmitted directly to the other users. In the past they had to be translated into numbers and then back into images - a laborious process that risked the loss of the original image. Users at each site can rotate, discuss and edit the images, supported by a videoconferencing link. These discussions can themselves be captured as QuickTime movies, edited and submitted to scientific journals.

12.2.4   Videoconferencing

The introduction of video PCs will create opportunities for new applications in the office. Although the quality of the early systems may prove to be disappointing, video on the desktop will eventually be used to enhance existing communications systems. Electronic mail packages, for example, will be extended to incorporate new data types. Audio mail is already available. In future users will be able to include photographs and video clips within mail messages that are sent to other users.

Present-day videoconferencing systems are expensive and often require special suites of rooms. By the late 1990s users will be able to open up a window on their desktop PC and talk directly to another user over an ISDN line. Users in decentralised work groups will be able to use multimedia to support collaborative projects. As one user modifies the document on-screen, the changes will appear on the copy of the document on the other user's computer. Multimedia will play an important part in software that supports such co-operative working, known as groupware

12.2.5   Multimedia in the home

The merging of home entertainment systems with multimedia and electronic home shopping facilities has already excited the interest of a wide range of suppliers from traditional retailers and manufacturers, through travel agents and mail order suppliers, to banks and companies that offer financial services. The development of the consumer market requires collaboration between these suppliers and the telecommunications companies. New consortia are being established to create the necessary infrastructure.

In the UK Videotron can already offer users of its Videoway cable system a choice of different camera locations for a televised sports event, thus allowing the viewer to exercise choice over the service he or she receives. BT has announced plans to provide 'video on demand' over standard telephone lines. Other mass market applications are likely to appear later in the decade as set-top boxes based on MPEG compression technology become available at competitive prices. These will be able to decode signals from satellites, to support applications such as interactive home shopping.

Summary

Multimedia is playing an increasingly important role in applications that range from simple information systems containing a few photographs and short musical clips to state-of-the-art medical imaging projects running on broadband networks. This range and variety is set to increase over the next few years. In the rest of Part III we look at some of these applications in more detail.

CHAPTER 13

Training and education

Multimedia is seen as one way of solving the growing problem of the gap between the skills and availability of the workforce and the increasing demands of technology in the industrialised countries. The early use of multimedia was largely for off-line training and education using interactive videodisk and standalone players. The introduction of digitised applications that can be stored on CD-ROM and delivered over networks will enable companies to achieve savings in staff time by turning to on-line training.

13.1   The need for training

Western governments are now agreed on the need for a skilled workforce. Changes in technology make work skills obsolete very quickly. The reduction in the life cycles of products means that new production techniques, skills and expertise are needed. Continuous training will become part of an employee's daily life.

Companies are faced with an inadequate supply of skilled labour due to poor educational standards and rapid turnover of staff. At the same time the workplace has become more knowledge and skills intensive. Building and maintaining a qualified workforce is one of the most important business issues of the day. Training is being transformed into a weapon of competitive advantage.

At the same time studies in some countries have found that there has been a reduction in the educational achievements of the workforce. A report by the Organisation for Economic Co-operation and Development highlighted the shortage of skilled labour in the United Kingdom. It criticised British managers for their slowness to adapt to a more competitive world market (OECD 1991).

Different types of training are needed for different types of worker. Blue collar workers typically need to acquire *hard* skills that include specific training for specific tasks, for example technical training on complex pieces of machinery. In contrast white collar workers need to develop *soft* skills, where ideas rather than practical tasks are taught.

The Commission of the European Communities (CEC) takes a close interest in the training needs of European companies. A report from the CEC's Industrial Research and Development Advisory Committee identified four different application groups:

1. Training in *on-the-job technical skills* takes place at or near the workplace. Staff learn how best to use their equipment in order to increase productivity.
2. Training in *on-the-job interpersonal skills* takes place at or near the workplace. Staff learn how to communicate and work with others both within and outside the organisation.
3. *Open learning* covers training away from the working area, in a designated training centre. Staff can work undisturbed and at their own pace.
4. *Training the trainers* helps trainers to understand the concepts, technologies and benefits of open and distance learning.

In each case training involves three stages. First trainees acquire information and skills. Next they need to practise these skills. Finally they need to reinforce their skills in the course of their daily activities. Multimedia is an effective way of acquiring information that makes use of all available means of communication. Because it is interactive, it is also a good way for trainees to practise what they have learnt in a supportive environment. When they return to work, on-line multimedia help can assist staff to resolve problems as they occur.

The traditional way to train staff was off-line. Employees were taken away from their jobs, often away from their place of work, in order to attend training courses that might last several days or even several weeks. Problems arise when staff miss a session for some reason. Employees often forget the skills learnt during training if these are not reinforced by frequent use.

An alternative approach is to train staff on the job. This flexible, continuous method of training can be supported by computer systems that can be accessed by the user at any time. Such just-in-time training allows the user to interrupt a task at any time in order to call up the training application for help. A prototype application has been developed by Nynex Science & Technology with the University of Massachusetts at Lowell. Using a simple logging machine, it shows how visual communications can speed the repair of automated factory equipment. Three different video services are provided: video mail, videoconferencing and remote access to video libraries.

Using a public switched multimedia service, the help desk can be somewhere else in the country. When a problem occurs on the factory floor, local staff call technical support. They can either use live videoconferencing to make contact with the remote service expert or leave a video mail message showing the malfunctioning machine for the expert to play back later. The machine failure is diagnosed by the expert who analyses the transmitted motion pictures of the problem. The expert can then decide whether to dispatch a repair specialist to the factory floor to guide the personnel already at the site through the necessary repair steps. Alternatively the video repair manual can be transmitted over the network to show the local personnel the relevant repair procedure with video and audio clips.

13.2   Multimedia in training

Computers have been used for training employees since the 1970s, using text-based and linear programs. They were followed in the 1980s by courses on interactive videodisks. These early CBT courses were developed to met the needs of a particular company. Some were developed by in-house teams, whilst others were commissioned from specialist companies. In either case a long development process was involved and costs were correspondingly high. Some of these customised or bespoke courses were later modified to create generic packages that could be sold to recoup these development costs.

Other generic courseware has been developed specifically for sale. Early titles were published on interactive videodisk, which is now being overtaken by the growing market for titles on CD-ROM. Of the 3,597 titles published on CD-ROM in 1993, about 12 per cent may be classified as education, training and careers. This is the most rapidly growing sector - up 160 per cent from the previous year (Finlay 1993).

13.2.1   Cost benefits

Using an interactive multimedia training system in the office will clearly provide significant savings in travel costs as well as reducing the amount of time for which staff are away from their desks. Are these savings offset by the cost of developing or purchasing the system? The second column in Table 13.1 shows the costs of sending 50 employees on a three-day training course in an off-site classroom. In the next two columns these are compared with those to be faced when buying a course off-the-shelf (a generic package) or having a customised (bespoke) course specially developed. It is assumed that these two CBT courses would take 10 hours to complete.

As the bottom line of the table shows, the cost per employee of using a generic package is as little as 330 ECUs (15 per cent of the cost of off-site training). With larger numbers of employees this cost will drop still further. In many cases no suitable generic package will be available. For 50 employees, the cost of developing a training package in-house will be approximately the same as sending the staff to an off-site course. If there are more employees, or the bespoke course can be reused in

Table 13.1   Comparative training costs

Type of cost	Classroom (in ECUs)	Generic course (in ECUs)	Bespoke course (in ECUs)
Salary	50,000	10,000	10,000
Development	30,000		100,000
Purchase		6,000	
Direct	30,000		
Use of workstation		540	540
Total cost	110,000	16,540	110,540
Cost/employee	2,200	330	2,211

Source: Multimedia Skills 1991

subsequent years, this approach will prove more cost-effective than conventional methods of training.

13.2.2   Qualitative benefits

In addition to the economic benefits just described interactive multimedia training systems may provide other benefits. Companies retain overall control over the training process. Courses will be prepared and 'delivered' on disk by the most effective trainers. The quality and content of training should thus be consistent throughout the organisation. The availability of courses is increased, as training is taken to the staff rather than the staff being taken to the training course. Courses can be individually scheduled at a time and place convenient to both employees and employers. Staff can be given realistic demonstrations of actual situations that they will encounter in their jobs, including some that are too expensive or dangerous to present live.

At the training session itself, control passes to the individual students who can pace the speed and quantity of learning to suit their abilities and work schedules. In addition, the system itself can be designed to adapt the material it presents to the knowledge and skills of each student. Content can be differentiated by depth or by style of presentation to suit different students. Key learning points can be made in a variety of ways to suit individual preferences. The system can also provide feedback, in the form of either test scores or indicators, to assist with self-assessment. Because training even in off-site courses is self-administered, teachers are free to spend more time to help those trainees who do have difficulties.

Trainees prefer active participation to the passive viewing of material. They retain more information, leading to a significant reduction in errors on the job and a consequential increase in confidence in their ability. There is a significant reduction in course retakes. American Airlines, for example, reported a drop of 40 per cent in the number of retakes for its flight attendants' course since it began using a multimedia system. Computer-based training systems can also offer non-biased validation and testing of a student's work.

13.2.3   Problems

Developing an interactive multimedia training application in house is an expensive business as the example in Section 13.2.1 shows. Development expenditure includes the costs of distribution (creating the disks) as well as the cost of specialist hardware and authoring tools. Specialist design skills are necessary, are unlikely to be available in house and must therefore be purchased. In addition there will be the cost of buying delivery systems or upgrading existing personal computers. Most companies plan to replace their desktop systems and networks over a period of time. It can therefore take several years before all staff have access to platforms that can support multimedia training.

Companies are naturally reluctant to invest in technology that may be obsolete within a few months, whilst training departments that invested heavily in interactive videodisk may not be able to justify scrapping this in favour of CD-ROM. Some managers suffer from technophobia, made worse by constantly changing technology and confusion over standards. Some suppliers may exploit this confusion by, for example, offloading single-session CD-ROM drives to purchasers who should really be buying multisession drives.

Careful consideration must be given to the environment in which the training system will be used. While JIT help is most appropriate within the relevant desktop application, many offices are unsuitable for sustained learning because of the level of background noise and the likely number of interruptions. It may be preferable to provide a quiet area within the building, without telephone contact, where staff can go to use training packages if they prefer.

13.2.4   Danish State Railways (DSB)

Because the capabilities of the existing railway signal systems in Denmark were becoming increasingly stretched, Danish State Railways (DSB) has introduced Automatic Train Control (ATC) on Danish railway lines to ensure their safety and efficiency. This in turn created a need for all 1,600 engine drivers employed by DSB to be trained to operate the new technology.

DSB's Consultative Service for Interactive Media (COSIM) was responsible for the development of a training programme based on an interactive videodisk that contains text, sounds, photos and video pictures. The course is carried out through the interaction of the driver, the videodisk programme, an ATC simulator and the teacher. Courses are held in two ATC training premises, each of which is equipped with six workstations. Each workstation consists of a personal computer equipped with a VGA colour display, a digital videographics card and digital sound card, a videodisk player, a bar-code box, bar-code pen and mouse.

The training programme is organised into five modules that cover:

1. Individual components of the ATC system.

2. Train data input panel and cap signal.
3. Simulation driving.
4. Practical test driving on lines equipped with ATC.
5. Multiple choice - final ATC certification.

The interactive video course can be held over two days, rather than the four days required for traditional methods. The driver is very much in control of his or her own learning speed and pattern. Each module has its own bar-code sheet. By moving the light pen over a bar code, the driver decides which module to see, how many times to work through a particular sequence and the overall order in which to work with the programme. As the light passes over the bar-code, commands are sent to the videodisk player, which is activated accordingly.

The advanced user interface enables the driver to learn at his or her own speed and in any order that he or she wishes, with constant feedback and testing facilities. The driver is thus able to repeat certain sections he or she may be unsure about, ensuring maximum benefit from the training. In Module 5, the driver is allowed to give a preliminary answer if he or she is unsure, rather than a final answer. The results list the type of answer for which the driver opted in order to highlight areas of potential weaknesses or general insecurities. The role of the teacher is modified to that of a consultant who can help with difficult subjects and guide the trainees.

The design of the programme involved DSB's teachers, technical experts and the Consultative Service for Interactive Media in defining the professional contents to be covered. Once the basic requirements had been identified, a prototype of the first three modules was produced and tested on a representative group of drivers.

One of the principal benefits of such a system is the reduction in the number of days required for training. The traditional approach would have included one day of practical training that would have required the presence of a locomotive instructor at additional expense. The total cost of the ATC training was DKK 8,447,115. Of this the development of the interactive video system cost about DKK 2 million, whilst the workstations cost a further DKK 1 million. In comparison the cost of traditional training was estimated at DKK 10,962,320. So using interactive video achieved a saving of around DKK 2.5 million or 23 per cent (Ljungstrøm 1992).

A further benefit is the overall improvement in the quality of the training received. The results of the target group test on the prototype, as well as other evaluation methods, showed clearly that the programme provided better learning and improved motivation.

Following the success of this project, DSB started work on a second system, designed to train fitters in fault-finding, diagnosing and troubleshooting in accordance with safety regulations. The cost of developing this program has been the same as the cost of providing a traditional course for approximately 300 fitters over two weeks. After completion of the 14 hours of scheduled training, the course will be available at any time to enable the fitters to brush up their knowledge and skills on the job using a JIT approach. This additional benefit has been achieved without any further cost to the company.

13.3   Multimedia in education

At first sight, interactive multimedia should offer the same benefits to school pupils as it does to adult trainees. Lessons can be structured to individual requirements, students can control their rate of learning and retention rates can be increased. Interactive videodisks have been used in European schools since the early 1980s. The first and best known project in the UK was the BBC's Domesday system - a set of two disks that contained data on the life of the United Kingdom in the 1980s. An optical disk player was developed, together with the LaserVision ROM (LV-ROM) format for interactive videodisks.

Despite this early interest the use of multimedia in schools remains low. The costs of hardware and software have been a deterrent. Early government-funded programmes, such as the Interactive Video in Schools (IVIS) project sponsored by the Department of Trade and Industry, have probably caused more harm than good by encouraging schools to invest in platforms that are now outmoded. More recently there have been government-sponsored programmes in France, Spain and the United Kingdom to get CD-ROM drives into schools. The National Council for Educational Technology (NCET), a government-funded body which promotes technology in education, is enthusiastic about the use of CD-ROM and multimedia to give pupils access to source material, such as newspapers from a particular period, so that they do not have to rely on opinions of teachers or text-books. However, the plethora of different compact disk formats will continue to confuse and dismay would-be purchasers.

In American schools videodisks are seen as a source of information, to be used with a remote control unit or bar-code reader to control the player, instead of a computer. This approach allows teachers and students to create and use interactive workbooks in the classroom, whilst avoiding the expense and complexity of the European systems (Looms 1992).

13.4   New developments in distance learning

Distance learning reverses the normal approach to training. Instead of the trainees travelling to a training centre to meet the trainer, the training is brought to the trainees who are remote from the trainers and source of training materials. Distance learning courses are based on text, supported by a wide range of other media - audio- and videotape, radio and TV broadcasts - and occasional meetings with tutors. In future wide area communications will also be used to give students on-line access to their tutors.

The teaching of surgery - like many branches of medicine - is heavily dependent on conveying visual information. One pilot project is designed to use facilities at University College London to enhance the teaching of surgery at other hospitals. SuperJANET is used to relay surgical demonstrations from the operating theatre and clinical demonstrations from the lecture hall. The project is also exploring ways to enhance existing courseware in a distance learning environment.

The Multimedia Teleschool

The CEC is encouraging the growth of training in Europe through the DELTA (Developing European Learning Through Technological Advance) programme. DELTA II has an emphasis on market-oriented projects. One of these is the Multimedia Teleschool (MTS) for European personnel development, whose aim is to develop a large, complex and realistic scenario for the application of advanced telecommunications technologies in corporate training.

The MTS project will merge traditional distance training techniques with *telematics* (the integration of computing and telecommunications technologies). Its first phase was based on existing telecommunications technologies - public networks and direct broadcast by satellite (DBS). For example, the Berlitz Teleschool project runs a course in English for telecommunications. A computer conferencing system on the host computer in Berlin delivers a series of regular study letters to each student's personal computer at their workplace. Students use the same system to return completed assignments to their tutors. This is supplemented once a fortnight by a live satellite broadcast by a panel of experts. The participants in their workplaces are linked with each other and with their tutors. Questions and contributions are sent on-line by the students to the tutors, who either respond on-line or pass them on to the experts at the TV studio. Students benefit from being able to communicate with fellow students and experts throughout Europe.

In the second phase of MTS these facilities are being extended to include basic rate ISDN to support facilities such as:

- a direct connection between the tutor's computer and that of the student for interactive remote tutoring;
- videoconferencing between the tutor and students at different sites for interactive distributed learning;
- delivery of CBT packages onto the corporate LAN via a training, delivery and administration server;
- remote distance control of local resources such as CD-ROM on end user machines.

The result will be a computer-mediated multimedia communication system with voice, images, video and data annotation. Students will be able to interact with their tutor and with each other.

University of Plymouth

In future distance learning by studio broadcast may also be combined with videoconferencing. The University of Plymouth, for example, provides courses via satellite broadcasts. Students can currently ask questions over standard telephone links or send them to the studio by electronic mail. The University is experimenting with the use of a PictureTel PCS 100 to allow students to make videoconferencing calls to the studio, or to a remote expert, over ISDN lines. Since SuperJANET supports ISDN-6 (384 Kbit/s), it will also be possible to provide videoconferencing links between academic centres.

Summary

Training is now seen as a priority at both national and organisational level. Multimedia can play a significant role in the development of cost-effective training systems. Managers must decide how best this can be achieved. They are faced with a choice of purchasing courseware off-the-shelf, which will be suitable only for very general skills, or with developing a system in house. Though more expensive, the latter can be tailored to the company's needs. They must further decide whether the course should be available on a disk in a standalone system or over the network in the desktop environment. It may be possible to combine specific off-site training in a particular skill with a just-in-time element that staff can refer to once they are back on the job.

References

[Finlay 1993] M. Finlay, ed., *Facts & Figures 1993: CD-ROM & Multimedia CDs*, TFPL Publishing.

[Ljungstrøm 1992] L. Ljungstrøm and L. Sørensen, 'Interactive video in the training of engine drivers at the Danish State Railways', *TIME Europe 1992 Conference Proceedings*, EPCO International, Eindhoven, pp. 65-73.

[Looms 1992] P. Looms, 'Interactive multimedia in education - a progress report', *TIME Europe 1992 Conference Proceedings*, EPCO International, Eindhoven, pp. 27-37.

[Multimedia Skills 1991] *Multimedia for Europe: the key to distance learning*, Multimedia Skills.

[OECD 1991] *Economic survey on the UK*, Organisation for Economic Co-operation and Development, 1991.

CHAPTER 14

Kiosks

This chapter describes the use of multimedia in point-of-information and point-of sale systems, collectively known as kiosks. Applications have been developed in a variety of sectors: tourism, museums and art galleries, local and national government, public relations and retail goods and services. Originally standalone, these applications are likely to be networked in future. This will make it easier to update the systems. Customers will be able to complete transactions electronically using smart cards. Eventually interactive television services will make it possible for customers to view information and make purchases in their own homes.

14.1   Multimedia for information and sales

14.1.1   Types of system

Multimedia is widely used in information systems that can be accessed by consumers to attract attention and promote interest in products and services. Point-of-information (POI) systems are used to inform the public about the facilities offered by organisations such as art galleries, museums, parks, hotels and airports. They use interactive multimedia to arouse the visitor's natural sense of curiosity. Once involved, users touch buttons and pictures in order to move freely about the system. Since the users determine what they see - and the level of detail involved - POI systems are suitable for both casual browsers and people with specific information needs. They provide consistent and up-to-date information in a range of different languages 24 hours a day - a service that staff cannot be expected to match.

Point-of-sale (POS) systems are used to support sales staff, disseminate information, encourage brand awareness, boost sales and promote new products. Transactional POS systems may in addition include card swipes to enable them to process credit card sales. It has been suggested that every shopping activity can be seen as a project to be carried out by the consumer, from the purchase of a tube of toothpaste to booking a holiday or buying a house. The role of the POS system is to guide the customer through all the steps required for the successful completion of the project.

For example, a customer who wants to purchase a conservatory might visit a DIY store where a POS system is available. This allows the customer to view a range of products, select the one required and print out its details. The use of automated systems in these circumstances helps to reduce pressure on the customer, who can browse at his or her own rate. The amount of space that is required for the display of products is reduced, as is the need for trained staff to offer advice. However, a POS system can do much more than that. Once the customer has decided on a design, it can promote a supplier who is able to fulfil the order. If the customer wants to carry out all or part of the work, it can calculate the materials needed and provide a shopping list with a plan of the store to show where each item can be found. It may even be possible to save video clips showing the assembly method on videotape for use whilst the job is in progress.

14.1.2   Benefits

From the point of view of retailers, the 1990s are a time of increasing competition - which means that they must reduce costs, increase flexibility and improve levels of service. The reduction of costs entails reducing staffing levels, inventory and floor space. Many retailers see the use of interactive multimedia as a way to achieve these reductions. Point-of-sale kiosks allow a retailer to reach a wide range of customers through the use of third party locations and 24-hour availability. They can extend the range of products offered, and provide faster and more convenient service. Retailers can ensure that the information provided will be consistent and accurate. During quiet periods, kiosks can be used for staff training.

Consumers expect to receive more information about products, and are seeking to save time as well as money. They are now familiar with a range of technologies from telephones to satellite TV and take it for granted that retailers will use technology to improve the speed and convenience of service.

Kiosks can also be used to capture statistical data on usage that enables in-depth market research to be carried out on consumer trends. This enables retailers to respond to rapidly changing market conditions and customer demands. They can position products accurately, adapt them for local needs and add or delete them easily. Experience shows that customers are more willing to answer personal questions when faced with an impersonal device such as a computer screen, so personal information gathered about individual customers and potential customers can be used to generate qualified leads from product queries for trained staff to follow up (IMR Group 1991).

14.1.3   Problems

There have been high failure rates in the past amongst retailers who have tried to develop multimedia systems. Typically these have occurred because the time and expense involved in the task have been underestimated, because the project was poorly conceived in the first place or was badly executed - especially in the selection of content and its presentation. Long development cycles make projects unattractive to marketing and merchandising managers who expect to move on before the project is complete. Inadequate and rapidly evolving technology has led to confusion and uncertainty about investment, especially during the recession.

The key factor for success in introducing a multimedia kiosk is to ensure that it is fully integrated with the retailer's business. The development of such an application is not simply an IT project - all business functions must be involved in order that the total impact of the system can be assessed. It is essential to establish the understanding and support of local staff before a kiosk is introduced.

In some cases inadequate promotion failed to create customer awareness and encourage customer usage. Poor terminal siting, with lack of privacy, may inhibit use of the system. The success of an installation may be limited by the number of terminals. Customers cannot normally share retail terminals - one person undertaking a lengthy session at a terminal may exclude many other customers.

Sources of material for content need careful consideration. In many cases retailers are using their own proprietary material so that questions of ownership and licensing do not arise. Where a system includes material supplied by third parties, as in electronic catalogues for example, the owner of the kiosk may become liable in law for the accuracy of all the information that it contains.

14.2   Point-of-information systems

Existing methods of communicating with the public rely on a mixture of notices, leaflets and personal contact with staff. Point-of-information systems replace or complement these methods, providing the means to deliver a consistent source of up-to-date information. They can be used by both commercial and public organisations.

Point-of-information systems, located in the reception area of company offices, can be used as an enhancement to traditional channels of corporate communication such as brochures. Visitors can be offered information about the company and its products and services.

Kiosks can also be used to inform the general public about local government services. In the UK, for example, Nottinghamshire County Council has installed

County Contact, a system that covers a range of general and specific information about the County Council's organisation and services. A number of more ambitious projects have been developed in the USA: Tulare County in California is using multimedia in conjunction with an expert system to allow self-qualification for welfare applicants, for example. The postal services in a number of countries including the UK have investigated the use of multimedia. The Italian Post Office commissioned PostaInforma kiosks for individual post offices to provide information in Italian, English, French and German on services, costs, advantages and availability. The kiosks, which are based on Apple computers with printers, can also dispense forms for driving and TV licences. The database holds all Italian postal codes and telephone area codes, as well as photographs and audio.

14.2.1   Museums and galleries

Arts organisations first used computer systems for administrative tasks in order to increase efficiency and reduce staff costs. Later computers were used to catalogue the collection, often adopting some form of hypertext. With the addition of multimedia features, POI systems have been developed to provide public access to some of this information.

Museo Amparo
In some public places users may wish to share information. Museo Amparo near Mexico City has installed a self-guided tour of its artefacts which combines audio, video, scanned images and text. There are 28 kiosks each of which supports up to three audio headsets. The soundtrack is available in four different languages. Six of the kiosks are also linked to large-screen projection televisions for group viewing. Users can choose a variety of options from a touchscreen which enables them to view any of the 175 artefacts covered. The system is a CD-I application, developed on a Sun SPARCstation. An Amiga 2000 and a PC were used for painting and titling. Apple Macintoshes were used for audio and video capture and for the creation of original graphics.

14.2.2   Tourism

Storyboards and audiovisual techniques are currently used to present information to tourists. However, these are limited by space in the quantity and depth of information which they can provide. The use of hypermedia allows the tourist to select the level of information which interests him or her, whilst disguising the full range and complexity of the stored data. The use of dynamic methods may also help to capture the interest of the younger generation who are used to interactive games. In addition language barriers can be overcome by allowing the user to select the language for text and audio playback.

Office of Public Works Heritage Guide
For these reasons the Office of Public Works (OPW) in Ireland commissioned a Heritage Guide for visitors to provide information about ancient monuments, national parks, inland waterways, and the flora and fauna to be found at 200 sites in Ireland. Information in several different languages can be accessed either by geographic area or by topics such as Early Christian crosses. A touchscreen gives access to text, colour photographs, sound commentary and in some cases short animations or video clips. The front end consists of maps and blank buttons. Data is held in a full relational database with pointers to external sources such as pictures and sound files. At present a new site can be inserted by adding one extra record, a task which the OPW staff can perform. Future plans are to use CD-ROM for sound and image, with records held on a hard disk updated over modems or ISDN lines. The first Heritage Guide, installed in Dublin Castle in June 1991, was followed by a special version developed for EXPO '92. The system is now located in six major centres around Ireland (Cromie 1992).

14.3   Point-of-sale systems

Electronic point-of-sale (EPOS) systems, linked to a store's order processing and stock control systems, are currently used by sales assistants to process orders or to answer queries about goods in stock. Text-based EPOS systems are used by retailers such as travel agents who offer booking services to the public. Customers can see information about flights and hotel accommodation on the screen and be given a print out to take away.

Multimedia can be used as a front end to this existing IT infrastructure. Graphics are employed in standalone information systems to represent products - it is intuitive for customers to touch the apple icon, for example, in order to get information about apples. Audio and video can be used to enhance EPOS systems. A video clip of a resort, photographs of hotel rooms and a map showing the position of the hotel can be displayed on the screen. However, the introduction of such electronic catalogues may involve legal issues and cultural changes.

14.3.1   Retail information systems

Information systems describe products and services, explain the benefits offered, show how they can be used, assist customers in making a choice and print out product and price information. They can include more information than paper catalogues, as the individual customer will decide how much he or she wants to read and ignore the rest.

Zanussi
In the UK one of the first multimedia information systems was Zanussi's Satellite

display system. It included information on 130 white goods appliances stored on interactive videodisk with a PC and printer. Zanussi's objective was to improve its presence at the point-of-sale - the network of 72 Satellite systems installed in large dealer showrooms since 1987 is said to have led to an increase of 30 per cent in sales. They were followed by Optima, a similar system for 500 smaller dealerships throughout the UK. These systems are designed to act either as sales demonstrators for staff or as standalone POI systems for users. They have a simple menu structure controlled by 10 large buttons. Customers can compare product features and prices, seek criteria for different product groups and key in their needs. They are then given recommended product options, dimensions and colours and further information about Zanussi.

Sears Childrenswear

As with all multimedia systems, the quality of the user interface is very important. Terms such as menu and button which come naturally to systems developers may not be intuitively obvious to customers. In the UK Sears Childrenswear has developed a generic framework called The Electronic Sears Store (TESS) that provides design guidelines - for screen layout, image size and text position, for example - that will be used in all the company's kiosks. The first of these - called MUM - has been installed in eight stores that sell goods to new and expectant mothers. The kiosk has therefore been designed to reassure the customer: it operates at seat height with comfortable chairs. As well as information about products, MUM provides 'stories' on topics about which the customer may feel some concern - what she needs take into hospital, for example. The system allows the company to extend its product range, offering the customer more choice whilst reducing the cost of stock holding. However, the system also includes an extensive audit trail so that the store can see the path taken by each customer and the time spent looking at each product. This information is transmitted to head office for analysis. In addition to assisting the buying teams, it can also be used to fine-tune the system itself.

14.3.2   Transactional systems

Point-of-sale systems can also accept orders, print receipts, process orders, update the host system, notify the distribution department and arrange delivery.

Florsheim

One of the best known *transactional* point-of-sale systems is that developed for Florsheim shoes in the USA. Florsheim Express Shops have been in use since 1985 in 550 outlets throughout North America, following research which showed that 35 per cent of customers walk out of the store because they cannot obtain the size they want. The Express Shops enable customers to select from Florsheim's complete range of shoes in all sizes - more than 23,500 sizes and widths in about 428 styles - from a video catalogue which is updated every six months. Customers can view shoes, choose the pair they want and order through the system. Orders are transmitted to the warehouse for direct shipment to the customers' homes within seven days. The system, which is based on interactive videodisk with touchscreen, keyboard and card swipe, now handles 30 per cent of Florsheim's business with an order cancellation rate of only 1.3 per cent.

HomeVision

Multimedia is also appropriate for companies specialising in one market sector such as fitted kitchens, travel agencies or estate agents. These often belong to a chain that can benefit from the consistency of information provided by such a system. HomeVision is an information system installed in 120 stores belonging to the Home chain of estate agents in Denmark. The customer enters the desired location, type of house, price and size and is presented with a list of properties that match these criteria. Each property is illustrated by photographs of the interior and exterior, floor plans and a map that shows its location. If a property is of interest to the customer, he or she can 'bookmark' it for further examination. As a result of the introduction of HomeVision, the average number of customer visits needed to select a property has been halved, whilst traffic through the stores has increased by 400 per cent and Home's market share increased from 15 per cent to 23 per cent during the two years after the system was introduced in 1990.

HomeVision has been developed on PS/2s with a touchscreen using IBM's Audio Visual Connection (AVC). It has to be updated on a regular basis - a service currently run by the developers using bar-code technology. Whenever a new house comes onto the market, its details are sent to the developers in a special envelope with a unique bar-code label which is used to register the property. Pictures and maps are then captured, floor plans redrawn and captured and a description and key figures entered under this bar code - a procedure which takes about 15 minutes per house. Update files are built once a week and distributed to the stores on disk - although in future it will be possible to update the system over an ISDN network (Jay 1992).

14.4   Networked kiosks

Careful supervision is required to ensure that information held in kiosks is up to date and that all POI systems contain the same material. Linking the kiosks by a network is the obvious solution to this problem.

Wigwam

A UK company, Wigwam, has developed an integrated information service that will provide estate agents with point-of-sale, front office and management information systems connected via telecommunications to a central database. Each subscriber has a PC in every office running a text and image database of properties for sale. The agent uses digitised Ordnance Survey maps to identify a precise geographic location with an applicant. The system then displays colour images (interior and exterior) and text describing a selection of properties in the chosen location that match the customer's specifications. The applicant can examine a wide range of properties in the agent's office and print out particulars of those that are of interest.

At the subscriber's office the system is based on a 486 PC, with an ISDN adapter or internal modem, running MS Windows and the Wigwam software products. Other PCs can access the database over a network with Novell NetWare. Each night after close of business the PC calls the Wigwam central system and uploads all new information generated that day over an ISDN or PSTN line. After midnight it makes a second call to retrieve new information relating to transactions in the subscriber's local area. Thus by the next morning full details of the latest properties on the system are available to all subscribers.

Banca Popolare di Bergamo

Banks and building societies already use networks of automated teller machines (ATMs) that customers access by using a plastic card. It is a natural step for these to be enhanced with multimedia interfaces. Banca Popolare di Bergamo, for example, has introduced interactive multimedia kiosks at its branches. From these customers can obtain up-to-date information on their accounts, loan-payment options and the bank's complete range of services. These kiosks are located next to the existing ATMs. A customer enters his or her ID code and uses a tracker ball to select the service required - to list transactions on an account, for example - to which the system responds with printed reports. Other options enable the customer to evaluate his or her financial situation before applying for a loan or to receive general information about the bank and its services. Each kiosk contains a Sun SPARCstation and a printer. The kiosk is a client-server application connected to a local area network which also supports workstations for bank teller and loan processing applications as well as the ATMs. The server at the branch bank is connected via an SNA gateway to the bank's main database on a mainframe.

AlphaServ

Telephone services are not the only way to update an information system - satellite may be cheaper for remote sites. ViewPoint, from a UK company called AlphaServ, is designed for the delivery of multimedia programmes such as POS marketing and customer information systems to remote sites. An American bank is using the system to support two applications broadcast by satellite to 50 sites. For the front office pre-recorded video is used for customer communications, whilst the back office uses live video for staff training. The content changes throughout the day.

Sales and marketing people prepare the programmes at a central site. Centralising the design means that the company can control the content and quality of its sales messages as well as keeping staff and customers informed about new product features and promotions, thus improving communications whilst cutting costs. The information is then broadcast for activation in real time or at a selected time slot.

At the receiving site, all that is required is a PC (just the processor box, with a satellite or ISDN interface and an MPEG-1 decoder card). Research showed that it was important for local staff to be able to get on with their jobs. All programme control is therefore carried out automatically. The system stops the current programme and starts a new one at the relevant time. It even controls the volume. Television is used as the display device because it is more cost-effective and reliable than a PC, and the customer can choose the screen size. Although the initial version is not interactive, a touchscreen version has already been implemented.

Electronic home shopping (EHS)

Electronic home shopping has attracted much attention recently. EHS will be most suitable for information-rich products and services, regularly purchased commodity items with convenient delivery and those for which information is required prior to purchase. It is most likely that EHS will be piloted in stores, places of work and other public access locations such as shopping centres, airports, railway stations and motorway service areas. These in-store applications will introduce the concepts and practicalities of electronic shopping to retailers, their staff and customers.

Generic shopping kiosks or terminals will provide consumers with access to an 'electronic shopping centre' offering a wide range of information, products and services all presented in a common easy-to-use format. They can be linked to payment systems and distribution channels. The development of telecommunications into the home and the merging of home entertainment systems with multimedia and electronic home shopping facilities will provide viable high-quality, two-way interactive communication in the home for EHS in the future (IMRG 1992).

Summary

Point-of-information and point-of-sale are the most active areas for multimedia development at the present time. Retailers are able to present consistent information, leading to improved customer confidence. At the same time they can cut inventory, reduce floor space and improve staff training. In future the development of wide area networks based on ISDN will permit retailers to update their kiosks on a regular basis, overnight if necessary. Customers will be able to carry out an increasing range of transactions using smart cards. Cable and satellite, as well as telephone lines, can be used to deliver information and retail services to the home.

References

[Cromie 1992] J. Cromie, 'Take 4000 years of Ireland's heritage, shake it up into multiple media, inject interactivity and beat into a kiosk', *TIME Europe 1992 Conference Proceedings*, EPCO International, Eindhoven, pp. 227-231.

[IMR Group 1991] *The IMR report: interactive services in the store, street, office & home*, The IMR Group.

[IMRG 1992] *Electronic home shopping: IMRG strategy document*, The Interactive Media in Retail Group.

[Jay 1992] A. Jay, 'HomeVision - a generic multimedia estate agency system', *TIME Europe 1992 Conference Proceedings*, EPCO International, Eindhoven, pp. 211-220.

CHAPTER 15

Image processing

Still images have been incorporated into many applications. These vary from the operational systems used to process document images by insurance companies, banks and building societies to the high-quality imaging needed for applications such as health care and publishing. Improvements in wide area telecommunications will enable image databases to be accessed remotely in the future.

15.1 The impact of image

Image processing (IP) is an enabling technology that allows users to manage information in the form of digital images. Developments in components such as image scanners, high-resolution screens, optical storage media and laser printers have combined to make IP systems economically viable.

In a multimedia system image is viewed as a data type in its own right. The potential for its use is the same as for any other type such as alphanumeric data, text or graphics. Every process that can be carried out on a conventional data item should be extended to handle images. No distinction should be made between the different uses of image, which may include:

- file folders (A4 documents);
- transaction processing (cheques);
- CAD (engineering drawings);
- publishing (manuals);
- medical imaging (X-rays);

- scientific imaging (satellite information).

Future multimedia systems will support all these applications. They will handle both those images that are acquired by capture from paper or microform and those that are created by the system itself, for example from graphics programs (CAD) or business programs (bar charts). This ambitious approach requires the integration of image support into the operating system in the form of sets of routines to input, manipulate, display, store and retrieve images.

Image processing systems already in commercial use may be regarded as a limited form of multimedia. *Operational systems* handle the distribution of high volumes of images where the quality of the image is not a high priority for the task being undertaken. Document image processing systems, for example, involve the extensive processing of paper documents such as insurance claims, mortgages and customer correspondence. In such automated procedural systems, image quality of between 200 and 300 dpi or less will usually be adequate.

In contrast *high-quality image processing* involves the distribution of low volumes of high-quality images such as satellite pictures showing geological and meteorological patterns, X-rays and fingerprints. For applications such as medicine and publishing the condition of the image is of paramount importance. Image quality of 1000 dpi and above is necessary.

Advanced image manipulation systems, such as security and surveillance, may also incorporate complex pattern recognition and motion detection algorithms. Video cameras have already been installed in shops, airports, railway stations and town centres. They have increasingly been used by the police following serious crimes such as bomb attacks or murders. Multimedia could be utilised for security protection in the home and in public places, though for obvious reasons this kind of application is rarely reported.

15.2   Operational systems

15.2.1   Document image processing

Existing data processing systems are limited in their scope. They lack the ability to handle the bulk of the information that an organisation receives - because it arrives on paper. It has been estimated that, in 1986, 95 per cent of all information in the USA was held on paper and that the use of paper was increasing at a rate of 25 per cent each year (Coopers & Lybrand 1987).

The term 'document image processing' (DIP) is used to describe computer systems that convert these paper documents to a digital form, which can then be processed electronically. The first generation of DIP systems was designed for specific paper-intensive applications in organisations such as building societies, public utilities, financial and insurance houses. Here it was used mainly as a replacement for traditional information and image management systems, which used microform for the storage of document images, whereas DIP systems typically (though not necessarily) use optical disk. Micrographics systems are best suited for archiving documents that are unlikely to be retrieved very often. In DIP systems on the other hand the emphasis is on the retrieval of information rather than on its storage. The most significant distinction, however, is that digitised images can be processed: that is, they can be transmitted from one user to another in a series of steps that make up a computerised business application.

Such an application must ensure that the users can process the image in a way that parallels the processing of the paper document. The processing can include:

- storing the digitised images in a database;
- retrieving the images for further processing;
- displaying the images on a screen, and possibly manipulating them;
- printing the images, or transmitting them directly by facsimile or electronic mail;
- management of the workflow.

Automating these processes means staff can be freed from tedious paper processing tasks, whilst service to the customer can be improved.

Amerada Hess
Other heavy users of documents are manufacturing and engineering companies. One oil exploration company, Amerada Hess, required a system to support site certification of welds in the conversion of a vessel into a floating production facility. The documentation had to be stored safely both on site and at sea when the facility was in operation. A DIP system based on personal computers was chosen for this project. Weld records were scanned into the system each day. The system eventually contained the images of 40,000 documents on 15 optical disks. During construction reference to the completed certificates was made easier by the use of image processing, whilst once the facility was off shore, there were savings in space and weight (Hales 1990).

Insurance claims processing
The concept of a document can also be extended to include information other than still images. Figure 15.1 shows a prototype application developed for an insurance company in the USA. This allows the customer's claim to be scanned and reviewed on-screen and audio comments added before it is sent to the regional claims centre. There, information such as X-rays of injuries or video of the damaged vehicle is added to the document. The claim is then verified and returned to the local office.

15.2.2   Geographic information systems

Geographic information systems (GIS) store and manipulate geographic data in a

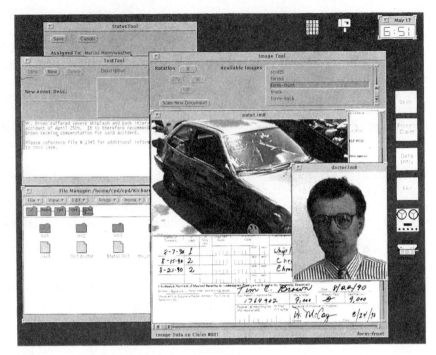

Figure 15.1   *Insurance claims processing system*

database. This database contains precise information on the location of large objects, either natural or man-made. The information is coded according to a system of co-ordinates, for example grid references, so that the objects can be shown in their correct spatial relation to each other.

GIS have traditionally been used by primary industries such as mining, oil and timber and by companies that want to combine maps with record-based information, complex calculations and processing routines. Public utilities and transport organisations find GIS helpful in integrating large amounts of information and modelling activities such as traffic routing. Environmental bodies see GIS as a useful tool in gauging the effects of pollution on the environment. Other industrial sectors are becoming aware of the potential benefits of GIS. Marketing specialists, for example, can combine geographical data with customer information, postcodes and market surveys to produce finely targeted data for mail shots and regional marketing campaigns.

The data held in GIS is a combination of digitised maps, text and numerical information. Image processing is used to capture, store and manipulate aerial or satellite photographs. Spatial information (such as maps) may be related to record-based data (such as the address of a householder) and the images (such as the deeds of the house) held in an image database. These can be retrieved and held in separate windows.

Fire, police and ambulance services need to co-ordinate resources over scattered geographical locations. An innovative project under development as part of the CEC's IMPACT programme is for a decision support system that will assist these agencies in dealing with major incidents. It is based on GIS that will include images that have been captured and stored using fractal compression.

15.3 High-quality imaging systems

15.3.1 Medical systems

Medical institutions face similar problems to the business community in the increase of paper-based documents and the complexity of managing them. The digitisation of medical records, including images, is likely to result in reduced storage costs, improved retrieval times and better access and distribution. Specialist medical services such as pathology are too expensive to be deployed at local level. In future facilities for remote consultation with experts may be provided over multimedia networks. Pathologists at Manchester University and University College London can already co-operate using an application called Pathnet on SuperJANET. The workstation at one end has a colour television camera connected to a conventional microscope. One pathologist can transfer a slide image in real time to a colleague in another location. The two can use videoconferencing software to be in visual and voice contact whilst they discuss the image, magnify certain parts of it, move the slide around under the lens and draw common conclusions.

Decision support systems for diagnosis and treatment planning will be able to make use of image libraries of diseased organs and access the latest medical information. Existing images can be enhanced by computer-based applications or combined to provide additional information. The ability to consult with specialists during diagnosis, treatment and treatment planning will lead to improved patient care and may help to limit liability, especially in small to medium-sized hospitals. There is also a great need for systems that can provide communication links between specialists at different locations for patient diagnosis and for videoconferencing support for training. This would not only improve administration for health care but also save specialists' time in travelling to and from consultations (Reis 1992).

Consultation and review (C&R) system

Brigham and Women's Hospital has developed a consultation and review (C&R) system for clinicians to handle CT and MRI images. Such film is owned by the organisation that performed the examination - BWH, in this case. As well as providing the primary interpretation, it is responsible for maintaining the film for seven years. At present there is a bottleneck in trying to access images after primary interpretation has been rendered. Clinicians, radiologists and specialists must review the scans, compare them with previous examinations, and discuss the interpretation and treatment. Problems arise in scheduling meetings and in making the results widely available. This bottleneck can be removed by delivering images, together with the radiologist's report, to the workstations of all those who wish to see them.

The use of radiology imaging takes place in five steps:

1. The clinician responsible for the patient's primary care orders a test.
2. The technicians perform the examination using CT or MRI.
3. A radiologist interprets the scans.
4. The results are communicated to the clinician, the patient and the appropriate specialists.
5. The next test or treatment is planned by the clinician and specialists.

Most recent activity in the development of imaging technology has been in the third (diagnostic) step. Picture archiving and communications systems (PACS) have been designed to assist the radiologist with the primary interpretation of the scans. In contrast BWH is concentrating on the last two steps - the post-diagnostic phase - because experiments with digital imaging systems for primary interpretation showed that radiologists preferred to work with film than with a digital image even on large (2,000 × 2,000 × 24-bit) displays. This preference is shared by medical insurers in the USA who are reluctant to cover claims arising out of misdiagnosis based on scanned images. In addition the technology is much cheaper since it costs as little as $5,000 to upgrade an existing PC in contrast to $150,000 or more for a special workstation. Because the data is orders of magnitude smaller it can be transmitted over Ethernet.

BWH has therefore decided to retain film for primary interpretation and to implement PACS that will concentrate on supporting consultation, review and treatment planning. This system will be integrated with the radiology information system (RIS).

The C&R system makes it possible for two or more of the people involved to consult together, either within the hospital over an Ethernet LAN, or from remote locations such as the on-call CT specialist's home.

After the interpretation has been rendered, the data is processed into little thumbnail versions. A clinician can go to a terminal and type in a request to see everything he or she has ordered over the last 24 hours. Security, patient and examination data are obtained from the RIS database. Once a specific examination is selected, the image file is transmitted and the images are displayed. From these minified images, together with the radiologist's report, the clinician can decide which frames to obtain in full resolution (Fener 1992).

This application formed part of the trials for the Media Broadband Service in Boston developed by Nynex between its various sites in the greater Boston area (Shuttleworth 1991). MBS can be used to support these teleradiology links, which enable specialists to respond more quickly than if they had to come into the hospital. Links can also be provided to one of the Harvard Community Health Plan neighbourhood health centres that BWH supports.

The provision of such facilities will enable major hospitals to improve the efficiency and productivity of their radiology departments, increase referrals from smaller hospitals and improve transaction processing and billing. Other opportunities for new applications are opened up, for example a 'telepathology' application that would permit the physician to send the images of blood or tissue samples for evaluation, rather than the samples themselves.

Surgical planning

In more radical applications such as surgical planning, image processing may be combined with visualisation and simulation. This will allow surgeons to practise complicated procedures such as brain tumour removal and reconstructive surgery beforehand on three-dimensional images created from an MRI scan of the patient's head. Surgeons can use these images to plan and simulate operative procedures. In patients suffering from bone deformities, the surgeon might experiment with the position of the eyes, for example, on the computer before the operation. Information on average face and bone structure may be stored and used as a reference point in future. It may even be possible to use a milling machine to make clear plastic templates, based on the computer image, that can be used during surgery to shape, say, the rims of the eye sockets.

In addition to pre-operative planning, the computer could be linked to the theatre during an operation. The surgeon could ask for a computerised simulation of a procedure before carrying it out on a patient. The surgeon could ask to see the position of an artery, for example. The 3D image can be rotated to the same position as the patient's head, part of the skull can be removed and the system can zoom in on the relevant area.

15.3.2   Pre-press publishing

Computer-assisted publishing (CAP) systems provide an environment that manages the content and structure of a publication in the pre-production phase of its life. Modern CAP systems need to be able to handle text, vector and raster graphics and image data types. They will also need to support larger structured data types, in the form of long documents. A key market is government agencies that need to develop voluminous documents from multiple sources, manage them and maintain them on a distributed basis.

Technical publications are particularly demanding, as they are more susceptible to change than other kinds of document. In this case the CAP system must be able to co-ordinate and maintain information produced by a number of originators in different forms at various times. CAP can be used in engineering, where complex documentation needs to be developed, maintained and updated in line with product design and manufacturing. Engineering documents usually form part of a group of related publications including specifications, parts catalogues, user handbooks and maintenance manuals. Efficient database management is essential to the successful maintenance of such documents.

Pre-press publishing relies on high-quality images in a time-critical production environment. By using multimedia and communications networks, document reviews and modifications can take place between different sites without the need for a hard copy. Pre-press production cycles can be shortened and archived elements can be retrieved and stored more efficiently.

Christian Science Publishing

The Christian Science Publishing Society in Boston has used MBS to transmit images throughout its headquarters. Pages of the Christian Science Monitor that were previously printed out for proof-reading are now reviewed on a high-resolution colour monitor. This saves about 10 minutes per page or 1 hour per day. Images from the newspaper were used as television graphics in the Society's daily TV news programme. This avoids having to reshoot, scan and digitise the images. Instead they are transmitted directly over a fibre optic network from the newspaper system to a computer graphics workstation in the television area.

The Society owns four different publishing media - a daily newspaper, a monthly magazine, a television channel and a radio station. Changes in the industry mean that news development and delivery must become independent. One reporter can be used to cover an event for all media for all the different delivery departments. A prototype video browser has been developed that can be used to show the layout or original text of any piece of copy that can then be cut and pasted. Copy can be selected by date, section, author or source. Frames can be grabbed from video retrieved from the library.

15.3.3   Image databases

Storing images electronically is a way to make them widely available, whilst protecting and preserving the originals. Image databases can be created for commercial, educational and research purposes.

Hulton Deutsch

Hulton Deutsch has over 15 million photographs and printed images - one of the largest collections in the world. It provides images to newspapers, advertisers, broadcasters and publishers. Selecting any one image from such a collection is a daunting task. In 1992 the company launched a series of picture archives on CD-ROM. The first disk contained more than 10,000 images of contemporary and historic personalities. It was followed by a series to cover each twentieth century decade, starting with the 1930s. Each disk contains a set of images held at medium resolution, together with search facilities for access and selection. These images are suitable for presentation purposes but not for reproduction. Customers who require hard copy can then order high-resolution images from Hulton in the usual way. By installing an ISDN line, images can also be sent electronically to clients (Cole 1993).

UK National Railway Museum

Specialist collections, such as early photographs in the form of glass plate negatives, must be stored in air-conditioned archives. The National Railway Museum in York has a collection of 750,000 photographs of trains dating back to 1866, which it wanted to make more accessible to the public. These are being scanned, digitised and compressed for storage on optical disk. Using JPEG compression, each disk can hold 1,000 images at 2,048 × 3,072 resolution. Once scanning is completed, the museum plans to let visitors view the images on screen. They may also be able to buy on-demand prints on a commercial basis (Electronic Documents 1993).

John Rylands University Library

Access to rare and valuable documents can be improved through a combination of high-quality imaging and a high-speed network. The John Rylands University Library of Manchester is using SuperJANET to make available its collection of Islamic manuscripts and the Genizah fragments. The latter, dating from the tenth to the thirteenth century, are a fundamental research source for Hebrew scholars all over the world. Cataloguing rare documents is made easier if scholars can compare them with documents in other collections. In the pilot application scholars with remote access can view the documents, enlarge them, print copies and discuss them with colleagues to assist in correct dating. There are plans to develop pattern recognition software that can be used to match scattered fragments so that whole documents can be recreated on the computer.

Summary

Image is the best established of the three important multimedia data types. Bitonal document images have been incorporated into operational systems, using fax compression standards. These systems may be extended to handle audio notation and video clips. Improvements in compression technology mean that colour images and high-resolution grey scale images may now be stored and transmitted in applications such as medicine and pre-press publishing.

References

[Cole 1993] G. Cole, 'Hulton Deutsch: application spotlight', *European Multimedia Bulletin*, vol. 3, no. 9, 1993, p. 8.

[Coopers & Lybrand 1987]. *Information & image management; the industry and the technologies*, Association for Information and Image Management.

[Electronic Documents 1993] 'Museum scans photos', *Electronic Documents*, vol. 2, no. 1, p. 11.

[Fener 1992] E. Fener and W. Hanlon, 'A functional model for PACS beyond radiology', *S/CAR 92*, Symposia Foundation.

[Hales 1990] K. Hales and J. Jeffcoate, *Document Image Processing: the Commercial Impact*, London: Ovum.

[Reis 1992] H. Reis, D. Brenner and J. Robinson, 'Multimedia communications in health care', *Extended clinical consulting by hospital computer networks*, Annals of the New York Academy of Science, vol. 670.

[Shuttleworth 1991] W. Shuttleworth, 'Health care and publishing applications for integrated broadband networks', *Broadband - The Ultimate Communications Network*, Blenheim Online.

CHAPTER 16

The multimedia office

This chapter looks ahead to some of the business applications that may be developed in the future. Information systems based on existing text retrieval software can be enhanced to handle image, audio and video. Alternatively, hypertext can be extended to include multimedia. The result - hypermedia - provides a new approach to information access. Project management tools can benefit from the introduction of hypermedia and multimedia in a number of ways. Decision support tools with audio and video links will allow workers in dispersed teams to discuss, modify and agree project documents. Electronic mail services can be used to distribute multimedia documents to project teams on remote sites in different time zones. The resulting improvements in communications will increase co-operation between staff working on large distributed projects, whilst reducing the time spent in communication.

16.1 Multimedia in the office

Multimedia data types can be used to enhance a wide range of office applications in the future. For example, voice annotation, photographs and video clips could be added to traditional business applications such as personnel databases and insurance claims processing. More importantly they make possible new applications, such as desktop conferencing. In the medium to long term, multimedia will support the next generation of office information systems. These multimedia office information systems will build on the infrastructure provided by document image processing and other imaging systems, and on communications facilities such as email. Office systems vendors are already supporting 'compound documents', which combine text, graphics, image and voice annotation, and can be sent as electronic mail messages.

Until recently the major problem for businesses and other organisations was to achieve efficiency in the performance of manual workers, clerical workers and others whose main function was to carry out routine tasks under supervision. Computer systems in organisations have evolved to support these workers, automating clearly defined tasks such as transaction processing. Meanwhile, as Peter Drucker has pointed out, the centre of gravity has shifted to the knowledge workers - 'people who have been schooled to use knowledge, theory and concept rather than physical force or manual skill' (Drucker 1970). Modern office systems have to support these knowledge workers, which means supporting the kind of business activities shown in Table 16.1.

16.1.1   Accessing information

Knowledge workers depend upon access to information. However, most data stored in computer systems at present consists of records holding small items - a name 'Smith' or an amount '23456' - that have no meaning on their own. In the real world, information takes many more forms than names and numbers. Databases that contain large amounts of text are already familiar to us in libraries and on-line information systems. Photographs, drawings, X-rays, fingerprints, voice commentary and video recordings will all be required in the database of the future, to be stored in digital form. Intelligent interfaces are needed to assist in tracking down the relevant information, wherever it is stored.

CD-ROM has now been established as a medium for the distribution of digital information in both commercial and consumer markets. A wide variety of training courses, business and financial information services are available commercially on CD-ROM. Many of these courses use hypertext for authoring and retrieval. Use within the computer industry includes the distribution of software and product

Table 16.1   The impact of multimedia on business activities

Task	Support now	Future support
Accessing information	Separate databases for records, text, image	Multimedia databases
Holding meetings	Audio telephony or dedicated videoconferencing	Desktop conferencing
Sending messages	Electronic mail (unformatted text)	Multimedia mail (audio and video)
Creating documents	Standalone word processing for text and graphics	Collaborative computing with shared workspaces, file transfer
Making decisions	Text-based decision support systems	Decision support systems combine knowledge-based reasoning and hypermedia

information. Microsoft now supplies some of its software - Windows NT, Word, Microsoft Works and Microsoft Office - on CD-ROM. Recent developments mean that limited numbers of CD-ROMs can be created in house economically using authoring software such as ToolBook. A recorder costs about £4,000, whilst disk prices are below £20 and are likely to fall still further, making CD-ROM a viable choice for corporate information such as conference proceedings. Photo CD, a related product from Kodak, can be used as a distribution medium for high-quality colour images.

On Demand Information

Information held on disk is difficult to update. An alternative approach is to hold all information on a central database and access it over ISDN lines. Such an information service for the construction industry service is being offered in the UK by On Demand Information (ODI). A CD-ROM version has been available in the past. This contained product literature from suppliers, including text, line art and photographs. In addition some 60 to 70 technical institutes, including the British Standards Institution (BSI) and the Building Research Establishment, provided information on topics such as building regulations and health and safety.

The On Demand version will include additional video and audio material such as video clips showing product features - a demonstration of a new power drill, for example. Subscribers will need a 386 or 486 PC with an ISDN interface and graphics card. The index, which is updated regularly, will be held locally on the PC. Knowledge retrieval, which includes 'fuzzy' searching methods to allow users to enter just the outline of a subject, is carried out off-line. When the subscriber has selected items, the system automatically dials the host, downloads the data requested and cuts off the line.

16.1.2   Holding meetings

In today's large international organisation, staff are often geographically dispersed. Conventional videoconferencing systems can be used to reduce travelling time and costs. However, these are expensive to install, complex to use and are mainly restricted to meetings between senior managers. Groups of knowledge workers require support for short informal meetings to encourage the ad hoc exchange of ideas and information.

Narrowband ISDN is already being used in conjunction with H.261 compression technology to support audio and videoconferencing over wide area networks. Chapter 5 identified a range of video PCs from companies such as IBM, Olivetti and PictureTel. These support services such as the ability to set up calls, share a portion of the screen, exchange text and images, fill in forms and transfer data.

The ODI service described above contains additional features that will enable users to view, edit, annotate (with text or voice messages) and route material to colleagues. The system will also support teleconferencing between suppliers and people such as architects and surveyors who specify products for construction projects. Architect and manufacturer will be able to look at the same page of the manufacturer's brochure on-screen, whilst discussing it over the phone. Videoconferencing links could be added in the future.

16.1.3   Sending messages

Where staff are separated by time as well as space, usually because they work in very different time zones, real-time communication may not be possible. At present such staff can only communicate through existing mail systems. Postal systems have largely been superseded by fax, electronic mail and voice mail. As with real-time systems, there is a need to enhance the electronic mail system to support the transmission of documents that contain multimedia data types. Users should be able to annotate these by recording comments using audio input devices. They may also wish to record video mail messages. Basic support for multimedia mail is now available on personal computers and workstations.

16.1.4   Creating documents

Documents are the outward and visible signs by which modern knowledge workers define their output. The creation of documents thus takes up a major part of their time. In all but very small projects, such documents will have more than one author. Increasingly documents can contain information in other forms than just text.

The MultiWorks workstation, exhibited at the 1992 ESPRIT Conference, is an advanced business computing system for capturing, communicating, authoring, publishing and retrieving multimedia documents across a range of media including CD-ROM and LANs. It will be available in different configurations for authoring and delivery. As part of the same project Bull has developed Multicard, which provides a hypermedia toolkit to allow programmers to create and manipulate distributed basic hypermedia structures, an interactive authoring and navigation tool, an advanced scripting language, a multimedia composition editor and a communication protocol (M2000). The objective is to allow the integration of various applications into a single hypermedia network (Rizk 1992).

16.1.5   Making decisions

Amongst knowledge workers, the key task that distinguishes executives from other staff is the need to make decisions. Such decisions may have a significant impact on the entire organisation. Yet very little support is provided for this task. In any decision-making process, considerable interaction is required between the participants in order to process information and arrive at decisions. This interaction involves the exchange of information and in particular the sharing of data. In future decision support software could be combined with multimedia to enhance basic project management tools through the sharing of documents and applications on workstations or personal computers.

16.2   Project management

As we have seen, multimedia can be used to enhance basic office software tools through the sharing of documents and applications on workstations or personal computers and through the use of multimedia communications on the desktop. Modern projects often need to manage large amounts of information that is typically complex in structure and diverse in form. In large inter-organisational projects the participants will be separated in space and may be in separate time zones, making collaborative work difficult.

There are a number of advantages from the use of multimedia in management tools for such projects. Firstly multimedia will make it easier for team members to communicate in a distributed environment. Participants can view, edit and process information jointly, working on shared documents. Secondly multimedia communications will also make it easier for teams to work effectively across sites. Finally the addition of graphics, animation, audio and video will improve the human-computer interface in applications such as training systems and on-line help desks.

Project managers might consider the development of a general purpose toolkit that will use hypermedia and multimedia to support decision making and planning. This toolkit might incorporate:

- the automation of decision support methodologies by allowing a range of algorithms to be incorporated, including customised ones;
- display of the methodological framework as 2D or 3D graphs, perhaps using animation;
- hypermedia facilities to allow users to add text or voice annotation to the framework;
- communications facilities to support real-time shared workspaces, with audio and video conferencing;
- tutoring and on-line assistance.

An alternative strategy is to develop individual modules that can stand on their own. These might include tutorial material on CD-ROM, an on-line help desk or a multimedia mail facility. ·

The remainder of this section reviews three groups of research projects that point towards ways in which project management tools can benefit from the introduction of hypermedia and multimedia. Collaborative computing tools with audio and video links will allow workers in dispersed teams to discuss, modify and agree project documents. Electronic mail services can be used to distribute multimedia documents to project teams on remote sites in different time zones. Hypermedia can be used to provide support for group decision making and for planning and scheduling.

16.2.1   Collaborative computing

Where staff are separated in space but not in time, they are currently able to communicate by voice telephony, either person-to-person or in conference calls. This support is now being extended via video telephony for person-to-person calls. Videophones allow participants to see each other but not to share and discuss documents. Videoconferencing systems are available for larger meetings, enabling participants at different locations to conduct face-to-face dialogues. However, research has suggested that participants at meetings generally spend as little as 20 per cent of the time looking at other participants. Instead, for most of the time, the participants' attention focuses on something else, such as notes, discussion papers and charts. Some videoconferencing systems allow document images to be transmitted, but these facilities are very expensive.

Multimedia workstations could be used to overcome these limitations. The added dimension will be the ability to share documents containing alphanumeric data, text and graphics. As well as documents users may want to share applications such as word processing, spreadsheets and drawing packages.

TeamWorkStation (TWS)
The TWS project is intended to provide an open shared workspace for real-time distributed projects. A prototype, developed by NTT in Japan (Ishii 1991), shows how the gap between personal computer, desktop (i.e. papers) and telecommunications can be bridged. The TWS prototype, based on Apple Macintoshes, provides each user with an individual screen, a shared screen (the open shared workspace) and live audio and video communication links for face-to-face conversation with other users. Users can move any application program between individual and shared screens just by dragging it with the mouse. They can share data on paper and books by bringing it under the CCD camera attached to a desk lamp. The shared screen is a strict implementation of the What You See Is What I See (WYSIWIS) design principle.

The system operates in three modes. In overlay mode, the overlay of video images is done by a video server and redistributed to the shared screens via a video network. Telescreen mode supports the non-overlaid remote display of individual screens, whilst teledesk mode does the same for individual desktops. For the prototype, four separate networks were integrated: a new video network (NTSC and RGB) controlled by a video server based on a computer-controllable video switcher and video effector; a new input device network; an existing data network (LocalTalk); and the voice (telephone) network. In future these will be integrated into a multimedia LAN and B-ISDN being developed by NTT.

BERKAPS

The use of desktop video will make it easier to get to know other people in large distributed projects, reducing the need for travel. Participants in a discussion can identify each other by sight. If there are more than two participants, video makes it easier to identify the person speaking. A multimedia conferencing system, BERKAPS (BERlin Konferenzfahige ArbeitsPlatzSysteme), has been developed by Telematic Services GmbH (Teles). The system supports and manages multimedia conferences which participants can join and leave as they wish. Each KAPS system allows a participant to join a conference and to monitor just the information in which he or she is interested. It also allows a participant to make private information from his or her own workstation available to other participants, should they wish to use it.

There is a centralised conference server, the KDE, which acts as a multimedia database and provides the control mechanism for the conference. Each workstation then needs a single add-in card, the KDT, which connects to the B-ISDN network and communicates with the KDE. Each user workstation can have windows displaying other participants as well as the usual applications (Stevenson 1991).

BERKAPS has been used as the basis of a prototype developed for RACE in the DIDAMES project (Schindler 1990). The field of application is the distributed industrial design and manufacturing processes of electronic subassemblies, including related distributed management activities. The prototype system will support up to eight users and is based on OSF/Motif and X Window System on UNIX platforms and MS Windows and Presentation Manager on DOS systems. The user interface (TELES-VISION) is designed for daily office use and supports: filing, retrieving, editing, case handling, electronic mailing, securing and conferencing.

16.2.2 Electronic mail

Electronic mail was developed for the transfer of unformatted alphanumeric and text-based data. The Multipurpose Internet Mail Extensions (MIME) can be used for exchanging a wide variety of objects, including image, audio and video, as well as applications such as PostScript. MIME has been implemented in commercial email software and does not break existing email systems.

Multimedia conferencing and mail systems were an active research area throughout the 1980s. For example, a prototype data-transfer service for multimedia data, called InternetExpress, was developed at Brown University (Palaniappan 1991). It was implemented in the Intermedia desktop environment, using TCP/IP point-to-point connection to send express packages to sites on the Internet. The service consists of desktop-independent and desktop-dependent components. The former services a local area network (implemented on a Sun workstation). The desktop-dependent component is responsible for packaging and unpackaging data and for mapping data to applications such as Lotus 1-2-3.

16.2.3   Decision support and hypertext

In the development of large, complex systems problems may be assigned to individual decision makers who are organised in a variety of ways with varying levels of authority. There may be no general method for tackling such unstructured problems with multiple conflicting goals. Computer tools based on hypertext can be used to support early unstructured thinking in problem solving or project design. They provide rapid response to a small collection of specialised commands.

IBIS

Issue-Based Information Systems (IBIS), an approach developed by Horst Rittel at Microelectronics And Computer Technology Corporation (MCC), was based on the principle that the design process for complex problems is fundamentally a conversation among the stakeholders (i.e. designers, customers and implementers) in which they pool their respective expertise and viewpoints to resolve design issues.

gIBIS, a graphical version of IBIS, was the first in a series of prototypes developed by the Software Technology Program at MCC (Begeman 1988). The user interface is divided into four windows: a graphical browser displays the IBIS graph structure with its nodes and links, the node-index window provides an ordered hierarchical view of the nodes in the current network, the control panel contains a set of buttons to access menus that provide additional functions, and the inspection window displays the contents of nodes. Within gIBIS a distributed group of users can browse and edit multiple views of the IBIS network.

rIBIS is a real-time groupware tool based on Germ, a generalisation of gIBIS to operate on a variety of problem-solving networks (Rein 1991), written in C and running under Unix on a network of Sun workstations. Users can switch between tightly coupled and loosely coupled interaction modes. In the former the group can see, discuss and edit an item together in real time. In the latter mode users work in parallel. Some of their operations are broadcast to other users, most are not.

Hypertext House (H2)

Other tools can be used to automate specific decision-making methodologies. One such tool is the Hypertext House (H2), a computer-based hypertext implementation of a manual framework called the 'House of Quality' (Hauser 1988), which allows individual decision makers to make their trade-off analysis explicit. H2 improves on this by allowing the communication of individual analyses among all the team members. Hypertext allows team members to attach their notes and models justifying each trade-off. It also provides the team co-ordinator with access to a wide range of models for combining the inputs of various team members into a team consensus.

In H2 the two-dimensional paper house described by Hauser is replaced by a three-dimensional Hypertext House. Every part of the picture can be activated by a mouse click that causes the appropriate series of cards to appear on the screen. Users can attach new requirements, supply attributes or estimates, or add comments, whilst the system keeps a record of every modification and the person responsible (Wolfe 1990).

Summary

Many advanced projects in computing and telecommunications have developed prototypes for the office of the future. In this environment, knowledge workers will have ready access to information in all its forms. They will be able to work in co-operation with others in different parts of the world to create and distribute compound documents containing many different types of data. They will be able to communicate at the desktop with these co-workers, both aurally and visually, either in real time or through electronic messaging systems. They will use decision support systems linked to these communications media to reach team decisions. Beyond these developments lie other projects, which may lead to the integration of multimedia communications with the fabric of the office, creating a world of ubiquitous computing.

References

[Begeman 1988] M. L. Begeman and J. Conklin, 'The Right Tool for the Job', *Byte*, vol. 13, no. 10, pp. 255-266.

[Drucker 1970] P. Drucker, *The effective executive*, Pan Books, London.

[Hauser 1988] J. R. Hauser and D. Clausing, 'The House of Quality', *Harvard Business Review*, vol. 66, no. 3, pp. 63-73.

[Ishii 1991] I. Ishii and N. Miyake, 'Towards an open shared workspace: computer and video fusion approach of TeamWorkStation', *Communications of the ACM*, vol. 34, no. 12, pp. 37-50.

[Palaniappan 1991] M. Palaniappan and G. Fitzmaurice, 'Internet Express: an inter-desktop multimedia data-transfer service', *IEEE Computer*, vol. 24, no. 10, pp 58-67.

[Rein 1991] G. L. Rein and C. A. Ellis, 'rIBIS: a real-time group hypertext system', *International Journal of Man-Machine Studies*, vol. 34, pp. 349-367.

[Rizk 1992] A. Rizk and L. Sauter, 'Multicard: An open hypermedia system', *Proc. ACM Conference on Hypertext*, pp. 4-10.

[Schindler 1990] S. Schindler and C. Heidebrecht, 'Broadband technology within the DIDAMES project', *Broadband Islands Workshop*, General Directorate XIII/F, Dublin.

[Stevenson 1991] I. Stevenson and S. Timms, *Broadband communications: market strategies*, Ovum.

[Wolfe 1990] M. Wolfe, 'A hypertext based decision support system to support team decision making', *Proc. IEEE Int. Conf. on Systems, Man and Cybernetics*, pp. 884-888.

CHAPTER 17

Multimedia in the home

The final chapter on applications considers the likely impact of multimedia in the home. It draws on evidence of past consumer behaviour to adduce the direction this may take in the future. Three possible platforms are identified: CD players, interactive television and home PCs. Applications for these platforms, though still largely speculative, are outlined.

17.1　Do consumers really want multimedia?

In contrast to the office, the need for multimedia in the home is unclear. So far most consumers have proved stubbornly resistant to its charms. The main reason for this lack of interest is almost certainly lack of money. The recession in North America and most European countries has discouraged consumer spending even on essential goods. Quality - or the lack of it - is also a key factor. Whilst people within the computing industry become wildly excited about digital video on PCs, because they are aware of the technological development that has gone into achieving it, consumers automatically compare it with TV - where full-screen, full-motion video means a 27-inch TV screen updated at least 25 frames per second. This comparison is not encouraging. Furthermore some of the people who create titles for the home market have more enthusiasm than design skill. The lessons that the film and television industries learnt over many years have yet to be applied to multimedia.

Surprisingly little research and market testing seems to take place to establish what consumers will and will not want to do with multimedia products. Instead suppliers draw false analogies with other products. Because, for example, audio CDs were successful, it is assumed that multimedia CDs will be equally so. Yet these products, superficially similar, meet very different personal needs. Listening to music is not the same as looking up information in an encyclopaedia or learning to play golf - two activities that now feature on CD. Instead of one relatively uniform activity we have a multitude of different ones, each with its own social setting. Multimedia for the home is a technology that enables a diverse range of applications, many of which may attract comparatively small markets.

Despite these caveats, many companies are interested in supplying the home market. A wide and confusing array of products have already been announced and more will follow. These products include:

- CD players;
- set-top converters;
- home PCs;
- personal information devices (PIDs);
- consumer videophones;
- electronic books.

Only the first three of these have the capability to support multimedia at present. This chapter will therefore concentrate on applications for these product groups.

17.1.1 Interacting with the television

Customers' interest in interactive multimedia will to a large extent be shaped by their past and present experiences with television. The first step towards viewer control of television was the introduction of the consumer version of the VCR. This device allowed viewers to time-shift - to record programmes that were broadcast at an inconvenient time or at conflicting times, and to watch programmes at a time of their own choice and as often as they wished. VCRs also introduced a set of features for the linear control of material, such as fast forward, rewind and pause, that provided the basis for future interaction.

The second step was the introduction of optical disks that could store large amounts of high-quality audiovisual material in analogue format for playback on a TV set. As Chapter 10 showed, linear videodisk was followed by an interactive version in which users could select topics, answer questions and control the order in which the material was presented. Too expensive to prove a commercial success in the home, most videodisks have been used for computer-based training and more recently for point-of-information or point-of-sale systems. Videodisk has been largely superseded by compact disk. It is significant for having introduced the basic concepts of non-linear interaction with multimedia information.

Early home computers also used the TV set as a display device. Users could program these systems as well as playing games. Products such as the Commodore Amiga scored an early commercial success. However, they were supplanted by systems from Sega and Nintendo with a dedicated console and video games on cartridges. By providing high quality at an affordable price, these have introduced a whole generation to interactive skills.

The next step is the move from standalone systems to ones available over networks. The standard television set, equipped with a set-top converter, can now support various levels of interaction. A simple cable-based system, such as the one that Videotron supplies in Canada and the UK, uses four TV channels, carrying related material, enabling the viewer to interact by using the set-top to choose among them.

An alternative approach being used by the Interactive Network in the UK adds interaction to an existing cable or satellite broadcast by injecting additional information into the broadcast signal in a similar way to teletext. This allows viewers to offer multiple choice answers to questions on a game show, for example.

In a true on-demand system, such as the one that BT is testing in the UK, each customer receives an individual signal, enabling him or her to choose from a menu of programmes. The choice is then signalled back to the head-end.

The 'Full Service Network' trial which Time Warner is planning for Orlando will offer a wide range of interactivity with the ability to send an individualised video stream to the customer. The system can be used to view interactive multimedia material of the sort that is available on compact disk as well as to access video on demand, home shopping and education applications.

17.1.2   The information superhighway

There are currently two models of how the market for networked information services should develop:

1. The restricted access or 'toll booth' model is very similar to existing cable and direct broadcast to home by satellite (DBS) services.
2. The open access or 'gateway' model is similar to existing telephony services and, especially, to the Internet - the impetus behind the Clinton-Gore vision of the Information Superhighway.

In the first case, the target market is residential households that currently take (or would like to take) cable television. Large amounts of centrally controlled information, geared to a mass market, would be distributed over cable networks to the domestic television and set-top box. The technology can support 500 channels, though providing a near video-on-demand service could take up a large part of this capacity.

In contrast, the target market for the second model is likely to include the upper range of residential customers and home offices. These customers will seek out information from a wide range of sources and download it over cable or telephone networks to a platform that can support a high level of user interaction. Instead of 500 channels there will effectively be a single channel, tailored to the customer's requirements. In future users should also be able to create and distribute information themselves.

This analysis suggests a bifurcation of the highway. Popular services with mass market appeal would continue to appear on television, whilst educational and informational services would be directed to those homes with PCs. Games, as at present, might well remain divided between the two.

17.2   Applications for CD players

Compact disk players were described in Section 10.5. Games and information are stored on disks, to be played back under user control with the standard television screen as the display device. Although many titles have been published, the early entrants - such as Commodore with CDTV (later CD32) and Philips with CD-I - have made comparatively little impression in this area. To date the players have sold in hundreds of thousands, rather than millions. Despite this experience, new players continue to appear. Rather than making a breakthrough, these have added to the confusion and will probably delay consumer acceptance still further. What is required by both developers and consumers is a single industry-standard platform that will play any title.

Interactive games
Sega and Nintendo continue to dominate the existing highly profitable market for video games. Both have expressed interest in the use of CD as an alternative to their existing cartridge systems. This will enable them to include video clips showing actors instead of or in addition to animation. However, whilst Sega went ahead with its CD system, Nintendo drew back because it did not believe that CD was yet a mainstream product. The cost of a CD player will have to drop to that of a cartridge system in order to create a viable market for video games on compact disk. The Multiplayer from 3DO, though backed with massive investment, has not yet made the looked-for breakthrough in this area.

Photography
One interesting and innovative product in this area is the consumer version of Kodak's Photo CD player, which might fit the slot in the market formerly occupied by slide projectors. Photo CD may also have some common features with the successful market for camcorders - consumers will provide the content but need editing facilities so that they can add titles and build up slide shows.

Movies
Compact disk could be a realistic alternative to videotape as a means of distributing movies. In 1993 a small UK company, Nimbus, demonstrated the ability to play back video from a compact disk on a special decoder. A CD to the Red Book specification could hold up to 79 minutes of full-motion video, using MPEG-1

compression, whilst up to 135 minutes could be held on a double density disk. More recently Philips has published its own specification for video on CD, the White Book.

Education

Compact disk is a natural platform for education in the home. Because it is interactive, it offers benefits over conventional audiovisual materials based on linear audio- and videotape. It can also hold much larger volumes of material, so that a whole language course, for example, could be held on a single disk.

Information services

Current CD-ROM players are designed for playback from disk and thus lack any communications capability. This will change under pressure from interactive television. Philips has developed a CD-I player that can control information on a remote disk, regardless of the transmission medium. Such a player could be used as an alternative to the set-top converter for applications like home shopping, providing access to electronic catalogues held on a central database.

17.3   Applications for interactive television

As we have seen, the term 'interactive' can be used to refer to a variety of different systems. An interactive TV system is one that has three basic components: a source of information, typically a server at the satellite uplink or cable head-end; a receiver that can be controlled by the customer, typically a television and a set-top box to receive and decode the signal; and a two-way transmission path between them.

Set-top converters

The set-top box, similar to existing cable and satellite converters, is connected to the cable, satellite and/or telephone network. The equipment will normally be rented from the cable or phone company as part of the annual subscription. The customer must be able to control the system and access information in the simplest possible way. The set-top converter will therefore support most of the following features:

- an addressable integrated receiver/decoder (IRD) for cable/satellite reception;
- a modem for a return telephony channel;
- a card reader for conditional access;
- a universal remote control device;
- a separate printer to enable the customer to keep a record of any goods ordered;
- on-screen menus and access to an electronic guide to the programmes available.

The current generation of converters are being built around a 386 or 486 processor with on-board memory, controlled by a real-time operating system kernel.

Servers

The server must be able to store and control very large volumes of multimedia information (images, music and speech, audiovisual). Most of this information is still in analogue form. Digitisation will greatly improve storage capacity (gigabytes now, terabytes in future) of the 'media libraries' involved and will enable the data to be loaded into fast disk storage for playout in multiple streams. A major debate has commenced, driven by a clash between Oracle and Microsoft, as to whether service providers should adopt a solution with a single, large centralised server running on a parallel processor or many small distributed servers that can be controlled by personal computers or workstations.

Content and applications

The most important part of an interactive television service is content, which can range from the Top 20 movies through specialised information services to material that consumers create for themselves. Content must be available on demand at economic cost to both customer and content provider - licensing arrangements for this information are a major issue. The system must be able to bill customers for the information received.

There are four main applications for interactive TV:

- entertainment on demand;
- commercial services;
- education and training;
- new communications.

Many very fanciful ideas have been put forward as to how these might evolve in the future. This section outlines some of the applications that have already been developed.

17.3.1   Entertainment

New entertainment services build upon pay-per-view (PPV) - a form of subscription television in which the customer places a phone call to a special number to order an individual item such as a movie or a major sports event. Technological improvements now allow the customer to order these items 'on impulse' by pushing a button on a remote control or cable converter keypad to select a programme just before or whilst it is being transmitted - a variation known as Impulse PPV. These new methods of selecting and paying for television, together with the greatly increased choice of programming, will alter the economics of television production.

Near video on demand (NVOD)

In North America cable services already use spare channels to permit limited amounts of customer choice. PPV services, available in hotel rooms, allow the guest to choose a movie from a list of those available and watch it at one of a number of start times. Cable links the set-top converter to a bank of VCRs for playout of the movie at scheduled intervals, typically 30 minutes apart.

These hotel services form the model for near video on demand (NVOD), an extended form of PPV in which each movie is retransmitted at intervals, perhaps as little as 10 minutes apart, so that the viewer need wait only a short time to see it. NVOD is limited to major movies and is of no use for live events. It is being provided on commercial DBS and cable services in the USA and in the UK from 1994 onwards.

Video on demand (VOD)

Full VOD will enable the viewer to select any item from a library of programmes and watch it at any time. In addition to this much wider choice of material, viewers should be able to carry out simple control functions similar to those available on a VCR (e.g. pause, rewind and fast forward). True VOD could more accurately be described as 'programming on demand' since the material chosen could be anything from an early episode of Star Trek to a complete opera or the latest news and weather, supposing that all this material is available on the server.

Providing a VOD service will require investment in infrastructure to support two-way communications, substantial expenditure on hardware and software for media servers, digitisation of existing material and copyright clearance. The last of these problems may prove the most intractable. In all the hype about VOD services, the need to negotiate a programming 'window' for this service has been widely ignored or overlooked. Movie distribution follows a recognised sequence of channels: cinema release, video rental, pay-per-view or NVOD, video sell-through and broadcast television. VOD must be slotted into this sequence. Since what is being granted is a right for the remainder of the movie's life, it is likely to go to the end of the queue.

Games on demand

Video games are currently sold over the counter and by mail order. Interactive TV will allow the viewer to order a game from an electronic catalogue, download it from the server, play it at a time of his or her choice and pay for it through his or her account. Sega Channel, launched in the USA in 1994, will provide video games on demand, 24 hours a day. Subscribers will be able to choose from a wide selection of popular games, special versions of soon-to-be-released titles, tips, news, contests and promotions. Once downloaded, the games can be played on Sega Genesis platforms.

Sport

Live sport has been used successfully on pay channels and for pay-per-view events. It is easy to add interaction: a choice of camera angles or commentary, control over action replays, access to background information or game statistics. In the USA, Prevue Interactive Systems' SportsVue service allows the viewer to choose from various text screens to look up the sports schedules, together with additional information such as updated scores, injury statistics and gambling odds on different events.

17.3.2   Commercial services

A range of commercial services is already available over electronic networks. Banks, for example, have used automated teller machines to handle transactions and account queries for years. Some have experimented with home banking services, using the telephone.

Home shopping

Home shopping channels have become increasingly popular in the USA and are now available in the UK. Viewers can use the phone to place orders for products that they have seen on these shows, whilst the programme makers get instant feedback about the commercial popularity of every item shown. Such programmes could be extended, using a remote control to select and a card reader to pay for impulse purchases.

As we have seen, service providers such as travel agents and estate agents are starting to use multimedia information systems to allow customers to plan holidays and buy houses. Such services could be expanded into the home. The estate agency service provided by Wigwam, described in Chapter 14, permits the applicant to examine a wide range of properties in the agent's office. In future it could be possible for families to view the information in the comfort of their own homes, over cable television.

Advertising

Commercial television already relies on advertising revenue. The current trend is to move away from general advertising aimed at the mass market, towards selective promotions. Where a choice of channels is available, viewers can be offered a choice of products. Another promising new area is local ad insertion, allowing an advertising agency to select a commercial and place it on a file server at a specific head-end in the demographic area best suited to its products. Prevue Interactive Systems has signed a deal with a major provider of discount consumer services in the USA under which subscribers will receive customised on-screen information about participating restaurants in their area. For example, subscribers will be able to use the service to view an on-screen menu, select restaurants in their area based on location and cuisine, read reviews and other customised real-time information about each restaurant. Similar arrangements can be made with any supplier of information that has local relevance.

News and information services

A range of information is widely available in Europe through teletext and videotex.

Teletext uses the vertical blanking interval - a set of lines between each frame in a video transmission - to provide additional free information to customers with compatible TV sets. Viewers use their remote controls to select from a series of numbered pages, which contain a variety of information - news headlines, weather forecasts, programme guides and advertisements as well as subtitles for foreign language films or the hard-of-hearing.

Videotex was developed in some European countries to provide information services, via the telephone, to subscribers with special terminals. France Telecom's decision to distribute terminals without charge guaranteed the success of its videotex service, Minitel. In the UK, in contrast, BT sought to charge for its equipment. As a result its videotex service, Prestel, failed to take off.

Information services for interactive television must offer improved quality and faster access at a competitive price. News is a perfect application for interactive television because it is already in modular form. Television news consists of a series of packages from which the editors of each news programme select the items they wish to broadcast. A news-on-demand service would permit viewers to select both the topics and the level of detail required from those held on the server, rather than sit through many items in which they had little or no interest.

In the UK IBM is developing a range of broadcast multimedia services including business TV and broadcast point-of-sale material. Together with Independent Television News (ITN), IBM has developed a News on Demand service for the desktop. The services are distributed via a satellite uplink facility at Warwick, with an optional terrestrial back channel. The company has a separate project for residential customers.

17.3.3   Education and training

Television is a natural medium for education and training. It allows students to proceed at their own pace and makes available additional material that reinforces the learning experience. Audiovisual material has been used for years to supplement courses at schools and universities, for adult education, business training and consumer hobbies.

Distance learning is already being merged with telematics. The Berlitz Teleschool project, described in Chapter 13, runs a course in English for telecommunications. This includes a fortnightly live satellite broadcast to which students can respond on-line to send in questions and contributions. Similar facilities could be developed for home subscribers.

17.3.4   Communications

High levels of interactivity will eventually enable customers to communicate with each other over the television network. Teleconferencing would support those who want to keep in touch with scattered family members by sending and receiving 'videograms'. Such communications services are currently a long way from commercial reality, since they require increased bandwidth from the home and specialised equipment such as video cameras. Text-based communications are a closer prospect. For example, the UBI Consortium in Canada plans to test an email service run by Canada Post, which will include the issuing of bills and bill payment services.

17.4   Applications for home PCs

The computer systems suppliers have been trying to get into the home market for a long time. Sales of home computers remained static as they were stubbornly associated with work rather than pleasure in most people's minds. As a way to play games, home PCs were expensive and cumbersome and compared unfavourably with Sega and Nintendo systems. As a way to read encyclopaedias, they were exceptionally cumbersome. This picture is changing. Falling prices, and the increased numbers of people who work from home all or part of the time, mean that personal computers have become a key factor in the home market.

The main barrier to the growth of multimedia on home PCs is now the lack of adequate network facilities. The telephone operators will be slow to provide ISDN to the home. An alternative would be a cable interface, such as that being developed by Microsoft, Intel and General Instrument. This will make available much greater bandwidth, which service operators could then use to introduce multimedia services to the home. These would provide a much greater level of interactivity and access to a far wider range of information than is likely to be available on interactive television.

Entertainment
Multimedia PCs are being purchased as a platform for entertainment and education programmes in the home. Applications on CD-ROM are designed to take advantage of familiar user interfaces such as Windows. Microsoft itself sells a number of multimedia titles including Encarta, a multimedia encyclopaedia containing more than 21,000 articles with sound clips, colour maps, animations, photographs, charts and graphs.

Office applications
Many professional people already have a computer for teleworking and home office applications. Combined with a modem that can handle voice, data and fax, and suitable desktop software, these can support limited services over public service telephone networks. Video PCs may be used by teleworkers in the home office when prices fall.

Information services

Anyone with a modem and a PC can now access a variety of free and commercial services. Compuserve, for example, provides basic services such as news and weather, as well as specialised financial information. Dial up access to the Internet makes it possible for the user to send and receive electronic mail, join discussion groups on thousands of topics, and download information from file servers on the other side of the world. Multimedia information can be sent over public networks, though very slowly at present.

Summary

Substantial investment in network infrastructure will open up opportunities for new consumer applications over the next 10 years. These applications will be a mixture of entertainment, education and information services. They will run on a variety of platforms. Television will continue to be the main source of entertainment in the home, in combination with a variety of different digital products including set-top converters, VCRs and CD players. Basic information services will also be provided via the television. Specialised information and personal communications are more likely to be accessed from the home computer.

Part IV

The impact of multimedia

The final part of the book focuses on a number of key issues for the development of multimedia systems. Early standalone systems were developed by training and marketing departments, often using outside skills. Data processing and IT departments have been slow to take up multimedia. Yet to be really useful multimedia must be integrated with existing technology. Managing a multimedia project is significantly different from managing conventional IT systems development. Project teams must bring together people with a wide range of skills A parallel stream of activities will be required to create the audio, video and image material that makes up much of the application's content.

One way to build a multimedia system is to use object technology. Objects, which encapsulate content with the procedures that handle it, are often thought to be a natural way to model multimedia data. Object-oriented databases can be used to store composite objects that combine image, audio and video data.

Whilst early systems allowed users to interact with a multimedia application running on a computer, future systems will enable them to interact with each other, using multimedia communications. Workflow management software can handle the movement of multimedia data between processes in office automation. Groupware will enable knowledge workers to share documents in real-time conferencing systems.

Most multimedia systems contain significant amounts of material that is likely to be subject to laws such as those that govern intellectual property rights. The book closes with a brief review of the legal issues relating to multimedia applications, to encourage managers to seek the appropriate advice at an early stage in the development process.

CHAPTER 18

Developing applications

Any multimedia project needs a comprehensive plan - based on a thorough analysis of user needs - that will identify all the necessary elements, many of which may be strange to most IT managers. These elements will include identifying and producing the text, graphics, image, sound and video material needed for the application. This process should proceed in parallel with conventional systems development. The satisfactory use of multimedia also requires a high level of skill in the design of the user interface. Training software engineers to understand design issues, although necessary, will not be sufficient. Managers need to build mixed project teams, with skills that range from graphics design to video production.

18.1   Introducing multimedia

Developing a multimedia system is currently a specialist and very labour-intensive activity. Early users and developers tended to underestimate the resources that would be required to create training and POI or POS applications. Managers overlooked both the complexity of the problems and the time that would be required to deal with them. Developers failed to identify the breadth of domain expertise that would be required. Both were unprepared for the sheer scale of the preparatory work that has to be undertaken. Whilst a well-designed system may appear deceptively simple, the design skills required to create effective high-quality user interfaces are likely to be missing in most organisations.

A key factor in ensuring success in building a multimedia application is realising the need to co-ordinate development with all the business functions involved.

Multimedia must be integrated as a normal routine business application - it should not be treated as an exclusively IT project. Managers should therefore build cross-functional teams. Such a team should always include representatives from the client or end user department, who will be experts in a particular domain such as the marketing of a range of children's clothes. It may also include a variety of other specialists - creative writers, artistic designers, psychologists, knowledge engineers - as well as software developers and hardware suppliers. A director with film or television experience will be needed if video material is to be specially shot. A production manager will be required to organise and control any large-scale operations for selecting and capturing image and audio material. The finance department may be involved if it is necessary to lease specialist equipment.

The integration of conventional data processing with multimedia is an important consideration in the design of many systems. If image, audio and video data are to be treated like alphanumeric data and text, then all the lessons that have been learnt in the development of conventional data processing systems must now be extended to multimedia data types. These issues cover the need for open systems to simplify integration, a standard architecture so that data can be exchanged between systems from different suppliers, multimedia databases to provide unified storage for different data types and communications systems that support image transfer across the enterprise.

Multimedia, like all new technologies, inspires fear amongst staff who may believe that their jobs are under threat. The implementation of a multimedia strategy must be executed in a manner that is in sympathy with a company's culture. Because it can potentially affect many areas of the existing operation, such a strategy needs to be driven from the top of the organisation - by a multimedia champion - and co-ordinated with other IT implementation plans.

18.2   Methodology

The existing process of systems analysis is neither appropriate nor sufficient for the development of multimedia systems. This is because building a multimedia application will involve parallel streams of activity, summarised in Table 18.1, to create the content and to develop the computer program that will control it. Extra time will be required to collect information about products and services, create text and photographs, record audio and get video sequences shot. These activities can be carried out in parallel with the software development, but require a different kind of expertise. The project plan should co-ordinate the start and end points for both activities.

18.2.1   Analysis and design

Both streams must start with a phase devoted to the specification of the system and

Table 18.1   Stages in developing a multimedia application

Stage	Main activities (content)	Main activities (IT)
Pre-production	Design concept	Project planning
	Storyboarding	Specification
	Building prototype	Analysis
	Scheduling	Design
	Budgeting	
Production	Image gathering	
	Audio gathering	Programming
	Video gathering	Unit testing
	Image preparation/creating artwork	Integration testing
	Recording live audio	
	Shooting live video	
Post-production	Mix/edit audio master	
	Edit finished artwork with graphics	
	Lay in final stereo audio	
	System emulation	System testing
		User acceptance testing
Completion	Transfer to other formats	
	Distribute copies of final product	
	Return hardware and software loans	Backup elements and
		storage
	Review	

project planning. During this phase the concept and scope of the design will be defined and major goals and deadlines will be established. A demonstration prototype can be built, using an authoring tool and some sample content material - off-the-shelf audio and video material can be used for this. At an early stage users will thus be able to assess the proposed navigational features, colours, style of presentation, fonts and quality of audio and video material.

The first important design activity is to describe the material the user will see or hear as he or she operates the application. In applications such as training this description is known as the storyboard: a detailed plan that shows each screen or element with the accompanying soundtracks. From the storyboard the authors will establish an outline of topics to be covered. This can be used to establish basic timings for sections of video, graphics and music. Other applications may adopt a different structure. Retail systems, for example, may involve the development of an electronic catalogue, in which each screen is the equivalent of a single catalogue page or entry.

A decision tree may be used to show the major menus in the system and proposed branches, loops and information flows. This might be accompanied by a screen design document that identifies each screen by name or number and functional category and indicates all other screens to which branching can occur. Screen types can include both the function of the screen (e.g. help screens, menus) and its contents (e.g. text only, text and graphics, animation, still image, video only). The type of content can be linked to the existing or potential sources of all external elements (e.g. scanned images, music) required to design that screen.

These documents can be used to generate a matrix that shows screen functions and features. Separate screens are enumerated according to their complexity. A precise count of the screens to be developed in each category is generated (e.g. text and simple menus versus graphics and animation with back paging and timing features). This can in turn be used to estimate times and costs for the development of the computer system (Szuprowicz 1991). It will then be possible to schedule activities for the production staff. These might include the days required to shoot video or carry out interviews. Supplies of videotape, videodisks and other computer storage media can be ordered. Rentals of videos, films and equipment can be arranged.

18.2.2   Content creation

During the production phase all the content required for the application must be selected from existing sources or created afresh for the project. It will be necessary for clients or end users to be closely involved in, and even to control, this stream of activities. It will include the selection of video clips from material available on videodisk or tape, of audio from records, tapes or cassettes and the choice of artwork for scanning. In most cases this content will have to be created specially for the application. A car showroom system, for example, must be able to display photographs of every model in the complete colour range. Manufacturers will not have complete sets of such photographs, which will therefore have to be specially shot under controlled conditions to ensure that the images are of consistent size and quality, and will thus scan well.

Woolworths MV+

The MV+ kiosk developed for Woolworths in the UK (Figure 18.1) provides a study in the problems that need to be faced and overcome in developing complex multimedia applications. The kiosk offers shoppers the opportunity to choose from the store's full range of music and videos - some 20,000 items - from a touchscreen kiosk. Different data media are used for different purposes. Voice is used for help messages, for example, whilst attractor videos play when the system is idle, to entice people to use it. Still images, such as the covers of compact disks, music and full-motion video clips are used to illustrate different items.

The user can choose either video or music. Several hundred videos are illustrated by 15-second full-motion video clips. Other videos do not have any suitable illustrations. In these cases the system displays just the database information (synopsis, running time, film classification and price), an image of the video cover, and perhaps a sample from the soundtrack.

Musical items on compact disk or cassette are illustrated by a 15-second sound sample from a representative track. The database information lists tracks, price, format (choice of cassette or compact disk), and the cover using scanned images.

Figure 18.1   *The MV+ kiosk*

A major issue for this project was the need to manage the identification and acquisition of all this material. For music this meant how to choose the track, or part of a track. A team of people used stop watches to capture audio samples from several thousand lines. For video this entailed a decision on which ones should be sampled - a choice that involved both the client and the development team. The material had to be innocuous as it would be playing in a public place. The team had to acquire the videos, identify the samples, and then create digital recordings. Production lines were set up in warehouses with videos, television sets, compact disk players, scanning workstations to capture the covers and digitising workstations to capture audio and video.

The developers liken this complex situation to process management. It involved artistic judgement, creativity and the application of fairly strict process rules. Everything was subjected to a quality audit.

18.2.3   Maintenance

Many applications will need to be updated on a regular basis. The method chosen will depend upon a variety of factors: the number and location of kiosks, the amount and type of data, the frequency of updating and the budget available. Updating may be uni-directional (when new data is supplied to the program) or bi-directional (when information is also collected by the system). The systems may be used to collect information on every key stroke and to identify both those areas of the system where users go most frequently and those they do not visit at all. The means of updating may include disks, local area networks, modems on switched telephone lines, ISDN connections and radio (Bucolo 1992).

Updating may be carried out by the developer or the client. Most clients prefer to do this themselves as this gives them greater control over the system as well as reduced costs. They will need tools and techniques to enable them to update the system (to incorporate price changes, for example) from the central mainframe overnight.

18.3   Design

The effectiveness of a multimedia application depends on the content of the information displayed, its presentation and the degree of interactivity between the user and the application. The successful display of information requires a degree of artistic flair. Many multimedia projects will therefore require team members with both a strong technical capability and a graphical design background.

The 'look and feel' of the application must also reflect the corporate image, being integral to the environment in which it will be used (for example, a department store). The use of an authoring tool will tend to determine the look and feel of the final application. Some managers may therefore wish to restrict the use of such tools to prototyping in the early stages of a project, leaving them free to develop the final version in their own in-house style.

There is widespread agreement that the interface between the user and the application is vital to the evolution of multimedia systems. Olivetti, for example, has gone to considerable lengths to produce a voluminous 'style guide' for its multimedia kiosk customers. The principles laid down in the guide have been applied by Olivetti itself in developing its Personal Communication Computer.

18.3.1   Kiosks

For kiosks a touchscreen is considered the most intuitive approach. However, the system must provide an instant response - if nothing happens, the user may lose interest or start pressing icons at random. The icons chosen must have universal meaning. The sequence in which information is presented needs careful attention in order to orient the user in the midst of a large amount of information. The quality of audio and video must be acceptable to users who are accustomed to analogue video on television and CD-audio standards. PC screen resolution still lags behind studio quality video. Limits to current compression and decompression methods mean that time-critical sequences need careful selection.

People choose to use kiosks because they want fast access to information. In general they will not have the means or the inclination to copy out screenfuls of information. In many cases therefore printed output will be required to supplement the display.

The design of the cabinet will depend on its location - indoors or outdoors - and whether it will be supervised. It is difficult to make touch-sensitive screens proof against vandals. In some locations alternative approaches, for example using a special keyboard that allows the system to operate inside a protective cabinet, may be necessary.

18.3.2   Human factors

An important aspect of developing multimedia systems is understanding of the physical, psychological and social aspects of human response. For example, the accurate reproduction of colour, using 16 bits, is more important than high resolution for consumer applications - the opposite is true for business applications. The eye is not so demanding when images are in motion, so it is possible to combine low resolution and full-motion video, whereas high resolution and good colour are required for a still image.

Multimedia, by its very nature, opens up new channels of communication via the computer. Whilst these new channels have the potential to increase our understanding of the information relayed and the speed at which we can process it, they may also bring further problems in their wake. New speech recognition facilities will mean that we can give verbal instructions to computers. And the computers will be able talk back, giving us audible help messages, for example.

Many offices now are open plan. In such offices there may be a constant background noise and activity that makes it hard to make a conventional phone call using a handset. The introduction of video PCs will mean that some of this background activity will be transmitted over the video link. This is likely to be distracting to the person receiving the call, as well as disrupting the quality of the transmission - limitations in compression technology mean that a static background is preferable. If the video PC is to be used for collaborative activities such as sharing documents, participants will need to use both keyboard and mouse in addition to the handset. If a speaker and microphone are used instead, there will be further problems with background noise. Headsets might be preferable - but not for short casual calls.

Summary

The development of successful multimedia systems requires a much wider range of skills than that of a conventional computer system. For this reason, managers must extend the project team to include people with a background in graphics design, television production, knowledge engineering and even psychology. The project plan must also be revised to incorporate a process management stream that will be concerned with the selection, creation and capture of content. These processes should be mainly or wholly within the control of end users.

References

[Bucolo 1992] M. Bucolo, 'Multimedia in the European tourist industry', *TIME Europe 1992 Conference Proceedings*, EPCO International, Eindhoven, pp. 195-204.

[Szuprowicz 1991] B. O. Szuprowicz, 'Designing a multimedia knowledge system', *Information Management*, Auerbach Publishers.

CHAPTER 19

Multimedia objects

Multimedia is not a standalone technology, but one of a number of significant developments in computing. The most important of these related technologies is object-orientation. Image, voice and video data can be encapsulated in objects. This mechanism ensures a clear distinction between the content of the object and the code that is used to access it. Object-oriented languages may be used to develop multimedia applications. Toolkits with multimedia objects can be used to ensure that these applications have a common look and feel. Multimedia data may be stored as binary large objects attached to a relational database or in a true object-oriented database.

19.1   Different kinds of object

The word *object* can be used in several senses. There are the objects that surround us in everyday life: letters, forms, brochures, magazines and computers. I shall refer to these as *real-world objects*. We can also use the word in two specific ways to refer to binary large objects (or Blobs) and to object-oriented languages, databases and tools.

Blobs are an extension to relational databases used to store large unstructured objects such as text, image or moving video. A point-of-information system that introduces the visitor to the contents of an art gallery might have a database that contains colour images of paintings, a voice commentary, a video showing a painter at work and a catalogue of the paintings. All of this information can be digitised and stored in the database as Blobs.

In an *object-oriented* system, in contrast, the data and its related procedures are packaged together as software objects that can be used to model real-world objects.

To illustrate this, think of an application such as a company's personnel database. The main objects of concern in the application are people - managers and staff. These can be modelled as 'manager' and 'staff' objects in the system. A software object that models a member of staff called Joe Brown may contain several different types of information about him, including records of his address, phone number and date of birth, copies of letters, a photograph and even an audio clip of his voice. These can be stored in the database as attributes of the 'Joe Brown' object. All information about a given person is thus related in a natural way.

In an object-oriented system there is a clear distinction between the content of the object and the way in which that content is manipulated by the code. This makes the system easier to maintain and update. Some developers have therefore chosen object-oriented languages such as C++ to develop multimedia applications. In the next section therefore, I will briefly outline the main features associated with object technology.

19.2   Object technology

19.2.1   Definitions

Object technology is a way to develop and package software that draws heavily from common experience and the manner in which real-world objects relate to each other. Formally I shall define an object-oriented system as one that combines four important features:

1. Data and procedures are combined in software objects.
2. Messages are used to communicate with these objects.
3. Similar objects are grouped into classes.
4. Data and procedures are inherited through a class hierarchy.

The basic building block of an object-oriented system is the object. At the simplest level an object in the real world is something that can be identified by a name. An object has certain properties that can be used to describe it: it has state. An object will behave in a given way in response to a given stimulus: it has behaviour.

Objects, messages and methods

A software *object* is the counterpart of one in the real world. It too has state and behaviour - packaged as data and the procedures which act upon that data, which are known as *methods*. The data and methods are stored and modified as an entity.

This mechanism for packaging data and procedures is known as *encapsulation*. Think of the object as a capsule, in which data is stored at the centre. Access to the data is via the methods, which in turn are accessed by *messages* from the consumer. The surface of the capsule is the interface with the consumer. It consists of public information containing the names (or selectors) and definitions of the methods. To initiate a method a message is sent to the object, which compares it with its list of selectors. If it finds a match, the corresponding method is activated and the appropriate response sent to the consumer. Otherwise an error message is sent.

Classes and instances

Classification is a familiar activity - it is the way in which we decide whether a given animal is a cat, dog or human being. In object-oriented system development, each real-world object is put into a class with other similar objects.

In formal terms, a *class* is an object that contains the definition of all data and methods that apply to its members. Some of this information applies to the class itself: in this case the data are known as *class variables* and the methods as *class methods*. Some applies only to the individual objects that are *instances* of the class: at the time of their creation they are initialised with specific data, or *instance variables*, which distinguish them from other objects in their class. The methods that can be applied to this data are known as *instance methods*.

Inheritance

Once real-world objects have been classified, a hierarchy of classes may be constructed by the techniques of generalisation and specialisation:

- Account is a class that encompasses both Savings Account and Current Account. The technique of creating a superclass from several existing classes in this way is known as *generalisation*.
- Gold Account is a special kind of Savings Account. The technique of creating a subclass of an existing class in this way is known as *specialisation*.

A hierarchy typically starts with a few abstract classes. Each new class is introduced as a subclass of an existing class from which it *inherits* data and methods - only the data and methods that are new to that class need to be defined and implemented.

So far we have assumed that each subclass inherits from only one superclass - single inheritance. Some languages support inheritance from more than one superclass - multiple inheritance. The results of this type of inheritance may be difficult to control. Strict rules must be provided to determine which features will take precedence.

Polymorphism

Polymorphism is a natural outcome of the encapsulation of methods in objects. Since the interpretation of a message is done by the object that receives it, the same message may be sent to any number of different objects. The + operator, for example, may be used to achieve a variety of results:

- addition of integers $1 + 2 = 3$;
- addition of floating point numbers $1.1 + 2.5 = 3.6$;

- addition of fractions $1/2 + 5/6 = 4/3$;
- addition of vectors $(1,2) + (5,6) = (6,8)$;
- concatenation of character strings   'abc' + 'def' = 'abcdef'.

On receiving the + method selector, for example, a vector object will check to see whether it has a method for this selector. If it has, it will execute that method. If it has not, it will return an error message.

Binding of message to method

The interpretation of a polymorphic message depends on the type of data involved. The binding of the message to a method must be made after the data types have been checked. However, languages vary in the degree to which they enforce the checking of data types and the time at which such checks are carried out. Type checking may be done by the compiler or at runtime. These options lead to two different approaches to the binding of message to method:

1. Static (or early) binding occurs when the data type of every object is known and can be checked during compilation.
2. Dynamic (or late) binding occurs when the data type is checked, and the link between message and method made, whilst the program is running.

The dynamic binding approach, adopted by Smalltalk, is sometimes said to be a key feature of object-oriented languages.

The choice of static or dynamic binding may be influenced by the type of data involved and by how much information is available about it. Tightly coupled collections of objects, such as computations with floating point numbers or vectors, whose behaviour is well known may be statically bound. In contrast, loosely coupled collections whose behaviour cannot be predicted require dynamic binding. For example, an office automation project might include a Container object called a Mailbox. This could contain an unknown number of objects of a variety of data types - a text message, voice mail, scanned image or even a video clip. The exact contents of the Mailbox at any given time cannot be predicted.

19.2.2   Tools for multimedia objects

A wide range of object-oriented tools is available to support software development. These vary from language compilers and interpreters, accompanied by simple support tools for programmers such as editors and browsers, to elaborate programming environments. Smalltalk has always provided an extensive library of classes that developers can use to build applications. Other libraries have been developed to support different languages. These have been particularly popular for building graphical user interfaces, where object technology can reduce development time. Using class libraries of basic components such as windows, menus, icons, buttons and scroll bars with rapid prototyping allows the interface to be developed separately from the application and tested on potential users and interactively refined. It is increasingly seen as a way of ensuring a standard interface to applications - creating a common 'look and feel'.

Existing toolkits can be extended by implementing new classes for multimedia objects (Niemöller 1993). Such a toolkit might provide templates for audio and video objects, for example. Panels are required for the interactive control (both editing and playback) of time-dependent data such as music or video. It is desirable that all such panels in an application or set of applications look the same and function in a similar way. This can be achieved through the development of a generic control panel - a class from which specific instances can be created.

19.3   Multimedia data management

User demand for multimedia is driven by the need to manage information that could not be integrated or even held electronically by other means. A database management system (DBMS) for multimedia should support:

- effective storage and retrieval of large multimedia objects;
- editing of text, image and voice data;
- sharing of multimedia objects between multiple users and applications;
- facilities to create, transmit and print or display multimedia objects.

Some of these facilities can be provided by adding binary large objects (Blobs) to a relational DBMS. Such an extended DBMS will be able to store and retrieve multimedia data items by name. This will be sufficient for applications such as document image processing where each image is stored and retrieved as a whole. More advanced facilities will be required in other applications. Text, image and voice processing will require the use of pattern recognition methods to retrieve parts of text, voice or image objects. Other applications such as the personnel database described above will need object technology to decompose complex objects into their component parts.

There are four possible approaches to data management in multimedia systems: a file system, a relational DBMS, an extended DBMS or an object-oriented DBMS. Custom file systems have been used for some early imaging systems, but will be superseded in the future as multimedia DBMSs come onto the market. In the rest of this section I will look briefly at the other three methods.

19.3.1   Using a relational DBMS

An existing DBMS may be used to hold record-based information, with a separate file system for image data. This is a common approach with geographic information systems (GIS). For example, IBM's Geographic Facilities Information System uses a layer called GeoManager on top of DB2. GeoManager provides geographical data manipulation functions, whilst DB2 handles storage of the data, backup and other DBMS functions.

Document image processing systems often use a relational DBMS as an index to documents that are stored as bitmapped images. For example, FileNet uses Oracle for the document index and its own document locator database to track images on optical disk.

19.3.2   Using an extended DBMS

The relational DBMS may be augmented in two ways. Firstly a semantic layer can be introduced to manage objects. Alternatively Blobs can be used to store images. Computervision's System 9 GIS, for example, use the Empress relational DBMS, which supports Blobs, as the underlying data management system. On top of this is an 'object management system' for complex data management, which can support aggregations (collections of similar objects) as complex objects in the database.

A Blob has no internal structure and may hold a variety of information - usually text or image, though voice and video are equally feasible. The DBMS does not need any information about the content of the Blob in order to manage it efficiently. Blob data types are therefore relatively easy to introduce, provided that all the normal DBMS functions including logging of transactions, archiving, copying of items, memory management and distributed data management are adapted to handle Blobs without degrading the performance of the system. However, an application that accesses the Blob does need to know about its contents in order to make meaningful use of them. The use of Blobs to store large unstructured data items such as image and text will not suffice for all multimedia applications. In some cases it may be necessary to access the internal structure and content of an object.

19.3.3   Using an object-oriented database

An object-oriented database management system (OODBMS) allows the developer to describe real-world objects in terms of software objects and classes and to store them in a database. It must therefore fulfil two key conditions:

1. It must support object-oriented concepts.
2. It must be able to manage persistent data.

The first condition may be achieved by adapting an object-oriented language such as C++ to support persistent objects. To fulfil the second condition the OODBMS must provide facilities for object management and for secondary storage management. The object manager will be a new component. Storage management may be provided either by interfacing the object manager to an existing DBMS or by developing a new component with all the features normally expected in a DBMS - security, recovery, query facilities.

So far there is no consensus on what detailed criteria an OODBMS should fulfil. In August 1989 a group of academics and researchers published the 'Object-Oriented Database System Manifesto' (Atkinson 1989) in an attempt to define these criteria. The authors report that, although there is a lot of experimental activity, the subject suffers from the lack of a common data model and the lack of formal foundations similar to those laid down for the relational model. They see the importance of agreeing on a definition of an object-oriented database management system and put forward characteristics that they believe such systems should possess.

The authors of the manifesto propose a number of mandatory and optional features, which are summarised in Table 19.1. Eight of the mandatory features deal with object-orientation and the remaining five with DBMS requirements. Any system that supports all 13 mandatory rules may be considered an object-oriented database management system.

There are other features that are felt to be important, though the authors do not agree whether they should be optional or mandatory. These include view definition and derived data, database administration utilities, integrity constraints and a schema evolution facility. Other issues, such as the choice of programming style, the best way of representing atomic types and constructors, the type system and the degree of uniformity, are felt to be the choice of the designer.

Table 19.1   The object-oriented database system manifesto

Type of criteria	*Rules*
Object-oriented	complex objects
	object identity
	encapsulation of objects
	types or classes
	inheritance through class or type hierarchies
	overriding, overloading and late binding
	computational completeness
	extensibility
DBMS	persistence
	secondary storage management
	concurrency
	recovery from hardware and software faults
	ad hoc query facility
Optional	multiple inheritance
	type checking and type inferencing
	distribution
	design transactions
	versions

Source: Atkinson 1989

19.4   The Object Management Group

The most influential player in the development of object technology is the Object Management Group (OMG), an international supplier organisation founded in 1989 to promote the object-oriented approach to software engineering. As part of this activity, the OMG has encouraged the definition of command models and a common interface for the development and use of large-scale distributed applications using object technology. Its aim is to build a set of standard specifications and to encourage the development of tools and software components that comply with those specifications. The OMG's first step was the publication of the Object Management Architecture (OMA) Guide (Soley 1990).

Object Management Architecture
The OMG's Object Management Architecture consists of the four major parts shown in Figure 19.1:

1. The Object Request Broker (ORB) enables objects to make and receive requests and responses.
2. Object Services (OS) is a collection of services with object interfaces that provide basic functions for realising and maintaining objects.
3. Common Facilities (CF) is a collection of classes and objects that provide general purpose capabilities useful in many applications.

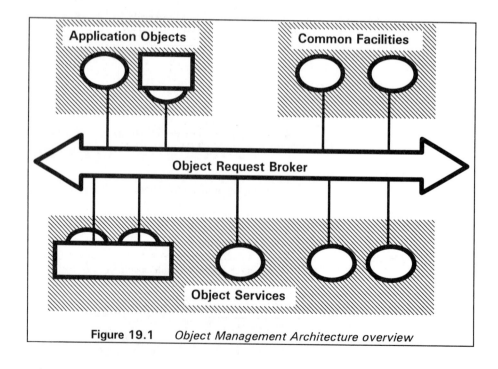

Figure 19.1   *Object Management Architecture overview*

4. Application Objects (AO) are specific to particular end user applications.

Application Objects and Common Facilities are application oriented, whilst the ORB and Object Services are concerned mainly with the system-level aspects of managing distributed objects.

An application that is OMA compliant will consist of a set of interworking classes and instances that interact via the ORB. Existing applications, external tools and system support software can be embedded as objects by using class interface front ends ('wrappers' or 'adapters').

Object Request Broker

The ORB provides the mechanisms by which objects make and receive requests. It allows applications on different machines in heterogeneous distributed environments to interoperate. It connects multiple object systems.

The fundamental mechanism for interaction is that of request and associated response. The ORB processes this request by identifying and invoking the method that performs the operation, using the parameters in the request. At the end of the operation, the ORB gives the results to the client that made the request.

The ORB is expected to provide the facilities such as name services to map object names in the request to equivalent names in the method, request despatch to determine which method to invoke, delivery to transport requests and results to the proper location and exception handling to report failures in object location and attempted delivery of requests.

Object Services

Object Services will be supported on all platforms. It provides basic operations for the logical modelling and physical storage of objects. It defines a set of intrinsic operations that all classes should implement or inherit.

These operations can include management of classes and instances, permanent and transient storage, query facilities on objects or classes and version control to support variants of objects.

Object Services may be implemented by components such as object-oriented DBMSs, transaction managers, query facilities, directory services and file services.

Common Facilities

Common Facilities is optional. It includes facilities that are useful in any application domains. These are intended to reduce the effort needed to build OMA-compliant applications. It provides a uniform approach to facilities that are shared across applications.

Facilities may include cataloguing and browsing of classes and objects, reusable user interfaces (text editors, for example), printing and spooling, help facility, electronic mail facility, tutorials and computer-based training.

CF classes represent common functionality that is adopted by the OMG as a standard.

Application Objects

An OMA-compliant application consists of a collection of interworking classes. Existing applications and data elements may be embedded in classes and applications. AO classes are more specialised than CF classes. They represent interfaces that are specific to an application domain and are not standardised by the OMG.

Most applications will be developed by value-added resellers (VARs). Examples include office applications such as word processing, spreadsheets, electronic mail as well as information access and query applications. Individual AO classes can migrate into CF classes if interfaces have enough in common. Applications may also cross boundaries, with some classes in the CF category and some in the AO category.

Summary

The development of multimedia applications is a difficult and expensive task. The use of object technology for system development can simplify that task in a number of ways. The encapsulation of data and procedures in objects is a natural way of modelling large quantities of digitised image, audio and video information that require special processing. Toolkits of multimedia objects can be developed or purchased for use in building consistent user interfaces. Object-oriented databases can be used to store complex objects that may consist of a variety of different types of data.

References

[Atkinson 1989] M. Atkinson, F. Bancilhon, D. DeWitt, K. Dittrich, D. Maier and S. Zdonik, *The object-oriented database system manifesto*, Rapport Technique, Altair 30-89.

[Niemöller 1993] M. Niemöller and U. Harke, 'Speeding up the process of multimedia application development', *Proceedings of the Multimedia Communications Conference*, Alberta.

[Soley 1990] R. Soley, ed., *Object management architecture guide*, Version 1.0, Object Management Group, Framingham, MA.

CHAPTER 20

Sharing multimedia

People need to interact with each other as well as with computer systems. Groupware products that enable this interaction must be integrated with multimedia technology. In the office of the future clerical workers will be able to handle multimedia data types as a matter of routine in office automation systems that are based on electronic messaging and workflow management. Knowledge workers will be able to work together on electronic documents, communicating in real time using audiovisual telephony or through mail messages.

20.1   Working in groups

As I have shown in Part III, multimedia systems are evolving from simple standalone products designed for single users to networked versions that enable those users to share applications. Most multimedia systems support interaction between the user and the system. However, many of our activities take place in a group. In the office of the future computer systems must be able to support interactions between groups of people, allowing them to work together on common tasks. If a group shares such a common task, it will need a common environment. Multimedia data types must move freely in this environment.

Studies in computer-supported co-operative work (CSCW) look at how groups work and seek to discover how technology can help them to work better. Considerations of time and place suggest the four categories of human interaction shown in Figure 20.1.

Computer-based systems that support groups of people engaged in a common

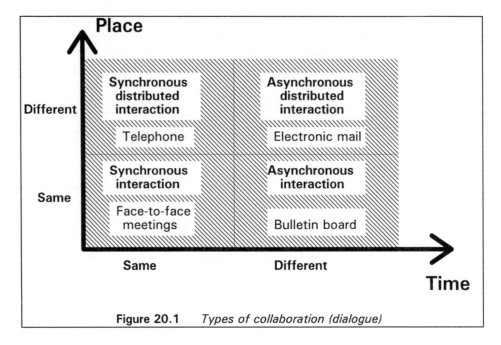

Figure 20.1   *Types of collaboration (dialogue)*

task (or goal) and that provide an interface to a shared environment are known as *groupware* (Ellis 1991). This definition encompasses a range of applications, some of which are in use now whilst others are still at the experimental stage. In the rest of this chapter I will look at the impact of multimedia in two classes of applications. Clerical workers are typically supported by office automation systems that incorporate image processing and workflow management. In contrast knowledge workers share information repositories supported by collaborative computing systems. Electronic mail provides links between all workers.

20.2   Workflow management

Co-ordination systems can be seen as a subset of groupware in which the work efforts of a number of individuals are integrated towards the accomplishment of a larger goal. Such systems are based on one of a number of different models that attempt to describe the way in which people co-ordinate their activities within organisations:

1. Forms-oriented models focus on the routing of documents (forms) in organisational procedures, which are modelled as fixed processes.
2. Procedure-oriented models view organisational procedures as progammable

processes, similar to software processes.

3. Conversation-oriented models are based on the belief that people co-ordinate their activities through conversations, which may be implemented through electronic mail, for example.

4. Communication-oriented models describe organisational models in terms of role relationships.

Of these, the forms-oriented model is probably the best known in practice, forming the basis for workflow management software.

Workflow management (WFM) is a pro-active system for managing a series of tasks that are defined in one or more procedures. The system ensures that the tasks are passed among the appropriate participants in the correct sequence and completed within set times, default action being taken where necessary (Hales 1993). A business process is defined as a procedure in WFM. Each time the procedure is invoked, a case is created. Thus at any given time there are a number of cases being processed, each case being at a given point in the procedure.

A procedure consists of a series of tasks, which are processed in a logical sequence. Cases are forwarded from task to task by the WFM software, usually by means of an electronic mail system. Data is gathered for each case from various sources. It may be input by participants, collected from other systems or databases, or derived within tasks. It can be of any type including text, image or voice. Data is stored within documents, which may also be of any type (e.g. word processor files, spreadsheets). Each case has associated with it a folder containing one or more documents. All data is normally stored within the system.

A further feature of WFM software is that it enables a variety of MIS information to be maintained such as audit trails, transaction logs, system usage statistics and user performance data. Workflow systems are already in use at departmental level and are expected to expand to meet corporate-wide applications.

Workflow management can be combined with other technologies, to handle multimedia data types. Document image processing, for example, relies on the idea that images can be substituted for the original paper document in a company's procedures. The flow of paper through the business is replaced by a flow of electronic images. For this to happen, there must be an established sequence of procedures through which a document will pass. For example:

1. A new document arrives in the mail room Here it is captured at a data entry station and routed to a particular clerk's work queue according to a set of rules specific to the application.

2. The clerk logs on to the system and the contents of the work queue are displayed. The queue contains items that the clerk has requested and any new items that have been routed to the queue.

3. The clerk selects items from the queue for processing. Such processes are specific to the application but may include searching for related documents, creating a new file folder for the document, attaching notes to a document,

accessing a mainframe application to read associated information, reading the document and keying alphanumeric data into another application, or using a word processing package to write a letter.

4. The clerk sends the document or folder to the next user or function. This routing is carried out automatically according to the rules built into the application.

Sources of WFM products include developers of original products such as Staffware (FCMC), suppliers of document image processing systems such as FileNet and office automation and systems suppliers such as IBM. Different combinations of products may be packaged together and sold as suites under names such as TeamLinks (Digital) or TeamWare (ICL). These WFM products are evolving to support multimedia data types, particularly document images. For example, ICL provides support for image processing and management (TeamVision) as part of its office information system (TeamOffice). This is combined with TeamFlow for workflow management and TeamMail for messaging transport. The underlying structure is based on distributed objects, using a client-server architecture.

20.3 Collaborative computing

Whilst workflow management is typically used to automate well-defined procedures for large groups of people, research into computer-supported co-operative work (CSCW) is most frequently aimed at workers in small self-directed professional teams. Social factors play a large role in this research, which frequently embodies a need to share, collaborate or co-operate with others in a joint project (Kling 1991). Multimedia has a significant part to play in the future in enabling and enhancing these activities through a variety of applications (Figure 20.2):

1. Multiuser editors can be used by members of a group to compose and edit a document, either in real time or asynchronously.
2. Decision support systems allow the exploration of unstructured problems in a group setting.
3. Computer conferencing systems support real-time communications between groups of people.
4. Electronic messaging systems allow team members to exchange messages asynchronously.

The real challenge for multimedia groupware is synchronous support for geographically dispersed groups to permit real-time conferencing or multiuser editing within shared workspaces. Such systems will require support for a variety of features, including:

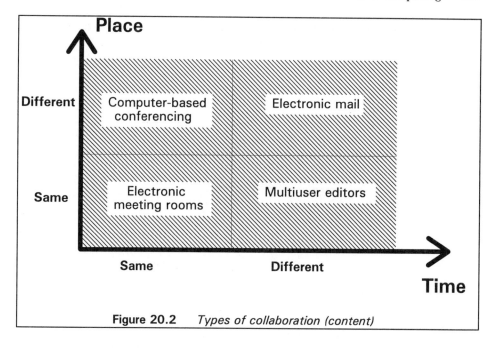

Figure 20.2   *Types of collaboration (content)*

- a set of objects where the objects (e.g. documents) and any actions performed on them are visible to a set of users;
- a view of some portion of the shared set of objects (e.g. an array of numbers presented as a graph);
- a collection of windows whose instances appear on different displays at the same time - changes in one window (e.g. scrolling it) appear in all the windows;
- a cursor that appears on each display and can be moved by different users.

These features, and others, are required to create a shared environment in which a key feature is likely to be the ability to be able to use familiar applications such as a word processor or spreadsheet.

Summary

Support for shared access to a limited range of multimedia data, usually document images, is already available within workflow management software. Multimedia mail, although technically feasible, is hampered by the lack of widespread acceptance of standards, such as Open Document Architecture, for electronic documents. Future groupware products will provide support for small groups of knowledge workers. These groups will be able to take part in desktop conferencing and collaborate on multimedia documents.

References

[Ellis 1991] C.A. Ellis, S.J. Gibbs and G.L. Rein, 'Groupware: some issues and experiences', *Communications of the ACM*, vol. 34, no. 1, pp. 39-58.

[Hales 1993] K. Hales, 'Workflow management: an overview and some applications', *Information Management & Technology*, vol. 26, no. 5. pp. 203-207 and 221.

[Kling 1991] R. Kling, 'Cooperation, coordination and control in computer-supported work', *Communications of the ACM*, vol. 34, no. 12, pp. 83-88.

CHAPTER 21

Multimedia and the law

Multimedia applications typically contain large amounts of information in a wide variety of forms. Even those that are apparently 'content-free' may be used to transmit information from one person to another. As a result they are likely to be subject to a number of existing laws that govern such questions as the ownership of information, responsibility for its accuracy and even the formation of contracts. The final chapter of the book focuses on a number of issues on which managers are urged to obtain legal advice.

21.1   Intellectual property rights

Commercial ideas and technology are protected by a variety of different legal rights, of which the most important for multimedia are copyright and patents. Some applications, particularly those in the retail trade, may require other intellectual property rights to be considered. Such systems may need to acquire the right to use third party trademarks or service marks, trade names and logos, for example.

Intellectual property rights may apply both to the content of the multimedia application and potentially to the application itself. Managers will therefore be concerned to ensure that they do not infringe the rights of others, particularly the owners of copyright, in any content acquired for the application. They may also wish to take steps to protect their organisation's own rights in the final system. Legal advice should therefore be sought at an early stage in any multimedia project.

The legal problems that inhibit the development of a broad marketplace for multimedia products and services are being tackled by the IMA Intellectual Property Project, which consists of five task groups:

- licensing paradigms and strategies;
- technical safeguards;
- publishing and library systems;
- collectives;
- legal and policy issues.

Amongst other activities, the Project will encourage the use of technical solutions for protecting intellectual property and the formation and growth of copyright agents.

21.1.1   Copyright

Copyright is the most important form of legal protection for multimedia applications. Originally designed to protect literary, musical, graphic and artistic works, copyright law arises without formality as soon as the work has been created. It now also protects such works as sound and film recordings, computer software, many compilations of information, broadcasts and cable programme services. If a developer reproduces the whole or a substantial part of a copyright work without the permission of the copyright owner, the owner can sue for damages. The owner may also seek to have the entire multimedia product withdrawn from the market.

International copyrights are protected by the Berne Copyright Convention, which is based on three principles:

1. A work that originates in one of the member states must be given the same protection in each of the other member states as the latter grants to the works of its own nationals.
2. This protection must be automatic and not be conditional upon compliance with any formality.
3. This protection must be independent of existing protection in the country of origin of the work.

As the USA was originally unwilling to join the Berne Convention, the Universal Copyright Convention (UCC) was created as a bridge between the USA and the Berne signatories. The UCC provides minimum terms of protection and limits formalities to a notice of copyright on each published copy. Its significance has been reduced by changes in US law to allow the country to become a party to the Berne Convention.

Managers may well seek ways to avoid having to deal with third party copyright owners. They might:

1. Create original materials by, for example, writing and recording a piece of music in house.

2. Rely only on works in the public domain in which copyright has expired.
3. Acquire the copyrights outright. Some large developers have purchased companies that own the copyright in collections of film, art or photographs, for example.
4. Use clip media - libraries of images, for example, that are supplied free of copyright.

If none of these routes are appropriate, managers will need to identify and contact all the copyright owners of any third party works they wish to use, and negotiate copyright licences with them.

Methods of licensing

Naturally developers will hope to acquire only the rights they need at a minimum cost. Difficulties arise in knowing what those rights are and what value they might have. Existing methods of licensing are based on models that work well in other sectors:

1. Per copy licensing is suitable for music on record, cassette or compact disk, for home videos and for books. It is difficult to apply this to multimedia applications on disk because there is no way of establishing the contribution of each content owner to the success or failure of the whole.
2. Per use licensing is suitable for on-line services. It requires a networked system that can be monitored so that customers pay for what they use. Many customers may prefer a flat rate fee that enables them to budget rather than face variable costs that they may not be able to control.
3. Concurrent use licensing is suitable for networked software. A flat fee is charged, based on the number of users who can access the service at the same time.

A fourth method called transclusion has been proposed in connection with Ted Nelson's Xanadu project - a unified literature environment on a global scale. This would ensure that once the user has paid to access an item, he or she has permanent access to it. The IMA has suggested that developers plan to license content in such a way that allows all forms of distribution.

21.1.2   Patents

A patent is intended to protect the owner of a new invention, by giving him or her the right to take legal action to prevent other people from exploiting it without consent. The inventor publishes details of the invention. In exchange the inventor gets a limited monopoly from the state for a period of 20 years. During this time the inventor pays annual renewal fees to keep it in force. After that the invention is available for the public to use freely (Bird 1991). Under UK law, there are four rules with which an invention must comply if it is to be patentable:

1. It must be new.
2. It must involve an inventive step.
3. It must be capable of industrial application.
4. It must not be excluded.

Computer programs as such are explicitly excluded by the UK Patents Act of 1977. It can, however, be argued that this does not prevent multimedia developers looking to patent law to protect their inventions. The test of patentability is that a computer-related invention should make a technical contribution to the existing knowledge in the computing field in question. If the program involves a new method of performing operations but no new technical result emerges this is not patentable. However, if the format of the program makes necessary some non-standard adaptation to the computer itself then this can be viewed as a new technical result even if it is internal to the computer (Rees 1992).

Patents are generally only effective in the country for which they have been obtained. However, the European Patent Convention (EPC) provides a mechanism that allows inventors to obtain patent rights in any one or more of the EPC Contracting States by filing a single application, which will designate the countries in which the patent is to take effect. A similar mechanism exists for those countries that are signatories to the Patent Cooperation Treaty (PCT).

Compton's patent

The US Patent Office, in contrast to the UK, has taken a very liberal approach towards granting claims for patents relating to software. In November 1993 multimedia developers were stunned when Compton's NewMedia, a leading title publisher, announced that it had been granted United States Patent Number 5,241,671. This identifies Compton's NewMedia as the owner of a 'Multimedia search system using a plurality of entry path means which indicate interrelatedness of information.' An abstract in the patent document further describes the invention as 'a database search system that retrieves multimedia information in a flexible, user-friendly system. The search system uses a multimedia database consisting of text, picture, audio and animated data. That database is searched through multiple graphical and textual entry paths. Those entry paths include an idea search, a title finder search, a topic tree search, a picture explorer search, a history timeline search, a world atlas search, a researcher's assistant search, and a feature articles search.'

The company applied for the patent in October 1989, immediately after the release of Compton's MultiMedia Encyclopedia. It has made clear its intention not to limit this invention to publication on CD-ROM. Rather it 'can be used with any information that can be stored in a database.' This would include applications available over a network such as the proposed 'superhighway', for example. Compton's sought to license the technology defined in this patent. The proposed programme gives developers several options including: entering into a strategic joint venture relationship with Compton's NewMedia, entering into a distribution arrangement with Compton's NewMedia Affiliated Label Program, developing a product using Compton's SmarTrieve technology, or complying with a royalty structure as set forth by Compton's NewMedia.

Following protests from the multimedia community, a request was made for examples of 'prior art'. The status of the patent is still under review at the time of writing.

MPEG Intellectural Property Rights

A further example of the complexities that may await developers of multimedia systems arises out of the success of the MPEG standard. There are said to be 1,500 patents related to the discrete cosine transform - one of the core elements of the MPEG compression algorithms - of which 33 may be significant.

An IPR meeting, held in Paris in March 1994 in conjunction with the MPEG meeting, attended by representatives of more than 50 companies who are among the manufacturers and users of digital compression technology world-wide. The group reached a consensus on a two-phase action plan for establishing a licensing entity:

- to identify which patent holders are willing to participate in this effort and whether they own rights necessary for the implementation of MPEG core technology;
- to determine an administrative structure that works with new licensees and licensers, the licensing structure, and the allocation of royalties.

The purpose of this group is to take advantage of MPEG's role as the digital television standard for the next century.

21.2   Errors and inaccuracies

Multimedia systems may frequently contain information whose accuracy must be ensured and maintained in order to protect users from financial loss or other harm. For example, as long as travel catalogues are displayed on shelves in a travel agent, legal responsibility for the accuracy of their content is borne by the companies that publish them. However, when the same information is transferred to a point-of-sale system in the shop, the travel agent may become liable for any errors. The agency may be able to limit its liability by including appropriate disclaimers, which should be clearly displayed to the customer before he or she enters any contract. Applications developers and their clients should therefore bear in mind the need for disclaimers when designing such systems.

There is a view current amongst some suppliers and developers that real-time multimedia over networks, being substantially free of content, is therefore also free of copyright problems and other legal hazards. Even where the application itself appears to be content-free, the fact that it is being used to give advice may involve its developers in a claim for damages. Some multimedia systems are designed to support remote consultations with experts. If the advice given turns out to be incorrect, is this the fault of the expert advisor or was he or she misled by defects in the hardware and software? It may be necessary to apportion liability between the service provider and the companies involved in the development and support of the multimedia system.

21.3   Electronic trading

Many of the networked multimedia applications that I described in Part III incorporate some form of business communication. Such communications can arise, for example, when a customer obtains services from an on-line insurance advisor in a kiosk, or when members of a project team pass documents between their personal computers. Problems can arise because the rules governing normal business transactions have not yet caught up with these new methods of communication.

Forming contracts
In law for a contract to be formed there must be:

- an offer from one party to another;
- an acceptance of that offer;
- a consideration by which each party obtains a benefit or potential benefit as a result of providing its obligations under the contract;
- an intention to create a legally binding agreement.

When is a contract formed by electronic means? With telex and telephone, the courts have decided that a contract is formed at the moment and at the place where acceptance is received. In the case of store-and-forward applications such as electronic mail that moment and place may be unknown or hard to determine. Companies that are planning to provide networked multimedia services need to be aware of this hazard. Furthermore some applications may allow users to form contracts. In this case, both the company providing the service and the users will need to know the moment at which they become legally bound.

In order to resolve disputes over contracts proof will be required of what happened between the parties. It will be necessary to:

1. Prove that a communication actually came from a particular party at a particular date and time.
2. Reduce the possibility that the contents of the electronic record could have been altered, deliberately or accidentally.

Because electronically stored information is inherently more volatile than written or typed information, there may be problems in establishing these proofs in law (Bird 1992).

Summary

Multimedia systems are breaking new ground in the law as well in the computing and telecommunications industries. Each system will typically involve dealing with a variety of different content providers. These may well be in different countries, subject to different laws. Many different regulatory bodies may be involved. Thus the creation of an application may involve numerous negotiations over a long period of time. Once the application is running, it will be subject like other computer systems to the laws governing the formation of contracts and legal liability.

References

[Bird 1991] *From idea to market place: an introduction to UK technology law*, Bird & Bird, London.
[Bird 1992] *Electronic trading, EDI and the law*, Bird & Bird, London.
[Rees 1992] C. Rees and A. White, 'Patents for software: how to find the holy grail of the software industry', *Copyright World*, issue 24.

Glossary

ADPCM (Adaptive differential pulse code modulation) a variation of DPCM which dynamically adjusts the range of amplitude values to match the data stream.

ADSL (Asymmetric digital subscriber line) a technique for sending a VCR quality picture over an ordinary telephone line.

Analogue a signal that varies continuously.

ANSI (American National Standards Institute) a non-profit-making organisation that serves as the national clearing house and co-ordinator for establishing standards in the USA.

API application programming interface.

ASCII (American standard code for information interchange) a standard table of 7-bit codes for the digital representation of letters, numbers and special control characters.

ASN.1 (Abstract Syntax Notation 1) an international standard language for describing structured information.

Aspect ratio the ratio of an image's width to its height.

Asymmetric compression an approach to the encoding and decoding of digital information in which the decompression process is not a step-by-step reversal of the compression process. The compression process typically takes much longer than the decompression process and needs a much more powerful computer.

Asynchronous information flow takes place in established services such as data communications on packet switching networks. It is typically bursty and packetised.

ATM (Asynchronous transfer mode) a transmission technique in which data is divided into fixed length cells that can be flexibly routed through the network.

AVI (Audio Video Interleaved) a file format for digital video under Microsoft Windows.

Bandwidth the amount of information, measured in kilobits per second (Kbit/s) or megabits per second (Mbit/s) that can be carried by a network. Bandwidth on an internal computer bus is measured in megabytes per second (MB/s).

B-ISDN (Broadband Integrated Services Digital Network) a planned enhancement of ISDN, which is expected to provide support for a 140 Mbit/s communications service by the second half of the 1990s.

Bitonal an image in which the picture elements have only two intensity values, 1 or 0, which usually stand for black or white.

Bursty packets of data that are transmitted in short bursts, rather than as a continuous stream.

Bus a network in which devices are logically connected in a line to a single cable. At any one moment, one device has control of the network and is allowed to transmit. (See also data bus.)

CAD (Computer-aided design) the automation of analysis, design and implementation phases in engineering projects.

CAM (Computer-aided manufacturing) the automation of such parts of the manufacturing process as numerical control, production planning and manufacturing resource planning.

CAP (Computer-assisted publishing) the automation of the development and publication of complex documents.

CAV (Constant angular velocity) a method of recording information on disks in which the rotation of the disk remains constant, whilst the length of track used to store a single item varies according to its position on the disk.

CBT (Computer-based training) the use of computers for education and training, in which computerised instruction forms the main component of the teaching process.

CCIR (Comité Consultatif International Radio) an international standard-making body (see ITU-R).

CCIR 601 a recommendation of the ITU-R (formerly CCIR) for digital video (704 lines with 576 pixels for PAL).

CCITT (Comité Consultatif International Télégraphique et Téléphonique) an international standard-making body (see ITU-T).

CD-DA (Compact disk-digital audio) the digital audio version of the compact disk developed jointly by Philips and Sony. The Red Book standard specifies a 12-cm disk capable of storing up to 72 minutes of high-quality sound encoded using 16-bit PCM at 44.1 kHz.

CD-I (Compact disk-interactive) a specification (the Green Book) proposed by Philips and Sony for a self-contained multimedia system that supports the simultaneous interactive presentation of video, audio, text and data.

CD-MO (Compact disk-magneto optic) a form of recordable compact disk specified in Part I of the Orange Book.

CD-ROM (Compact disk-read only memory) a version of the compact disk for the storage of digital data. The Yellow Book specifies a 12-cm disk which can store up to 550 MB of text, still images, graphics and audio.

CD-ROM XA (Compact disk-read only memory extended architecture) an extension of the CD-ROM specification (the Yellow Book) which is compatible in some respects with CD-I. It supports the interleaving of sound and picture data for animation and sound synchronisation.

CD-WO (Compact disk-write once) a form of recordable compact disk specified in Part II of the Orange Book.

Chrominance the colour information part of a video signal.

CIF (Common Intermediate Format) an ITU-T recommendation for digital video with a resolution of 352 pixels per line, 288 lines per frame.

CLV (Constant linear velocity) a method of recording information on disks in which the rotation of the disk varies whilst the length of track used to store a single item remains constant.

Codec (coder/decoder) a processor that can code analogue audio or video information in digital form and decode digital data back into analogue form.

Component signal a colour signal in which luminance and chrominance information are transmitted separately.

Composite signal a colour signal in which luminance and chrominance information are combined in a single signal and transmitted across a single wire.

Compression the process of reducing the number of bits required to store or transmit information in digital form.

Continuous tone an image that has shades of grey or colour.

CSCW computer-supported cooperative work.

Data bus a group of conductors, operating in parallel, that transfer data from one part of a computer to another.

DCT (Discrete cosine transform), a relative of the fast Fourier transform, is one of the main components of several compression algorithms. Low spatial frequencies, to which human beings are more sensitive, are coded more accurately than higher frequencies.

Decompression the process of decoding a compressed image and expanding the data to its original length.

Digital a signal that varies discretely.

DIP (Document image processing) the use of computer systems to convert paper documents to a digital form, which can then be processed electronically.

DPCM (Differential pulse code modulation) a variation of PCM in which the differential of the signal is encoded rather than the signal itself.

Dpi the number of dots per inch, used as a measurement of image resolution in documents. A dot is equivalent to a pixel.

DTP desktop publishing.

DVI a trademark of Intel Corporation for products based on the Digital Video Interactive (DVI) technology originally developed at the Sarnoff Laboratories.

ECMA European Computer Manufacturers Association.

EISA (Extended industry standard architecture) an extended version of the ISA bus that can support improved performance and a choice of a 16- or 32-bit data path.

Erasable an optical storage medium that can be rewritten after data has been erased.

Ethernet a local area network initially developed by Xerox and made into a formal standard by ECMA and the IEEE 802.3 committee. It implements the bottom two layers of the OSI seven-layer model.

ETSI (European Telecommunications Standards Institute) consists of equipment manufacturers, service providers and large users. It was established to create Europe-wide standards and strengthen Europe's role in international standard making.

FDDI (Fibre distributed data interface) an ANSI and ISO standard for fibre optic LANs.

Fractal Image Compression a proprietary image compression technology developed by Iterated Systems. Fractal transform codes derived from the image are stored instead of the image itself.

Frame a single complete image in a film or moving video recording.

FSFM (Full screen full motion) video can be played back at the same speed as broadcast TV or video (25 or 30 frames per second).

Genlock a synchronisation generator lock (genlock) is a way of combining video signals from different sources (e.g. external video source with computer-generated graphics).

Grey scale an image whose pixel values represent shades of grey.

GUI graphical user interface.

H.261 an ITU-T recommendation for video codecs for audiovisual services at $p \times 64$ Kbit/s where $p = 1,2,..,30$. It is intended for videoconferencing and videotelephony.

Halftone an image that creates the illusion of continuous tone on a bitonal display.

High Sierra Group a standards group set up to establish nominal data format and compatibility for CD-ROM.

Hypermedia a term used to describe hypertext which contains a large proportion of non-text information (e.g. graphics, image, video, sound).

Hypertext non-sequential information, consisting of linked pieces of text or other media (nodes) joined together by a network (of links). The hypertext reader navigates through the network of information, choosing when to follow a link.

HyTime (Hypermedia/time-based document structuring language) an ISO standard for hypermedia that allows a complete application to be encoded in a linear stream.

ICR (Intelligent character recognition) the use of artificial intelligence and other techniques to read and encode a wide range of characters, including all typefaces and some handprinted characters.

IEEE (Institute of Electrical and Electronic Engineers) a US organisation with an extensive standards programme.

Interframe compression the removal of redundant information which is repeated from one frame to another in a moving video sequence.

Interlace a technique for doubling the vertical resolution of a video image by broadcasting two sets of alternating lines. Even-numbered lines are drawn in one pass, odd-numbered lines in a second pass. Because the eye averages similar values, the image remains clear.

Intra-frame compression the removal of redundant information within an image or within a single frame of a moving video sequence.

ISA (Industry standard architecture) a 16-bit bus for the IBM PC/AT and compatible PCs.

ISO (International Organisation for Standardisation) the world-wide co-ordinating standards body with a membership composed of national institutions for standards in individual countries such as the British Standards Institution (UK) and ANSI (USA).

ISO 9660 a standard for the format of the directory on CD-ROM, for use under different operating systems, originally developed by the High Sierra Group.

Isochronous information flow takes place on circuit switching networks for applications such as telephony. Isochronous channels strictly maintain the timing relationships between successive bursts of information supplied to them.

ISDN (Integrated services digital network) a series of ITU-T recommendations related to the transmission of voice and data down the same digital line.

ITU-R (International Telecommunication Union - Radiocommunication Sector) one of the bodies of the United Nations specialised agency dealing with telecommunications (formerly the CCIR).

ITU-T (International Telecommunication Union - Telecommunications Standards Sector) another of the bodies of the United Nations specialised agency dealing with telecommunications (formerly the CCITT).

IV (Interactive video) the name for systems that allow analogue information stored on videodisks to be accessed interactively by users through a computer.

JBIG (Joint Bitonal Image Group) a collaboration between the ITU-T and ISO to develop an international standard for bitonal (black/white) images.

JIT (Just-in-time) an approach to training in which help and information are given to the user as required.

JPEG (Joint Photographic Experts Group) a collaboration between the ITU-T and ISO to develop a general purpose compression standard for continuous tone still images.

LAN (Local area network) a communications system for workstations and computer systems (nodes) within a local site to enable passing of data between nodes on the network and the sharing of peripheral devices such as printers.

Line art a bitonal image or mode of scanning that generates a bitonal image.

Linear videodisk the name for systems that allow analogue information stored on videodisks to be accessed sequentially by users, in playback mode only.

Lossless any form of compression in which the original data can be recovered without loss.

Lossy any form of compression in which the data is not exactly recoverable.

Luminance the brightness of an image.

MCA (Micro channel architecture) a proprietary bus developed by IBM for its high-end PS/2s.

MCI (Media command interface) allows Windows-compatible applications to control multimedia devices such as CD-ROM drives.

MHEG (Multimedia and Hypermedia information coding Experts Group) is an ISO activity concerned with co-ordinating the specifications of higher layers of the multimedia application development process. Its aim is to allow bit stream specifications for multimedia and hypermedia applications on any platform.

MIDI (Musical instrument digital interface) a standard published by the International MIDI Association that defines communication between musical devices.

MO (Magneto-optic) a technique used for the storage of data on erasable optical disks. Information is stored and erased by the combination of a laser to heat the surface and a magnetised coil to reverse the polarity of the medium locally.

MPC (Multimedia PC) the (trademarked) name for a minimum specification for a personal computer to run multimedia applications.

MPEG (Moving Picture Experts Group) an ISO activity to develop a standard for the storage of video and associated audio on digital media.

MUI Multimedia user interface.

NTSC (National Television Systems Committee) the standard for colour video in the USA, Canada and Japan established by the National Television Systems Committee. It specifies a 525-line screen updated at 30 frames per second.

OCR (Optical character recognition) a technique by which characters printed in a standard typeface can be automatically read and encoded.

ODA (Open document architecture) an ISO standard to allow the interchange of documents containing text, image and graphics between systems supplied by different manufacturers.

OLE (Object linking and embedding) a Microsoft technology that will allow users to insert multimedia elements into software programs.

OMF (Open media framework) a standard, developed by Avid Technology, for transferring digital video and audio over networks in a way that is independent of both device and system type.

Optical disk a disk on which information is read and written using a light, usually a laser.

OSI (Open system interconnection) is an ISO standard for data communications that uses a seven-layer model of interworking between computers.

Overlay the technique of placing computer-generated graphics (e.g. titles) over standard video.

Overscan a method of display in which an image is extended to fill the whole screen, as on a television set.

$p \times 64$ a short way of referring to the H.261 standard for visual codecs.

PAL (Phase alternation line) the standard for colour video used in most of Europe, Africa, Australia and South America. It specifies a 625-line screen updated at 25 frames per second.

PCI (Peripheral component interconnect) a new motherboard architecture for personal computers proposed by Intel.

PCM (Pulse code modulation) the standard method of encoding digital audio signals. The input wave form is sampled at regular intervals and the amplitude converted to a binary code.

Photo CD a type of CD-WO disk called a 'hybrid disk'.

Pixel a picture element forming the basic element in a digital image.

POI Point-of-information.

POS Point-of-sale.

QCIF (Quarter Common Intermediate Format) an ITU-T recommendation for digital video. It is a quarter of the CIF resolution - 176 pixels per line, 144 lines per frame.

Quantisation the technique of determining the value of a signal to some arbitrary degree of accuracy.

RACE (Research in Advanced Communications Technologies in Europe) a research programme funded by DGXIII of the Commission of the European Communities.

RAID (Random arrays of inexpensive disks) a storage concept developed at the University of California in which data is stripped across several physical drives.

Resolution the number of dots per unit length measured in one of two directions. The number of pixels measured across and down the screen is also frequently referred to as its resolution.

RGB (Red-green-blue) an output signal and image-encoding scheme for colour displays on computers that consists of separately controllable red, green and blue elements.

RISC reduced instruction set computer.

SDH (Synchronous digital hierarchy) a set of ITU-T standards for the implementation of SDT.

SDT (Synchronous digital transmission) a way of allowing individual channels within a multiplexed signal to be retrieved without fully demultiplexing the whole signal.

SECAM (Système électronique couleur avec mémoire) the TV standard developed in France. It specifies a 625-line screen updated at 25 frames per second.

SGML (Standard generalised markup language) an ISO standard for the content and logical structure of an electronic document.

SMSL (Standard multimedia/hypermedia scripting language) an international standard to enable cross-platform compatibility and portability of multimedia scripts.

Sonet (Synchronous optical network) an ANSI standard for the implementation of SDT.

Spatial redundancy the repetition of patterns within a two-dimensional image.

S-VHS (Super VHS) an improved version of the VHS half-inch videotape format that stores brightness and colour information separately rather than combined in one video signal.

Symmetric compression an approach to the encoding and decoding of digital information in which the decompression process is a step-by-step reversal of the compression process. The two processes thus take the same length of time.

Temporal redundancy the repetition of patterns between frames in motion video.

TIFF (Tagged image file format) An industry-standard format for the exchange of image files developed and controlled by Aldus and Microsoft.

Token Ring a local area network based on technology developed by IBM in 1985, and made into a formal standard by the IEEE 802.5 committee. It defined a ring architecture, in which the network takes the form of a closed loop with all the devices attached to the ring.

UTP (Unshielded twisted pair) the standard cable used for telephone lines and now a popular way to connect PCs to a local area network.

VCR (Video cassette recorder) a device that can record and play back video signals using removable tape cassettes.

VHS (Video home system) a trademark for the half-inch videotape format developed by JVC and Matsushita.

Videodisk an optical disk that can be used to store analogue video and audio information. Some forms may also be able to store digital audio.

WFM (Workflow management) a pro-active system for managing a series of tasks that are defined in one or more procedures.

WORM (Write once read many) a form of optical storage in which information can be recorded once and read many times, but not erased.

Bibliography

Technology

Systems development

Buford, J. F. K. (ed.) (1994) *Multimedia Systems*, New York: ACM Press.
Khoshafian, S., Baker, B., Abnous, R. and Shepherd, K. (1992) *Intelligent Offices: Object-oriented Multi-Media Information Management in Client/Server Architectures*, New York: John Wiley and Sons.
Minoli, D. and Keinarth, R. (1994) *Distributed Multimedia Through Broadband Communications Services*, Boston, MA: Artech House.
Waterworth, J. (1992) *Multimedia Interaction with Computers: Human Factors Issues*, Chichester: Ellis Horwood.

Hypermedia

Berk, E. and Devlin, J. (eds) (1991) *Hypertext/Hypermedia Handbook*, London: McGraw-Hill.
Howell, G.T. (1992) *Building Hypermedia Applications: A Software Development Guide*, London: McGraw-Hill.
Woodhead, N. (1993) *Hypertext and Hypermedia*, Reading, MA: Addison-Wesley.

Specific platforms

Amiga, PC, Macintosh, Next

Burger, J. (1993) *The Desktop Multimedia Bible*, Reading, MA: Addison-Wesley.

CD-ROM

Botto, F. (1992) *CD-ROM and Interactive Multimedia: A Guide for Users and Developers*, New York: John Wiley and Sons.
Sherman, C. (ed.) (1992) *CD-ROM Handbook*, London: McGraw-Hill.

CD-I

Hoffos, S., Sharpless, G., Smith, P. and Lewis, N. (1992) *CD-I Designers's Guide*, London: McGraw-Hill.

Philips Interactive Media Systems (1991) *Introducing CD-I*, Reading, MA: Addison-Wesley.

Philips Interactive Media Systems (1992) *The CD-I Production Handbook*, Reading, MA: Addison-Wesley.

Philips Interactive Media Systems (1992) *The CD-I Design Handbook*, Reading, MA: Addison-Wesley.

DVI

Bunzel, M. and Morris, S. (1992) *Multimedia Applications Development Using DVI Technology*, London: Intel/McGraw-Hill.

Luther, A. (1991) *Digital Video in the PC Environment*, London: McGraw-Hill.

Macintosh

Apple Computer (1993) *Inside Macintosh: QuickTime*, Reading, MA: Addison-Wesley.

Apple Computer (1993) *Inside Macintosh: QuickTime Components*, Reading, MA: Addison-Wesley.

Apple Computer (1993) *Inside Macintosh: CD-ROM Handbook*, Reading, MA: Addison-Wesley.

Windows

Desmarais, N. (1993) *Multimedia on the PC: A Guide for Information Professionals*, Westport, CT: Meckler.

Microsoft (1993) *Windows Multimedia: Authoring & Tools Guide*, Redmond, WA: Microsoft Press.

Microsoft (1993) *Windows Multimedia: Programmer's Reference*, Redmond, WA: Microsoft Press.

Microsoft (1993) *Windows Multimedia: Programmer's Workbook*, Redmond, WA: Microsoft Press.

Applications

Falk, D.R. and Carlson, H. (1993) *Multimedia in Higher Education: A Practical Guide to New Tools for Interactive Teaching and Learning*, Westport, CT: Meckler.

Hodges, M.E. (1992) *Multimedia Computing: Case Studies from MIT Project Athena*, Reading, MA: Addison-Wesley.

Saffady, W. (1993) *Electronic Document Imaging Systems: Design, Evaluation and Implementation*, Westport, CT: Meckler.

Waterworth, J. (ed.) (1991) *Multimedia: Technology and Applications*, Chichester: Ellis Horwood.

Supplier information

The most comprehensive information on suppliers and products, together with background articles and interviews, is contained in an annual publication:

Multimedia Ventures (ed.) *European Multimedia Yearbook*, London: Interactive Media Publications.

Journals

These publications are mainly for technical readers:

IEEE Multimedia, quarterly, Los Alamitos, CA: IEEE Computer Society.
Multimedia Systems, bi-monthly, Berlin: ACM Press/Springer International.
Electronic Documents, monthly, Oxford: Learned Information.
Information Media & Technology, bi-monthly, Hatfield: Cimtech.
Multimedia Review, quarterly, Westport, CT: Meckler.

Newsletters

These publications are mainly for non-technical readers:

Inside Multimedia, 10 issues a year, Derby: John Barker.
Interactive Media International, monthly, London: Interactive Media Publications.
Multimedia Week, weekly, Potomac, CT: Philips Business Information.
European Multimedia Bulletin, monthly, London: Digital Vision International.
OII Spectrum, monthly, Twickenham: Technology Appraisals.

Market studies

These publications, which contain market forecasts, are mainly for marketing managers:

Hales, K. and Jeffcoate, J. (1990) *Document Image Processing: the Commercial Impact*, London: Ovum.
Jeffcoate, J. and Matthews, J. (1994) *Interactive Television: the Market Opportunity*, London: Ovum.
Jeffcoate, J. and Templeton, A. (1992) *Multimedia: Strategies for the Business Market*, London: Ovum.
Jeffcoate, J., Li, M. and Timms, S. (1993) *Networked Multimedia: the Business Opportunity*, London: Ovum.

Standards

ISO standards

These may be purchased from your country's national standards body. In the UK this is the British Standards Institution, 2 Park Street, London W1A 2BS.

ITU Recommendations

These may be purchased from the International Telecommunications Union, Information Services Department, Place des Nations, 1211 Geneva 20, Switzerland. In the UK they are also available from OmniCom PPI Ltd, Forum Chambers, The Forum, Stevenage, Herts, SG1 1EL.

Compact disk specifications

The Red, Yellow, Orange, Green and White Books are available to developers from Philips and Sony.

MPC Specifications

These are available from the Multimedia PC Marketing Council, 1730 M Street N W, Suite 707, Washington, DC 20036, USA.

IMA Compatibility Project

Further information is available from the Interactive Multimedia Association, 48 Maryland Avenue, Suite 202, Annapolis, MD 21401-8011, USA.

Object technology

Further information is available from the Object Management Group, 492 Old Connecticut Path, Framingham, MA 01701, USA.

Index